STUDIES IN THE HISTORY
OF CHRISTIAN MISSIONS

R. E. Frykenberg
Brian Stanley
General Editors

STUDIES IN THE HISTORY
OF CHRISTIAN MISSIONS

Susan Billington Harper

*In the Shadow of the Mahatma: Bishop V. S. Azariah
and the Travails of Christianity in British India*

D. Dennis Hudson

Protestant Origins in India: Tamil Evangelical Christians, 1706-1835

Brian Stanley, *Editor*

Christian Missions and the Enlightenment

Kevin Ward and Brian Stanley, *Editors*

The Church Mission Society and World Christianity, 1799-1999

Cover Illustration

'The Cession of Matavai' by Robert Smirke, R.A., 1799.

This picture was commissioned by the Directors of the London Missionary Society and presented to Captain James Wilson, commander of the *Duff*, which took the first LMS missionary party to the South Pacific. It depicts the cession to the LMS on 16 March 1797 of land at Matavai in Tahiti, though the missionaries later discovered that the ceremony was intended as a gesture of hospitality and an invitation to share the produce of Matavai rather than as a grant of freehold rights in perpetuity. Those shown in the picture include: Pomare I, paramount chief of Mo'orea (standing center-left, naked to the waist); his son, Pomare II, paramount chief of the Porionu'u (the left-hand of the two figures carried on men's shoulders); the priest, Ha'amanimani (front left, depicted addressing Captain Wilson and making the act of 'cession'); Captain Wilson (right, holding the hat); his nephew, William Wilson, first mate of the *Duff* (immediately to the left); Elizabeth Hassell, wife of LMS missionary Ralph Hassell, and her two children (beneath the Wilsons); and William and Sara Henry, LMS missionaries (far right).

The picture is reproduced by kind permission of the Council of World Mission.

CHRISTIAN MISSIONS
and the
ENLIGHTENMENT

Edited by

Brian Stanley

WILLIAM B. EERDMANS PUBLISHING COMPANY
GRAND RAPIDS, MICHIGAN / CAMBRIDGE, U.K.

CURZON PRESS LTD
RICHMOND, SURREY, U.K.

Published jointly 2001 by
Wm. B. Eerdmans Publishing Co.
255 Jefferson Ave. S.E., Grand Rapids, Michigan 49503 /
P.O. Box 163, Cambridge CB3 9PU U.K.
www.eerdmans.com
and by
Curzon Press Ltd.
15 The Quadrant, Richmond, Surrey, TW9 1BP, U.K.

Printed in the United States of America

06 05 04 03 02 01   7 6 5 4 3 2 1

Library of Congress Cataloging-in-Publication Data

Christian Missions and the Enlightenment / edited by Brian Stanley.
p.   cm.   — (Studies in the History of Christian Missions)
Includes bibliographical references.
ISBN 0-8028-3902-9 (cloth: alk. paper)
1. Missions — Theory — History of doctrines — 18th century.
2. Protestant Churches — Scotland — Missions — History — 18th century.
3. Protestant Churches — Great Britain — Missions — History — 18th century.
4. Enlightenment.   I. Stanley, Brian, 1953-   II. Series.

BV2420.C47   2001
266′.009′033 — dc21

2001018479

British Library Cataloguing-in-Publication Data

A catalogue record for this book is available from the British Library.
Curzon Press ISBN 0 7007 1559 2

Contents

v

Preface

This book owes its origin to the North Atlantic Missiology Project (NAMP), an international collaborative scholarly venture based at the Centre for Advanced Religious and Theological Studies, Faculty of Divinity, University of Cambridge, and funded by The Pew Charitable Trusts of Philadelphia. The project was established early in 1996 to promote research and publication at the highest level into the interaction between theology, theory, policy, and practice in the Anglo-American Protestant missionary movement in the period from 1740 to 1968. It has been concerned with all regions of the globe to which Protestant missionaries from the North Atlantic world were sent.

The chapters of this book were all originally given as papers at conferences or seminars organized by NAMP in Britain or the United States between 1996 and 1998. The majority were given at the opening NAMP consultation held in Cambridge in September 1996. Subsequent volumes in the Studies in the History of Christian Missions series will publish further papers given at NAMP events. Since January 1999 NAMP has continued in a second phase under the new name of "Currents in World Christianity," which is concerned with the transformation of Christianity in the twentieth century into a truly global religion. The CWC project will continue until December 2001. Further details of project activities may be obtained from the project office at Westminster College, Cambridge, CB3 0AA, or from the project web site, whose URL is http://www.divinity.cam.ac.uk/carts/cwc.

Grateful acknowledgment is due in the first place to The Pew Charitable Trusts, without whose generous support this volume would never have been written. The opinions expressed in the chapters that follow are, of course, solely those of the authors and do not necessarily represent the views of The Pew Charitable Trusts. Acknowledgment is also due to the Council for World Mission for permission to cite extracts from the CWM (London Missionary Society) archives. I also wish to thank Dr. David Thompson, Director of the Centre for Advanced Religious and Theological Studies, for his unfailing support for the project. My fellow general editor of the series Studies in the History of Christian Missions, Professor R. E. Frykenberg of the University of Wisconsin–Madison, has given continual encouragement and guidance. Without the vision of William B. Eerdmans, Jr., of Wm. B. Eerdmans Publishing Company, and Malcolm Campbell and Jonathan Price of Curzon Press, this series would not have seen the light of the day. Particular thanks is due to the staff of Eerdmans for their work in preparing the volume for publication and to Liesl Amos for preparing the index.

BRIAN STANLEY
University of Cambridge
October 1999

List of Contributors

Brian Stanley is Director of the Currents in World Christianity Project at the University of Cambridge and a Fellow of St. Edmund's College. From September 2000 he is Director of the Henry Martyn Centre for the study of mission and world Christianity, in Cambridge. His publications on the history of Christian missions include *The Bible and the Flag: Protestant Missions and British Imperialism in the Nineteenth and Twentieth Centuries* (Apollos, 1990) and *The History of the Baptist Missionary Society, 1792-1992* (T&T Clark, 1992).

Andrew F. Walls is Curator of Collections at the Centre for the Study of Christianity in the Non-Western World, University of Edinburgh, and an Honorary Professor of the University. He is also Guest Professor of Ecumenics and Mission at Princeton Theological Seminary. His numerous publications on the missionary movement and non-Western Christianity include *The Missionary Movement in Christian History* (Orbis Books and T&T Clark, 1996).

Penny Carson teaches history at Malvern College, England, and writes on early Protestant missions in India. She gained her Ph.D. from the University of London in 1988 for the dissertation "Soldiers of Christ: Evangelicals and India, 1784-1833."

D. Bruce Hindmarsh is the James M. Houston Associate Professor of Spiritual Theology at Regent College, Vancouver, British Columbia, Canada. He was awarded the D.Phil. from the University of Oxford in 1993 for a dissertation on John Newton. His publications include *John Newton and the English Evangelical Tradition* (Eerdmans, 2001).

Jane Samson is an assistant professor of history at the University of Alberta. She has published on the maritime and imperial history of the Pacific islands, including *Imperial Benevolence: Making British Authority in the Pacific Islands* (University of Hawaii Press, 1998).

Ian Douglas Maxwell is a Church of Scotland minister at Kirk o' Field Church in Edinburgh. He was awarded the Ph.D. by the University of Edinburgh in 1995 for the dissertation "Alexander Duff and the Theological and Philosophical Background to the General Assembly's Mission in Calcutta to 1840."

Natasha Erlank is lecturer in history at Rand Afrikaans University, Johannesburg. She was awarded a Ph.D. by the University of Cambridge in 1999 for a dissertation entitled "Gender and Christianity among Africans Attached to Scottish Mission Stations in Xhosaland in the Nineteenth Century."

Daniel W. Hardy was formerly Director of the Center of Theological Inquiry, Princeton, New Jersey, and before that was Van Mildert Professor of Divinity at the University of Durham. He has written widely on modern theology, including *God's Ways with the World: Thinking and Practising Christian Faith* (T&T Clark, 1996).

List of Abbreviations

BL   British Library
BMS   Baptist Missionary Society
CMS   Church Missionary Society
CWM   Council for World Mission
EUL   Edinburgh University Library
FCS   Free Church of Scotland
FMC   Foreign Missions Committee
GMS   Glasgow Missionary Society
IOR   India Office Records
LMS   London Missionary Society
NAMP   North Atlantic Missiology Project
NLS   National Library of Scotland
SMS   Scottish Missionary Society
SOAS   School of Oriental and African Studies, University of London
SPCK   Society for Promoting Christian Knowledge
SPG   Society for the Propagation of the Gospel in Foreign Parts
SSPCK   Society in Scotland for Propagating Christian Knowledge
WMMS   Wesleyan Methodist Missionary Society

CHAPTER ONE

Christian Missions and the Enlightenment: A Reevaluation

BRIAN STANLEY

The theme of this volume is embedded in the language that is conventionally applied to the past two hundred years of Christian missionary activity. We speak of "the modern missionary movement," or, more significantly still, of "the modern missionary enterprise." At least tacitly, our terminology suggests that it is possible to identify a distinctively modern Christian project for "enlightening" the globe by means of a highly organized investment, and transfer from West to East and North to South, of funds, personnel, literature, and institutions. The relation of Christian missions to modernity is now a topic of intense debate both in the scholarly community and, in less obvious ways, in the churches. The recent explosion of writing by historians and anthropologists on the missionary impact has concentrated on the role of missions in propagating the values, disciplines, and economic relationships characteristic of modern Western societies. The missionary movement has been portrayed as one of the earliest forces of "globalization," creating networks and new media of communication no less powerful than those established by the global market and information technology revolution of the late twentieth century. The American anthropologists John and Jean Comaroff (undoubtedly the most influential exponents of this recent scholarship) have graphically described nineteenth-century overseas missions as "nodes in a global order, their stations pegging out a virtual Empire of God no less ether-

---

1. John L. and Jean Comaroff, *Of Revelation and Revolution*, vol. 2: *The Dialectics of Modernity on a South African Frontier* (Chicago and London, 1997), p. 12.

real than is cyberspace today."[1] From a different intellectual perspective, Christian theologians and mission theorists have been no less concerned with questions of mission and modernity. For them, the close approximation between the missionary movement and patterns of modernity raises a question mark over the appropriate forms, or even the fundamental legitimacy, of Christian mission in a postmodern world. The contemporary crisis of confidence in the validity of Christian mission has its roots, according to the late South African missiologist David J. Bosch, in the collapse of the Enlightenment inheritance and the emergence of a postmodern worldview.[2]

These debates over mission and modernity focus more sharply on Protestant than on Catholic Christianity. Two reasons may be adduced for this. First, the rapid expansion of Christian missionary activity in the eighteenth and nineteenth centuries was, in its original impetus, largely a Protestant evangelical phenomenon. Roman Catholic missions, which had dominated the field from the sixteenth century, were in the doldrums following the suppression of the Jesuit order in 1773 and the vicissitudes of the papacy during the Napoleonic era; only gradually, in the course of the nineteenth century, did the Catholic missionary enterprise revive. Second, the Roman Catholic Church, in the aftermath of the French Revolution, set its face firmly against the values of modernity throughout the nineteenth century, whereas the Protestant churches, with varying degrees of enthusiasm, appropriated the intellectual legacy of the Enlightenment. Protestant missions, therefore, were in the nineteenth century much more active apostles of modernity than Catholic ones, and hence in the late twentieth century they have felt more acutely the challenge of disintegrating confidence in modernity. This volume concerns itself only with Protestant missions.

The eighteenth-century Protestant missionary awakening was intimately associated with the birth of evangelicalism. Evangelical Christianity, for long regarded by historians as an enthusiastic, heartwarming, and experiential reaction against the aridity and skepticism of the Age of Reason, has in recent years been increasingly interpreted as a movement whose origins and contours owe an immense debt to the philosophical and cultural patterns of the Enlightenment. "The evangelical version of Protestantism," writes David Bebbington in what has become the standard work on evangelicalism in Britain, "was created by the Enlightenment."[3] W. R. Ward has shown how the

---

2. David J. Bosch, *Transforming Mission: Paradigm Shifts in Theology of Mission* (Maryknoll, N.Y., 1991), pp. 2-7, 349-67.

3. D. W. Bebbington, *Evangelicalism in Modern Britain: A History from the 1730s to the 1980s* (London, 1989), p. 74; see also D. W. Bebbington, "Revival and Enlightenment in

"heart religion" of Count Zinzendorf, father figure to much of the eighteenth-century awakening, was indebted in various paradoxical ways to Enlightenment thought.[4] Similar work by Mark Noll and others on American evangelicalism has demonstrated its essential congruity with Enlightenment ideals and patterns of thought.[5] While recent studies of popular religion in eighteenth-century Britain have emphasized the extent to which ordinary people responded to the evangelical message in ways that did not conform to Enlightenment norms of order, reason, and individual choice,[6] evangelicalism as a theological system can no longer be dismissed as intrinsically anti-intellectual or irrational. On the contrary, the particular blend that evangelicalism achieved between the doctrines of grace and the canons of empiricism and common-sense philosophy has come to be widely recognized as the key that unlocks not simply the distinctive tenets of evangelical theology itself but also such wider mysteries as early nineteenth-century political economy or the character of the dominant intellectual tradition of the United States in the antebellum era.[7]

It is no surprise that this trend has been carried over into studies of the missionary movement, that most vigorous and arguably unruly of the offspring of the eighteenth-century Protestant awakenings. David J. Bosch devoted one of the most substantial chapters of his seminal textbook on historical missiology, *Transforming Mission,* to the subject of "Mission in the Wake of the Enlightenment." Bosch was not afraid to make sweeping claims about the nature of the relationship, asserting that "the entire modern missionary

---

Eighteenth-century England," in *Modern Christian Revivals,* edited by Edith L. Blumhofer and Randall Balmer (Urbana and Chicago, 1993), pp. 17-41.

4. W. R. Ward, "Enlightenment in Early Moravianism," in W. R. Ward, *Faith and Faction* (London, 1993), pp. 95-111.

5. For an excellent brief summary of Noll's extensive writings on this theme, see his *A History of the Churches in the United States and Canada* (Grand Rapids and London, 1992), pp. 154-57; see also n. 7 below.

6. For examples see Deborah Valenze, *Prophetic Sons and Daughters: Female Preaching and Popular Religion in Industrial England* (Princeton, 1978); David Luker, "Revivalism in Theory and Practice: The Case of Cornish Methodism," *Journal of Ecclesiastical History* 37 (1986): 603-19; David Hempton, *The Religion of the People: Methodism and Popular Religion c. 1750-1900* (London, 1996).

7. Boyd Hilton, *The Age of Atonement: The Influence of Evangelicalism on Social and Economic Thought, 1785-1865* (Oxford, 1988); Mark A. Noll, "The Rise and Long Life of the Protestant Enlightenment in America," in *Knowledge and Belief in America: Enlightenment Traditions and Modern Religious Thought,* edited by William M. Shea and Peter A. Huff (Washington, D.C., and Cambridge, 1995), pp. 88-124. For a recent judicious assessment of the extent of evangelical indebtedness to Scottish common sense philosophy see Harriet A. Harris, *Fundamentalism and Evangelicals* (Oxford, 1998).

enterprise is, to a very real extent, a child of the Enlightenment"; and, similarly, that "The entire western missionary movement of the past three centuries emerged from the matrix of the Enlightenment."[8] According to Bosch, emphases derived from the Enlightenment provided *the* defining or paradigmatic features of the Protestant missionary movement from its origins in the eighteenth century until the collapse of Enlightenment rationality in the postmodernist crisis of the late twentieth century. The Methodist scholar Kenneth Cracknell has applied the same theme to the fiercely contested question of Christian attitudes to world religions. The radical denial by nineteenth-century missionaries of salvific significance to other religious traditions was due, writes Cracknell, "not only to their mediaeval and reformation inheritances but to the new rationalism which was becoming prevalent in both Europe and America."[9] Although Cracknell admits that the legacy of both medieval and Reformation thought played its part, the dismissal of non-Christian religions as idolatry or superstition is for him explicable primarily in terms of the preeminent value placed on rationality by evangelical Protestantism in the Enlightenment era.[10]

These recent approaches to the intellectual framework of evangelical Protestantism and its missionary expressions have proved extremely fertile, not least in stimulating new perspectives on the mental culture of missionaries and their domestic supporters. This book seeks to reinforce, and in no way to undermine, the central contention of such writing that the modern Protestant missionary movement cannot be understood unless full attention is paid to the intellectual milieu within which evangelicalism was shaped. Moreover, it broadly supports the now established consensus that this milieu was essentially one formed by the intellectual contours of the Enlightenment. In chapter two, Andrew Walls demonstrates convincingly that the origins of the modern Protestant missionary movement lie not, as conventional wisdom would have it, in late eighteenth-century English evangelicalism but in a continental and primarily Germanic Pietist tradition stretching back a century earlier to the era in which the Protestant *Aufklärung* first made its protest against the rigidities of confessional orthodoxy.[11] Those isolated dissenting voices that have recently claimed that, on the contrary, early nineteenth-

8. Bosch, *Transforming Mission*, pp. 274, 344.

9. Kenneth Cracknell, *Justice, Courtesy and Love: Theologians and Missionaries Encountering World Religions, 1846-1914* (London, 1995), p. 14.

10. Cracknell, *Justice, Courtesy and Love*, pp. 14-20.

11. For the essentially religious nature of the Protestant Enlightenment in Germany see Joachim Whaley, "The Protestant Enlightenment in Germany," in *The Enlightenment in National Context*, edited by Roy Porter and Mikuláš Teich (Cambridge, 1981), pp. 111-12.

century evangelicalism should be viewed as a counter-Enlightenment Romantic ideology have not, in the view of the contributors to this volume, advanced a persuasive case.[12] Yet the fact that such voices are beginning to make themselves heard suggests that it is time to pose some questions to what has become the historiographical orthodoxy on this subject. Historiographical orthodoxies develop their vigor on the basis of innovative research and writing, in their maturity spawn further creative interpretations, but then in their scholarly middle age run the risk of becoming overweight and ponderous, bloated with a surfeit of conference papers and publications dedicated to ever more meticulous analysis of their central preoccupations. The study of evangelicalism and the Enlightenment has, thankfully, not reached that stage. This volume is to be read as a sympathetic contribution from those who are concerned to ensure that this profitable line of inquiry is kept lean and hungry by the discipline of challenge and questioning.

In certain circles in both historical and theological scholarship, "the Enlightenment" is in danger of becoming a term of abuse, a trend that needs no definition but only repeated censure. As Richard Bernstein has complained, postmodernist writing essentializes and universalizes the Enlightenment that it attacks, and thus ironically falls prey to the very intellectual fashions that it professes to deplore as characteristic of Enlightenment discourse.[13] In the churches, this habit of mind may be due in some measure to the popularization and oversimplification of the extremely important writings of the late Lesslie Newbigin, who cogently identified the Enlightenment separation of fact and value as lying at the root of the malaise of Christianity in contemporary Western society.[14] We are all post-Enlightenment people now. For Christians, the consequent temptation is to identify theologies of which they disapprove with the Enlightenment, and then to employ the identification as a facile device for cutting loose from moorings that may turn out to be more deeply embedded in the banks of Christian tradition than such an equation would suggest.

Among historians of modern Protestant mission, a similar temptation rears its head with peculiar force, in part because many of them remain woe-

12. For example, Doug Stuart, "'Of Savages and Heroes': Discourses of Race, Nation and Gender in the Evangelical Missions to Southern Africa in the Early Nineteenth Century," Ph.D. thesis, University of London, 1994.

13. Richard J. Bernstein, "Are We beyond the Enlightenment Horizon?" in Shea and Huff, *Knowledge and Belief in America*, p. 338.

14. See especially Newbigin's *The Gospel in a Pluralist Society* (London, 1989). For a recent study of Newbigin's missiology see George R. Hunsberger, *Bearing the Witness of the Spirit: Lesslie Newbigin's Theology of Cultural Plurality* (Grand Rapids, 1998).

fully ignorant of the earlier Roman Catholic missionary tradition, and in part because the scope for finding a genuinely pre-Enlightenment model of Protestant mission as a control against which to measure the Enlightenment missionary paradigm is necessarily rather limited. Bosch's chapter on "The Missionary Paradigm of the Protestant Reformation" is predictably much shorter than his following chapter on "Mission in the Wake of the Enlightenment," and it begs some large historical questions by placing the origins of Pietism in the former rather than the latter.[15] It is no surprise that Bosch had to concede that "the Enlightenment macro-paradigm remains elusive and manifests itself, at best, in a variety of sub-paradigms, some of which appear to be in tension, even conflict, with others."[16] Whether this assortment of frequently contradictory subparadigms remains in any meaningful sense a "paradigm" is clearly open to debate. Bosch's admission that mission in the Enlightenment era "was much more diverse and multifaceted than ever before" may point to the conclusion that the Enlightenment ought rather to be understood as an emancipation of the individual reason from paradigmatic ways of thinking.[17] Certainly one does not have to dip very far into the scholarly literature on the impact of the Enlightenment on Western views of the non-Western world to realize that, in the hands of different writers, "the Enlightenment" is wheeled out as an interpretative device to explain mutually contradictory trends. The Enlightenment has been blamed by many for making Westerners more arrogant and racist; yet it has been credited by others with making them more tolerant and open to learn. Some authors have identified the Enlightenment confidence in progress as one source of the missionary imperative, while others have seen Enlightenment values as fundamentally subversive of the Christian missionary project.

The great majority of Anglophone nineteenth-century evangelicals, had they been able to eavesdrop on this scholarly conversation, would, of course, have been totally mystified. According to Owen Chadwick and the *Oxford English Dictionary*, the term "Enlightenment" as an English rendering of the German term *Aufklärung* first appears in 1865, followed in 1889 by the first use by Edward Caird of the phrase "the Age of Enlightenment."[18] Even if late

---

15. Bosch, *Transforming Mission*, pp. 252-55. Bosch argued on p. 276 that Pietism *later* succumbed to the influence of the Enlightenment, but, for a convincing case that Pietism and the Enlightenment were closely related from the outset, see W. R. Ward, "Orthodoxy, Enlightenment and Religious Revival," reprinted in his *Faith and Faction*, pp. 16-37.

16. Bosch, *Transforming Mission*, p. 285.

17. Bosch, *Transforming Mission*, p. 339.

18. Owen Chadwick, *The Secularization of the European Mind in the Nineteenth*

Victorian evangelicals had heard the term, they would have taken it to refer to the religious skepticism of the French encyclopedists and reacted with indignant incomprehension to the implication that their brand of godliness had anything in common with the thought of Voltaire or Rousseau. In the period of the Evangelical Revival, as Chadwick points out, British Protestant writers placed themselves in a national tradition that conceived of the relationship between religion and progress in terms that were diametrically opposed to the views of that relationship held by those French writers whom a later generation came to regard as the fathers of the Enlightenment.[19] The fact that past generations of Christians would not have understood the charge that is now being leveled against them may, of course, be taken as clinching evidence of how all-pervasive their intellectual conditioning actually was, but it ought at least to alert us to the difficulties involved in taking a term introduced into the English language in the late nineteenth century with one quite precise meaning in mind, applying it to a far broader and more diverse spectrum of intellectual and cultural trends, and then invoking that term as an explanation of why this tradition of Christians believed what they did about the world and their role within it.

Note should be taken of the protests that leading historians of ideas have recently made against the very term "The Enlightenment." J. G. A. Pocock has advocated the dropping of the definite article, on the grounds that its continued use presupposes that there was a single unitary process displaying a uniform set of characteristics in Europe and North America. We should rather remind ourselves, argues Pocock, that the term "Enlightenment" is simply a tool "which we use to isolate a variety of phenomena which we suspect were similar, were interrelated, were the product of a shared history; after which we may proceed to enquire into how far our suspicions may or may not be justified."[20] Bernstein agrees: "There is no single platform, no set of substantive claims, no common essence that the thinkers of the age of Enlightenment share."[21] If there was a common element in Enlightenment trends, according to Lester Crocker, it consisted less in *what* people thought than in *how* they thought, since Enlightenment people thought many irreconcilable things in pursuit of inquiries and proposals that were "often wildly

---

Century (Cambridge, 1975), p. 151. *Aufklärung* itself was used from the 1780s, but only widely from the nineteenth century.

19. Chadwick, *The Secularization of the European Mind,* p. 148.

20. J. G. A. Pocock, "Enlightenment and Revolution: The Case of English-speaking North America," in *Transactions of the Seventh International Congress on the Enlightenment* (Oxford, 1989), p. 252.

21. Bernstein, "Are We beyond the Enlightenment Horizon?" p. 336.

different from one another," yet shared a common determination to rethink everything free from the constraints of authority.[22] Even that definition is arguably too tight, since it brands Enlightenment thinking with the imprint of radical free thought, an equation that cannot be sustained in every case, nor even, arguably, in the majority of cases. In many parts of Europe, and even in North America, Enlightenment people were just as likely to extol the conservative virtues of order, harmony, balance, and discipline as the contrary principles of radicalism.[23]

The chapters that follow discuss the various features that are most frequently held to be distinctive of the conduct of Christian mission within the modern Protestant tradition, principally in relation to the eighteenth and early nineteenth centuries. Among these various features five impress themselves on the present-day observer with particular clarity. First, an almost universal belief that non-Western peoples were "heathens," lost in the degradation of sin and in need of salvation through the gospel of Christ. Second, a parallel tendency to dismiss other religious systems either as "heathen idolatry" or as at best superstitions and not religions at all, and hence as devoid of any trace of the presence of God. Third, a belief in the manifest superiority and liberating potential of Western "civilization," in both its intellectual and its technological aspects. Fourth, an unshakable confidence in the regenerative capacity of rational knowledge, always provided this was linked to Christian proclamation. Fifth, an assumption that the Christian message was addressed principally to individuals, calling them to undergo a conscious and identifiable inner experience of personal "conversion" to Christ. Of these five central features, however, only the fourth and fifth can be "explained" with any semblance of plausibility by primary reference to the Enlightenment, and even in these cases the argument can be sustained only with considerable subtlety and qualification. Each of the first three, and in lesser measure even the fourth and fifth, can be shown to be rooted in older, pre-Enlightenment traditions. In the case of all five features, however, it can be maintained that certain philosophical emphases current in the Enlightenment were partially, or in some instances even wholly, responsible for the *way* in which missionaries in the modern period reworked these long-established Christian patterns of thinking about the Christian encounter with non-Christian faiths and cultures. What cannot be supported, however, is any simple ascription of the

22. Lester G. Crocker, "Introduction," in *The Blackwell Companion to the Enlightenment*, edited by John W. Yolton (Oxford, 1991), p. 1.

23. Bebbington, "Revival and Enlightenment in Eighteenth-century England," p. 27; Noll, "The Rise and Long Life of the Protestant Enlightenment in America," pp. 102-6.

patterns themselves to a supposedly unitary body of philosophy labeled "The Enlightenment."

The conviction of evangelical missionaries that non-Christians were lost in their sin and dependent on the gospel of Christ for salvation was one that evangelicals shared with both their Catholic and their Protestant forbears. It was grounded on the theology of the Pauline epistles and the Augustinian tradition that mediated that theology to Catholic Christendom. If evangelicals reiterated these emphases with greater passion and urgency than did their predecessors, it was because they were unambiguously people of the Book, men and women whose consciousness was soaked in the Bible and whose own experience confirmed the scriptural testimony to the natural depravity of humanity and the sovereignty of divine grace. These convictions flew in the face of the confidence that most Enlightenment thinkers placed in natural moral capacity and the autonomy of reason.[24] For evangelical missionaries, therefore, as Jane Samson demonstrates in chapter five with reference to the Pacific, observation of non-Western societies was always refracted through the lens of the biblical testimony to the nature and condition of unredeemed humanity. Evangelicals were predisposed to reject those eighteenth-century thinkers who projected an ideal image of the "noble savage," and instead to locate the peoples they encountered on a theological map drawn by the apostle Paul in the first chapter of the letter to the Romans.[25] Nevertheless, as Samson points out, this repudiation of Enlightenment optimism about the state of humanity did not entail an equal repudiation of the current enthusiasm for classifying and ranking the range of human societies: evangelical missionaries found it possible to combine a biblical insistence upon the unity of humanity in sin and grace with an interest in ethnographic classification and racial genealogy.

Second, the identification of non-Christian religious systems as idolatry is at least as old as Tertullian, since it was rooted in the biblical tradition urging Israel to maintain uncompromising opposition to the religion of the Canaanites. Determination to extirpate "pagan idolatry" was a dominant motif in the sixteenth-century Spanish conquest of Central and South America. Although there was a disagreement between those, such as Bartolomé de las Casas, who saw idolatry as a natural product of post-Babel human religiosity, and the majority of Spanish exegetes, who believed idolatry to be demonically

24. Noll, "The Rise and Long Life of the Protestant Enlightenment in America," pp. 96-98.

25. On this theme see Andrew F. Walls, "Romans One and the Missionary Movement," in Andrew F. Walls, *The Missionary Movement in Christian History: Studies in the Transmission of Faith* (Edinburgh and Maryknoll, N.Y., 1996), pp. 55-67.

inspired, the application of Old Testament categories of Canaanite idolatry to indigenous religions was, if anything, even more sweeping than in later Protestant missionary thought.[26] The differences between Catholic and Protestant delineations of heathen idolatry have relatively little to do with the Enlightenment and much more to do with Protestant anti-Catholicism, which led missionaries to find analogues in non-Christian societies for the "priestcraft" that they abominated at home. Neither can the further option, common to many early nineteenth-century missionaries in southern Africa, of denying that traditional religionists possessed any "religion" at all be attributed simply to Enlightenment preconceptions: claims of the total absence of religion among the inhabitants of the New World were quite widely made by the earliest European voyagers.[27]

Third, Europeans have believed in the intrinsic superiority of their civilization from classical times and have consistently located that superiority in their supposedly unrivaled capacity to "improve" the natural world by technological innovation. During the eighteenth century, as Penny Carson shows in relation to India in chapter three, that belief was increasingly cast in terms of the ability of European civilization to bestow the benefits of rationality, progress, liberty, and happiness. The terms were distinctive to the Enlightenment era, but the confidence that lay behind them was not. The Enlightenment creed of human progress was constructed on the foundation of a Renaissance confidence in human creative capacity grounded in the philosophy of Aristotle.[28] It was also, as Andrew Walls points out in chapter two, bolted on to a concept of Christendom as a European territorial entity that was first established by the conversion of the tribal peoples of northwest Europe from the eighth century onwards. Those nineteenth-century Christians in Britain and North America who equated (and not all of them did so) the adoption by non-Western peoples of Western civilization with "progress" made that equation not just because they were Enlightenment people but also because they were heirs to this tradition that made little conceptual separation between the expansion of Europe and the expansion of Christendom.

The fourth point is closely related to the third. Medieval Christian apolo-

---

26. Pierre Duviols, *La lutte contre les religions autochtones dans le Pérou colonial: "l'extirpation de l'idolâtrie" entre 1532 et 1660* (Lima, n.d.), pp. 21-23.

27. David Chidester, *Savage Systems: Colonialism and Comparative Religion in Southern Africa* (Charlottesville and London, 1996), pp. 11-12. Chidester concedes that such denial of the presence of religion was not universal, being impossible to make in the case of the Aztecs or Incas, for example.

28. Anthony Pagden, *European Encounters with the New World: From Renaissance to Romanticism* (New Haven and London, 1993), p. 6.

getic against Islam had made much of the supposed rational superiority of Christianity, particularly after the Aristotelian revolution of the thirteenth century. Thomas Aquinas's *Summa Contra Gentiles* (1264), written as a manual for Christian missionaries in Islamic Spain, employed Aristotelian categories of reason to demonstrate the truth of Christianity. Such categories, mediated through Aquinas in particular, established the intellectual parameters for the first encounter between European Christian "civility" and non-Western "barbarism" in the New World of Spanish America in the sixteenth and early seventeenth centuries.[29] The disjunction between "rational" European and "irrational" "savage" was thus no invention of the eighteenth century. The *philosophers* of the French Enlightenment took a dim view of Africans, regarding them as barbarians without rationality or industry.[30] What was, however, new about eighteenth-century thought was its increasing tendency to assert the *intrinsic* unity and equality of all humanity and to explain the manifest differences between "primitive" and "civilized" peoples in terms of the impact of the environment. If a tropical climate and deprivation of rational influences explained the degraded state of the African, then it followed that a change of environment and, above all, the inculcation of rational principles through education had the potential to raise even the most degraded specimen of humanity to the heights of civilization.[31]

This body of assumptions had two extremely important consequences for evangelicalism. The first was that evangelical Christians were much more inclined than their predecessors in Christian history to insist on the fundamental unity of humanity as a foundational principle of biblical teaching. Evangelical apologetic for missions appealed to the basic humanity of the "heathen" as constituting in itself a reason for seeking to restore to them those dimensions of a fully human existence that had been supposedly lost as a result of sin. "Can we as men, or as Christians," asked William Carey in his *Enquiry,*

> hear that a great part of our fellow creatures, whose souls are as immortal as ours, and who are as capable as ourselves, of adorning the gospel, and contributing by their preaching, writing, or practices to the glory of the Redeemer's name, and the good of his church, are inveloped in ignorance and barbarism? Can we hear that they are without the gospel,

29. Pagden, *European Encounters with the New World,* pp. 53-55.
30. William B. Cohen, *The French Encounter with Africans: White Response to Blacks, 1530-1880* (Bloomington and London, 1980), p. 67.
31. Cohen, *The French Encounter with Africans,* pp. 73-79.

without government, without laws, and without arts and sciences; and not exert ourselves to introduce amongst them the sentiments of men, and of Christians?[32]

The centrality of this conviction of the unity of humanity to evangelical missionary discourse goes some way towards justifying Bosch's bold claim that "the entire modern missionary enterprise is, to a very real extent, a child of the Enlightenment."[33] Chapter eight will return to this theme at greater length.

In the second place, the literature of the early missionary movement displays an immense confidence in the elevating and illuminating capacity of knowledge and rational argument — a confidence that is explicable only in terms of the philosophical environment of the eighteenth and early nineteenth centuries. Evangelicals could never concede that the regenerative capacity of knowledge was absolute. Their continuing adherence to the biblical insistence that a lost humanity could be redeemed only through faith in Christ implied that the role of education and other instruments of "civilization" could be no more than auxiliary to the central task of communicating the gospel of the cross. Thus even that most "Moderate" of the Scottish evangelicals, Alexander Duff, set his face in India against the separation of Western education from the teaching of Christianity.[34] Nevertheless, it was in the Indian subcontinent more than any other mission field that evangelicals were forced by the paucity of response to their call for conversion to place more and more reliance on the supposed ability of both education and rational polemic to lighten the darkness of the "heathen" mind. Confronted by obdurate Hindus or Buddhists in India or Ceylon (now Sri Lanka), evangelical missionaries engaged in verbal and written polemic in what inevitably proved a futile endeavor to convince their audience of the truth and reasonableness of Christian doctrine.[35] As the discussion in chapter eight of the relationship between Christianity and civilization in the missionary movement will suggest, field experience could push mission theory towards forms of orthodoxy that conformed more closely to the canons of the Enlightenment than to the canons of Holy Scripture.

32. William Carey, *An Enquiry into the Obligations of Christians to Use Means for the Conversion of the Heathens . . .* , new facsimile ed., edited by Ernest A. Payne (London, 1961), pp. 69-70.

33. See n. 7 above.

34. See below, p. 140. For a full discussion of Duff's view of the inadequacy of Western knowledge to undermine Hinduism in isolation from Christianity see Gauri Viswanathan, *Masks of Conquest: Literary Study and British Rule* (London, 1990), pp. 52-64.

The fifth marked feature of the modern Protestant missionary tradition sheds further light on the precise nature of the intellectual reshaping wrought during the Enlightenment era. It has been powerfully argued by Peter van der Veer and Peter van Rooden that the "privatization" of religious belief and conversion characteristic of evangelical Protestantism was articulated as a solution to the political dilemmas posed by confessional conflict in post-Reformation Europe. The increasing acceptance by European states from the late seventeenth century onwards of the reality of religious pluralism dictated the withdrawal of religion from the public to the private sphere. The obverse of the Enlightenment's insistence on religious toleration was the claim that religious belief must be left to the individual. Formerly a matter of public allegiance to the religious establishment, it now became a voluntary act of the individual will. A separation between formal religious profession and authentic personal commitment was the necessary price of civil stability and progress. The "conversion narrative" recording the experimental nature of the subject's acquisition of true faith thus became common in the seventeenth century as a sign of this distinctively modern view of religion. The missionary movement, according to van Rooden, was both the product and promoter of this voluntarization of religion. The locus of Christian commitment had moved from the state church to the voluntary society of "true," converted believers, and such societies pursued the goal of the dissemination of true Christianity both within formal Christendom and beyond it: the public sphere could be regenerated only indirectly, through the associated power of regenerated individuals. The distinction between the public and the private spheres became accepted as a mark of "civilization" because on such a distinction rested the ability to identify "true" conversions. Evangelical missionaries therefore sought to transform "heathen" societies by means of procuring genuine individual conversions, and they anticipated that on the mission field, as at home, such private acts of religious commitment could be divorced from issues of communal identity and public allegiance.[36]

---

35. See especially R. F. Young and S. Jebanesan, *The Bible Trembled: The Hindu-Christian Controversies of Nineteenth-Century Ceylon* (Vienna, 1995); R. F. Young and G. P. V. Somaratna, *Vain Debates: The Buddhist-Christian Controversies of Nineteenth-Century Ceylon* (Vienna, 1996).

36. Peter van der Veer, ed., *Conversion to Modernities: The Globalization of Christianity* (New York and London, 1996). The above paragraph summarizes the argument of van der Veer's introduction (pp. 1-21), and especially of the chapter by Peter van Rooden, "Nineteenth-century Representations of Missionary Conversion and the Transformation of Western Christianity" (pp. 65-87).

This is a compelling argument, and one that is substantially supported by Andrew Walls's analysis of the voluntary missionary society in its European context in chapter two and by Bruce Hindmarsh's study of early evangelical conversion in chapter four. Professor Walls agrees that the predominantly voluntarist model of Protestant missionary agency, foreshadowed by the Pietists and the Moravians and developed more fully in Britain from the 1790s, enabled evangelical Christians to combine acceptance of the framework of Christendom with an Enlightenment confidence in individual responsibility, tempered by the Pietist emphasis on the fellowship of the "renewed." It also facilitated a union of missionary zeal with assumptions about the indispensability of mechanisms of corporate organization, logistical support, and printed information that owed much to Enlightenment confidence in human capacity.[37] It is symptomatic that the publication that is frequently (but, as Walls shows, quite misleadingly) interpreted as the herald of the Protestant missionary awakening, William Carey's *An Enquiry into the Obligations of Christians to Use Means for the Conversion of the Heathens* (1792) should rely on a process of rational inquiry to convince his fellow Baptists that a set of coordinated voluntary measures — "means" — could and should be employed by a company of "serious Christians" in order to achieve a divinely prescribed goal. Hindmarsh similarly suggests that the evangelical conversion narrative flourished "when Christendom, or Christian civil society, had eroded far enough to allow for toleration, dissent, experimentation, and the manifestation of nominal and sincere forms of adherence to faith, but not so far as to elide a traditional sense of Christian moral norms and basic cosmological assumptions."[38] Evangelical Christians saw conversion as an intense drama culminating in conviction of sin and a free and conscious choice by the individual (albeit under the persuasive influence of the Holy Spirit) to yield his or her sphere of individual sovereignty to the lordship of Christ. This conception of religious change to "real Christianity" was formed against the backcloth of the formal Christianity of confessional Christendom, whether in Lutheran, Reformed, or Anglican guise. When mission experience beyond the boundaries of Christendom began to throw up instances of decisions to adopt the Christian faith in which collective indigenous perceptions of what was good for the community (including what was good in material terms) played a greater part than individual awareness of guilt, evangelicals struggled to find acceptable criteria for evaluating the authenticity of the resulting conversions. As Vanessa Smith has recently argued with reference to the Pacific,

37. See below, pp. 29-30.
38. See below, p. 97.

early nineteenth-century missionaries were haunted by the fear of insincere conversions spawned by the false attractions of material improvement or the acquisition of the supposedly occult power of literacy.[39]

Walls's chapter helps to answer those questions that are left unanswered by the thesis of van der Veer and van Rooden. The apparently protracted time lapse between the emergence of conversionist Protestantism in the seventeenth century and the general appearance of voluntary societies committed to global mission at the close of the eighteenth century should not perplex us overmuch, for Anglophone writing of Church history has exaggerated the novelty of what Carey "began" in 1792 and obscured the indebtedness of British missions to earlier continental models. Similarly, the question, raised implicitly by van der Veer and van Rooden's thesis, of why substantial segments of evangelicalism in England and Scotland should have remained strongly committed to the maintenance and propagation overseas of religious establishments becomes less problematic when we take account of Walls's argument that the distinctiveness of the Evangelical Revival lay in its ambiguous and inherently unstable amalgam of an Anabaptist commitment to voluntary religion with a desire to reinforce national, territorial Christianity by means of its spiritual renewal.[40] Hence nineteenth-century Protestant missions tended to oscillate between continuing admiration for the territorial vision that had animated European Christendom in its first encounter with the non-Western world in the sixteenth century — a vision of unitary Christian polities governed by a partnership of church and state dedicated to the overthrow of "heathen idolatry" — and a separatist vision of a church set apart from the structures of an apostate world, seeking to renew society by the evangelism of individuals rather than by imposed structural change. On the whole, however, somewhat contrary to the implications of van der Veer's and van Rooden's theory, it was the former model that predominated. What the Enlightenment did was to transform the Anabaptist concept of voluntary religion from its previous status as a threat to the stability of Christian society into a means of preserving that stability amid the disruptive forces of confessional conflict and challenges to Church authority. The paradox of much evangelical Christianity was that it sought to use the model of the believers' church to shore up the creaking structures of Christendom in Europe and even reconstruct them overseas.

Wherever the Enlightenment creed of toleration was transposed to a con-

39. Vanessa Smith, *Literary Culture and the Pacific: Nineteenth-Century Textual Encounters* (Cambridge, 1998), pp. 1-3, 53-81.
40. See below, pp. 30, 41.

text in which Christianity was a minority religion, ambiguities surfaced that began to unravel the inconsistencies within the amalgam of the evangelical version of the Enlightenment. Gauri Viswanathan's study of the development of English literature in British India argues that Alexander Duff's opposition to the secularist policy of the East India Company stemmed from fear of the moral and social consequences of any attempt to divorce the educational process from the teaching of religion.[41] As Penny Carson discusses in chapter three of this volume, the demands of religious and moral "improvement" in India after 1813 ran counter to that other Enlightenment ideal of the religiously neutral state. Thus Anglican evangelicals opposed the *de facto* religious establishment of Hinduism by the East India Company by deploying two arguments that were ultimately inconsistent: on the one hand, they decried such establishment as an infringement of the free toleration that ought to be bestowed on Christians in the company's territories; on the other hand, they claimed, in terms derived from historic European Christendom, that the company government owed an obligation to God to give distinctive and official support to the tenuous Christian missionary presence. Furthermore, their campaign for an Anglican episcopate, which gained its object in the renewal of the company charter in 1813, argued either explicitly or implicitly for the extension of religious establishment from England to India. Carson has demonstrated that in 1813 Anglican evangelicals stayed aloof from the radical petitioning campaign mounted by the nonconformist churches to secure entrance for missions into India; the libertarian language of natural rights employed by the campaign was alien to their thinking, even though at heart they shared the desire of their dissenting brethren to see full toleration for mission activity.[42] Evangelicals of different denominational persuasions thus reacted with varying degrees of enthusiasm and caution to the political vocabulary of the Enlightenment. Elsewhere, notably in the island kingdoms of the Pacific, even dissenting evangelicals often attempted to re-create on the mission field the monolithic Protestant establishments that they had dismissed as nominal or oppressive at home.

It is increasingly accepted that there was not one Enlightenment but several during the eighteenth century. In what ways the distinctive features of the German Protestant Enlightenment were mediated to the CMS and LMS by the large number of their early missionaries who were Germans or who trained at Berlin or Basel remains an intriguing question for further research. Walls notes one such area of intellectual importance in chapter two by point-

41. Viswanathan, *Masks of Conquest,* pp. 7-8, 36-37, 46-49, 64-65.
42. See below, pp. 66-67.

ing out the seminal role played by German CMS missionaries such as J. F. Schön or S. W. Koelle in the pioneering of African linguistics.[43] Nevertheless, the Enlightenment that did most to mold English-speaking evangelicalism in general and the missionary movement in particular was that in Scotland. Various scholars have demonstrated the peculiar importance of Scottish "common-sense" philosophy in shaping the intellectual milieu of American Protestantism in the period up to 1865.[44] The same Scottish intellectual tradition that gave birth to common-sense philosophy also exercised a disproportionate influence on mission theory. In India it was mediated through the commanding figure of Alexander Duff. In South Africa, it was represented by leading missionaries such as John Philip or David Livingstone and educational institutions such as the Lovedale institution, founded by the Glasgow Missionary Society in 1841. In the Pacific, its leading early representative was John Love, secretary of the LMS, who endeavored to model the Tahiti mission on the civilizing principles he had learnt from the Scottish Moderates. Perhaps the dominating concern of the eighteenth-century Scottish Enlightenment was with the creation of the conditions for individual and collective virtue through an educational process dedicated to the imparting of rational knowledge, especially knowledge of the history of human social development.[45] It was this body of ideas that proved so determinative in shaping the thinking of nineteenth-century missionaries — from England and America as well as Scotland — on the central question of how the "heathen" were to be civilized.

Chapter six introduces this theme by analyzing the debate conducted within the Church of Scotland from 1750 to 1835 between "evangelical" and "rational" Calvinists over what was the correct sequence to be followed in propagating the gospel to "uncivilized" people: should one begin with apostolic preaching, or was it necessary first to inculcate rationality by educational means? This debate set the parameters for the educational mission enterprise adopted by Alexander Duff in Calcutta, a venture that established the direction of Protestant mission policy in India for the best part of a century. What emerges from Ian Maxwell's analysis is a sense that in the missions of the

43. See below, pp. 38-39.

44. E.g., Henry F. May, *The Enlightenment in America* (New York, 1976); Noll, "The Rise and Long Life of the Protestant Enlightenment in America," pp. 93-94, 99-106; Mark A. Noll, *Princeton and the Republic, 1768-1822: The Search for a Christian Enlightenment in the Era of Samuel Stanhope Smith* (Princeton, 1989); Douglas Sloan, *The Scottish Enlightenment and the American College Ideal* (New York, 1971).

45. See David Allan, *Virtue, Learning and the Scottish Enlightenment: Ideas of Scholarship in Early Modern History* (Edinburgh, 1993).

Church of Scotland the long-established confidence in the superiority of European knowledge within the Christian inheritance was molded according to the specific contours of the Scottish Enlightenment in three particular respects. One was the understanding of Christianity as a form of superstructure that depended on a foundation of the principles of natural religion. A second distinguishing feature of the Scottish Moderate tradition was a confidence that divine providence worked as much through rational argument and the dynamics of economic and social progress as through more obviously spiritual means. A third emphasis, formed by a union of the other two, was the assumption that there was a providential moment inclining a nation or society to accept the superiority of Christianity, a moment that was defined by that nation or society's stage of "civilization." It was this belief, Maxwell demonstrates, that inspired the General Assembly's project of an educational institution in Calcutta, which Duff was appointed in 1829 to initiate.

The intellectual categories of the Scottish Enlightenment equally fixed the parameters of missionary expectations of African progress towards the goal of civilization, as Natasha Erlank's study of the Scottish mission to the Xhosa demonstrates in chapter seven. They also, crucially, inhibited the development of that mission, since Erlank indicates that the lack of enthusiasm in Scotland for the South African mission (relative to that shown for India) was rooted in Scottish Moderate skepticism about the capacity of "savages" to respond to the gospel without the preparatory leaven of Christian education. Only from 1863 to 1864 did the fortunes of the Xhosa mission revive, following Duff's visit to Xhosaland, his assumption of office as convenor of the Foreign Missions Committee of the Free Church of Scotland, and the subsequent concentration of resources on the formation of an educational elite at Lovedale under the principalship of James Stewart.

The English missionary movement was also deeply affected by the Scottish intellectual tradition. Significant numbers of Scots served with English societies, particularly the LMS: in its first one hundred years, 183 of the 1,023 missionaries sent out were Scottish.[46] Furthermore, most English nonconformist missionaries were trained in seminaries whose curricula were influenced more by Scottish than by English models. Nearly 40 percent of the LMS missionaries sent out in the first thirty years of the society's history (and 70 percent of those sent to India) were trained at the Gosport Academy and Missionary Seminary, whose principal was David Bogue, born and bred a Scottish Presbyterian. Though a convinced evangelical, Bogue was clearly influ-

46. James M. Calder, *Scotland's March Past: The Share of Scottish Churches in the London Missionary Society* (London, 1945), pp. 5, 10.

enced by the Scottish Moderate tradition, believing that missions should be directed first to civilized people who were more amenable to rational argument.[47] After Gosport, perhaps the most influential of the seminaries that trained missionaries for the LMS was the Glasgow Theological Academy, established in 1811. Students at the academy usually took science and philosophy classes at the University of Glasgow, and the academy's first tutors, Greville Ewing and Ralph Wardlaw, did much to shape a Scottish school of mission theory that combined evangelical zeal with confidence in the capacity of reason to support the claims of revelation.[48] Ewing was first secretary of the Edinburgh Missionary Society and the primary architect of Scottish Congregationalism. However, as a student at Edinburgh University under the principalship of William Robertson, he had been taught by leading Moderates such as Dugald Stewart.[49] Wardlaw, while a determined opponent of David Hume and all theories of the sufficiency of natural virtue, was one of the most influential writers persuading early nineteenth-century evangelicals of the harmony of inductive empirical science and biblical revelation.[50]

Chapter eight examines the various ways in which the originally Scottish debate about the relationship between evangelistic proclamation and "civilization" was conducted by missionaries in English societies in the late eighteenth and early nineteenth centuries. It seeks to relate this analysis to some of the illuminating recent writing from anthropologists and intellectual historians who have attempted to transcend the excessively periodized approach adopted by many historians of mission. It argues that, although missiological theory in the English societies from the 1820s onwards was almost uniformly hostile to the Scottish rational Calvinists' insistence on the priority of civilization, mission practice generally adhered to a working partnership between gospel proclamation and educational or economic improvement that undercut the consistent claims of evangelical rhetoric that the gospel was itself the divinely appointed engine of civilization. These themes will be exemplified by reference to the Pacific, and to the figure of Samuel Marsden in particular.

---

47. F. Stuart Piggin, *Making Evangelical Missionaries, 1789-1858: The Social Background, Motives and Training of British Protestant Missionaries to India* (Abingdon, 1984), pp. 156-57, 180.

48. Piggin, *Making Evangelical Missionaries*, pp. 164, 167-68.

49. J. J. Matheson, *A Memoir of Greville Ewing* (London, 1843), pp. 15-16. Other Moderates who taught Ewing included Andrew Dalzel, James Finlayson, and Thomas Hardy; see Richard B. Sher, *Church and University in the Scottish Enlightenment: The Moderate Literati of Edinburgh* (Edinburgh, 1985), pp. 139-40.

50. W. L. Alexander, *Memoirs of the Life and Writings of Ralph Wardlaw, D.D.* (Edinburgh, 1856), pp. 185-86, 327-28; see Hilton, *The Age of Atonement*, pp. 86, 180, 210-11.

The European "discovery" of Pacific populations had an analogous impact on the late eighteenth-century Western imagination to that exerted by the "discovery" of the New World of America on the European mind of the sixteenth century. The chapter goes on to show how evangelical variants of Scottish Enlightenment theories about the relationship of commerce and civilization to Christianity shaped the English mission enterprise through such channels as John Philip (a major influence on Sir Thomas Fowell Buxton) and David Livingstone. The chapter should thus make some contribution towards the historiographical task of identifying the longer-term contrasts and continuities between the patterns of conceiving religious and cultural difference exhibited by Protestant missionaries in the Enlightenment era and those apparent in their predecessors.[51]

Daniel W. Hardy's final chapter in this volume serves to remind readers whose interests lie more in the sphere of history than that of theology that the issues analyzed in this volume remain of more than merely academic interest for Christians today. The inclusion of a theological essay in a primarily historical collection is itself a post-Enlightenment statement: the academic disciplines of history and theology, formerly so rigidly separated by the canons of modernity, are now showing signs of renewed mutual recognition and even interpenetration. Hardy reflects on the fundamental theological issues raised for Christian mission by the implications of previous mission theory and practice in the intellectual frameworks of modernity. As a theologian, Hardy is interested in elucidating the criteria that determined the missionary movement's understanding of orthodoxy — and hence the application of theological norms to the experience of those to whom the missionaries went. He notes the various ways in which Christians reacted to the challenge of the Enlightenment. Of the models that he lists, this volume suggests that the majority of Protestant missionaries in the eighteenth and nineteenth centuries adhered either to what Hardy terms an "Enlightenment-reconstituting" position or to an "Enlightenment-instrumentalizing" one. By this he means that missionaries either embarked on a conscious defensive strategy of reconstituting Enlightenment norms of rationality in terms that were fully supportive of Christian orthodoxy or adopted a highly selective and purely instrumental approach that put Enlightenment methods at the service of Christian faith. These theological positions were inherently unstable amalgams. On the one hand, evangelical theology adhered to a doctrinal position that was antecedent to the Enlightenment and in fact openly hostile to the challenges that

51. See the comments of Nicholas Thomas, *Colonialism's Culture: Anthropology, Travel and Government* (Cambridge, 1994), p. 68.

some Enlightenment thinkers raised to the supreme authority of the Christian revelation. On the other hand, evangelical missionaries maintained philosophical or strategic stances that were essentially congruent with the Enlightenment in its more Christian forms, especially as manifested in Scotland. Such amalgams came under mounting strain in the course of the nineteenth century as mission experience called into question Enlightenment assumptions about the superiority of Western knowledge and, to some extent also, evangelical assumptions about the Christian claim to unique religious truth. After the First World War, these amalgams dissolved almost completely, as the increasingly polarized and newly defined "liberal" and "evangelical" sectors of Protestantism pursued divergent paths leading away from the Enlightenment inheritance. At the end of his chapter, Hardy outlines a proposal for constructing a new "Enlightenment-surpassing" foundation for Christian orthodoxy capable of sustaining the inescapable missionary imperative of Christianity in the context of a postmodern world.

CHAPTER TWO

The Eighteenth-Century Protestant Missionary Awakening in Its European Context

ANDREW F. WALLS

Christian history is the story of successive transformations of the Christian faith following its translation into a series of diverse cultural settings. Our topic, the Protestant missionary movement, is intimately related to one of these transformations that helped to change the demographic balance and cultural milieu of Christianity within a couple of centuries or so. When the movement began, the vast majority of those who professed and called themselves Christians — certainly more than nine out of ten — lived in Europe or North America. At the end of the twentieth century something like six out of ten of professing Christians live in Africa, Asia, Latin and Caribbean America, or the Pacific, and the proportion who do so rises year by year. The accession to the Christian faith that has taken place in the southern continents has been accompanied by a recession from it in Europe and North America. In the course of the twentieth century, Christianity has become a mainly non-Western religion. The implications of this for the future of Christian theology and liturgy, for Christian intellectual development and Christian impact on society, and for the relations of Christians with those of other faiths have hardly yet come into mature consideration.

This transformation of Christianity clearly arises from the impact of the Western upon the non-Western world. This is not the same as saying that it arises from the rise of the European empires or the establishment of European hegemony. Its relationship to the Western empires is a highly complex question. The Christian impact on the non-Western world sometimes preceded, sometimes followed the imperial structures, and the accession to

Christianity has become most noticeable since their collapse. We can now see that in the very period in which Christianity was taking hold in Africa and Asia, it was also being quietly but surely eroded in Europe. It is also possible to argue that the Western contact with the non-Western world, and the attempt to establish hegemony over it, contributed significantly to dissolving the special form of relationship between church and society that we call Christendom, that phenomenon that grew out of the early encounters with Christianity of the European peoples before the Roman Empire and that persisted long enough to be thought of as characteristic alike of Europe and of Christianity.[1] Experience taught that the religious settlements, achieved with such pain in so many European countries, could rarely be reproduced overseas, and that realization may well have hastened the decay of Christendom. Yet Christendom — the concept of Christianity as territorial — which lay at the heart of the European Christian experience, was not essential to the future of Christianity, and new expressions of the Christian faith have developed, and continue to develop, beyond Christendom in African and Asian societies. Africans, Asians, and Australasians became Christians for African and Asian and Australasian reasons. The most vigorously growing sector of contemporary Christian studies, the area of most potent discovery, is that which uncovers those processes and their subsequent manifestations within African, Asian, and Australasian Christianity.

All this indicates that African and Asian and Latin American Church history is not the same as missionary history; in itself, the missionary movement is a product of Western Church history. Nevertheless, the missionary movement is the terminal by which Western Christianity was connected to the non-Western world, and as such it has special importance as an object of study. It was both the principal medium in which Western Christianity made its impact on the non-Western world and the principal sense organ by which Western Christianity itself felt the impact of the non-Western world. There is therefore a good case for regarding it as one of the most permanently significant topics of Western Christian history. To understand it would be to understand better the present and perhaps the emerging state of the Christian faith, and yet, considered as an object of study, the missionary movement is by no means a well-worked field. Excellent standard treatments of the history of the Church in the modern West hardly mention it, and in this they accurately reflect the principal concerns of Western Christianity. The truth is that for most of the period of its existence, the missionary movement was not a major pre-

---

1. Cf. Andrew Walls, "Christianity in the Non-Western World: A Study in the Serial Nature of Christian Expansion," *Studies in World Christianity* 1.1 (1995): 1-25.

occupation of the Western Church. Those were periods, certainly, when the work of missions was celebrated and acclaimed in the West, but even then it was a marginal activity for all but a minority of Western Christians. There were other times when suspicion or contempt, or lukewarm recognition, or simple indifference, was the prevailing sentiment within the Western Church towards the missionary movement. Yet for most of the time that Church was simply too busy about its own local concerns to take much notice of what was known as "the mission field." Throughout their history, whether we are thinking of the leadership of the Western churches or of their membership, missions were the province of the enthusiasts rather than of the mainstream.

In the conventional historiography of the Western missionary movement, Roman Catholic writers, after due acknowledgment of such early figures as Ramón Lull and St. Francis, highlight the Iberian voyages of the late fifteenth century. They see the flowering of the movement in the early seventeenth century, followed by a loss of impetus and partial stagnation by the middle of the eighteenth century, then new life and vigor bursting out in the nineteenth to produce an unprecedented *plantatio ecclesiae*. Protestant writers ponder the question why the sixteenth-century Reformers say so little about the evangelization of the world, point to a dawning missionary consciousness among the Puritans, especially in their American manifestation, hail new signs of activity in the Moravian missions and in eighteenth-century India, and then describe the "real" Protestant awakening in the last years of the eighteenth century. This is symbolized (and many see as initiated) by William Carey's *Enquiry into the Obligations of Christians to Use Means for the Conversion of the Heathens* (1792) and by issues in the emergence of the early British missionary societies, following broadly denominational lines. This development in Britain, on this interpretation, is followed by an analogous movement in America and by another crop of societies in continental Europe. Bringing the basic elements of these stories together, one arrives at a picture of the missionary movement (and the author must confess to having written in such terms)[2] with two cycles, rather like the two cycles of imperialism, centered respectively on the Americas and on Asia, identified by D. K. Fieldhouse.[3] Of the equivalent cycles of missionary enterprise, the first is seen as originating in the last years of the fifteenth century and fading in the course of the eighteenth. This cycle is essentially one of Roman Catholic ac-

2. *Theologische Realenzyklopädie*, 4-Auflage, Bd XXIII (Berlin, 1994), s.v. "Mission VI," pp. 40-50.

3. D. K. Fieldhouse, *The Colonial Empires: A Comparative Study from the Eighteenth Century*, 2nd ed. (London, 1982).

tivity, though with a burst of Protestant growth in the later part of the period. The second cycle is identified in the second half of the eighteenth century, and gathers momentum in the nineteenth. This cycle, beginning in a period of decline for Catholic missions (symbolized by the suppression, through the influence of Catholic powers, of one of the most effective Catholic mission agencies, the Society of Jesus), is predominantly a Protestant movement in its origins, and its motor is the Evangelical Revival. New movements within the Catholic Church, however, produce a missionary revival during the nineteenth century, and the age of imperialism heightens the competition between traditionally Protestant and traditionally Catholic powers. Refinements of this model indicate how, by the mid-nineteenth century, all shades of Protestant churchmanship had endorsed the missionary movement, so that it was no longer an evangelical monopoly, and how from a point early in the twentieth century, North America progressively replaced Europe as the base of the missionary movement from the West. We need follow the second cycle no further into the period of decolonization and ecumenism, which also reflects decline and confusion in Western Christianity. Some would now see a new cycle of missionary movements emerging outside the West; no country now has a more focused missionary consciousness than Korea, nor has any other country mobilized a greater proportion of its population as missionaries, and this despite the fact that Korea's modern Christian history commenced only late in the nineteenth century.

The topic allotted to me requires an attempt to read the history of the missionary movement in a European context; and this exercise raises questions about the two-cycle model, and in particular its stress on the initiatives of the late eighteenth century. In the first place, a European context causes the Catholic and Protestant movements to be taken together, as representing the interaction of the peoples of Europe (including their descendants settled in North America) with those of the non-Western world. From a Western viewpoint, the issue of Catholic or Protestant missionary proclamation might be one about whether the authentic faith of Christ was transmitted to the non-Western world, or a perverted and destructive misrepresentation of it. For those who heard these proclamations, however, the differences, with roots deep in the intellectual and religious life of Europe, were — both in their attractive and in their repellent aspects — often less significant than what the proclamations had in common. In the modern debates about gospel and culture that have arisen out of the manifestations of Christianity in the southern continents, Catholic and Protestant theologians work on similar agendas. A recent study has shown that the conceptual problems in Andean languages faced by modern Protestant evangelists are precisely those that faced the

Spanish friars who constructed the first Quechua catechisms in the sixteenth century.[4] The crucial questions for the communication of the Christian message were the same. We have become used to the idea that Christianity exists in three modes, Catholic, Protestant, and Orthodox. That distinction is rooted in European cultural history. In the non-Western world these modes still have significance as indicators of affiliation and organization, but they are becoming less and less helpful as descriptors; and huge areas of non-Western Christianity cannot be meaningfully comprehended under any of the three modes. One wholly unexpected effect of the missionary movement has been the diversification of Christianity, with the prospect of whole new traditions of Christianity, as clearly reflecting historical and cultural developments in the southern continents as the Catholic, Protestant, and Orthodox modes reflect those of Europe.

Regarding the European experience of encounter with the non-Western world, the demographic basis of European Christianity, for all its inheritance from the Christian Roman Empire, lay in the conversion of the tribal and semisettled peoples beyond that empire's frontiers. Here it was that the concept of Christendom developed, as the gospel was gradually adopted as the basis and undergirding of customary law. Christendom, the total body of Christian princes and their subjects, all (whatever their actual, often highly dysfunctional, relations with one another) owing allegiance to the King of Kings, notionally represented unbroken Christian territory, subject to the law of Christ, from the Atlantic across the European landmass. All born within that territory were born under the law of the King of Kings; within that territory idolatry, blasphemy, or heresy should have no recognized place. East and south of Christendom lay another realm, and the only other one of which Western Christians had much close knowledge before 1500. The lands ruled by the Turks included lands once Christian and the lands where Christ had walked, which *ought* therefore to be Christian, but which were beyond immediate reclamation. By 1500, the period when European maritime expansion began to open contact with worlds hitherto outside European consciousness, Europe had become Christian territory in a way it had never been before. The last pagan peoples (apart from some in the extreme north), the populations of the Baltic region, had been dragged within the orbit of Latin Christendom. Still more significantly, the most successful of all the crusades had recently removed the open Muslim presence from southern Spain. At roughly the same

4. William Mitchell, "Language and Conquest in Early Colonial Peru: The Ambivalent Dialectic of the Appropriation of the Andean Language," in *From Christendom to World Christianity*, edited by L. Sanneh and A. F. Walls (forthcoming).

period, Christianity became more European than it had ever previously been. Other Christian centers faded. The long-lingering second Rome on the Bosphorus collapsed, the once vigorous Christianity of central Asia was eclipsed, the Christian presence in China disappeared from view, the Nubian Christian state folded, the Ethiopians stood in mortal danger, and the old Christian populations living under Muslim rule saw steady erosion. The remaining Christian populations in Asia and Africa impinged little on European Christian consciousness, unless in confused impressions such as fueled the stories of Prester John. For all practical purposes there was Christian territory, which was subject to the rule of Christ, and pagan territory, which was not. This representation was, if anything, strengthened by observation of the other realm, which recognized the lands of Islam and the lands of warfare. The only model of Christianity that western Europe knew was the Christendom model, the model of Christian territory. Faced with accessible territories where Christ was not known, the manifest duty of Christians was to bring their peoples into the sphere of Christendom, to make those lands Christian territory. The fact that God had so significantly and recently blessed the use of the sword in reclaiming Granada could only reinforce the conviction. Conquest and conversion belonged naturally together.

There is no need here to pursue the Spanish story through Peru, Mexico, and the Philippines. This is a story of the expansion of Christendom, but it is not the story of the origins of the missionary movement. The modern missionary movement began not in the Spanish territories but in the Portuguese, and in those great Asian empires to which the Portuguese trading settlements were neighbors or customers. The Portuguese, with exactly the same theology as the Spanish, and the same inherited experience, found the task of expanding Christendom by the sword all but impossible. They tried; but only in the small enclaves under their direct control, and then often imperfectly, could they enforce it. Hindu and Buddhist and Islamic traditions refused passive surrender. New Christian populations did emerge in Asia, but there was no parallel to the events of Mexico and Peru. There was not the remotest hope of bringing about the conversion of the Moghul or the Chinese empires by the means adopted in the Americas; the strange story of Japan's "Christian century" simply served to underline the point.[5] It was necessary to accommodate the Christendom idea to political and military reality.

That reality laid a new requirement upon those for whom the universal claims of Christ's kingship overrode all other considerations. It was necessary to develop a new category of Christian personnel, whose function was to

5. C. R. Boxer, *The Christian Century in Japan, 1549-1650* (Berkeley, 1976).

commend, explain, and illustrate the Christian message without the power to coerce acceptance of it. Further, in order to attain this uncertain end, those involved must adapt themselves to the modes of life of another people, acquire another language at a fundamental level, and find a niche in another society that enables them to function within it. This is the style of life exemplified in the Jesuit missions at the Moghul and Chinese courts and in far humbler situations in many other places. It is a new development, one born out of frustrated colonialism. It was far from new in the total Christian history and not without precedent in Western Christian experience, but it was counter to the natural first instincts of Western Christianity and to its domestically developed patterns. The idea of living on terms set by other people, which lies at its heart, remained the expression of the essential missionary experience, the missionary ideal for both Catholics and Protestants for centuries to come. It was perhaps the first learning experience that European Christianity received from its contact with the non-Western world.

For its accomplishment this missionary ideal required a combination of three factors. First, it needed a substantial corps of persons with the degree of commitment capable of sustaining such a life and with the intellectual equipment to further it. Second, it needed a form of organization that could mobilize and maintain such a force. Third, it needed sustained Western access to specific locations, with reasonable expectation of continued communication. Throughout its history, Western missionary enterprise depended on these three factors, and the presence or absence of one or more of them has brought about its upswings and its downswings. These factors account, among other things, for the periods when Western Christians talked of missions but did not establish them, as well as for the periods when they did not even talk of them.

The first factor, the corps of competent personnel, implies powerful religious influences, informed by a tradition of mental training. The second, organizational viability, implies political and ecclesiastical conditions that allow for innovation and flexibility. The third, the logistical factor, implies maritime capability, with access to transoceanic bases and communications, and a certain level of public consciousness about such things. The logistical factor in the Western missionary movement requires more attention than it has so far received. The earliest missionary concern arose from the new Iberian maritime consciousness; the Jesuit missions in India, China, and Japan depended on the Portuguese enclaves in Asia for their communications and supplies. When control of maritime access passed from the Portuguese to the Dutch, the Netherlands assumed, though without great enthusiasm, the Portuguese role of the extenders of Christendom. It was the only Protestant power to make the attempt. With the accession of the British to maritime leadership, all pretense of responsibility for the extension of Christendom as the aim of public policy (if we except a brief period under the English Commonwealth) came to an end. However, the logistics of the missionary movement, the business of getting its personnel to viable overseas stations, still depended very much on the use of British facilities. In what follows an attempt will be made to show that the significance of the institution of missionary societies in Britain lies not in their initiating the Protestant missionary movement (an impression created by much earlier writing), nor solely in their initiating a British missionary movement, but in the logistical support and expanded outlets they provided for a preexisting continental missionary movement. We may note that among smaller European nations none maintained a higher level of missionary consciousness than Norway, an incorrigibly maritime nation; while the Protestant population of landlocked Hungary produced only a couple of missionaries — and those from the German minority — in the whole of the nineteenth century, and no mission agency before the twentieth.[6]

Maritime access in itself, however, was not enough to promote missionary consciousness. This question is worth considering in relation to the sources of personnel for the early missionary movement, and to the organizational means used to recruit missionaries and maintain missions. For the early Catholic missions the organizational models were already to hand in the orders; the religious and political conditions of the Catholic Reformation favored their adaptation and development for missionary purposes, enabled the emergence of new custom-built orders and societies, and provided the motivated personnel for both the older and the newer. Protestants had no ready equivalent of the orders to provide the backbone of a mission force or sustain one if provided. It is frequently said that it was the Evangelical Revival that provided the committed corps of personnel for the Protestant missionary movement; it can be further argued that the eighteenth-century development of the voluntary society provided Protestants for the first time with a focused and flexible form of organization such as the orders had provided for Catholics.[7] The evangelicalism that emerged from the revival in Britain and North America provided a highly successful form of Christian adaptation to the European Enlightenment. It reconciled the developed consciousness of

6. See A. M. Kool, *God Moves in a Mysterious Way: The Hungarian Protestant Foreign Mission Movement, 1756-1951* (Zoetermeer, 1993).

7. Cf. Andrew F. Walls, *The Missionary Movement in Christian History* (Edinburgh & Maryknoll, N.Y., 1996), pp. 79-85.

individual responsibility, so characteristic of Enlightenment thought, with Christian faith, while the development of close fellowship that it fostered among the like-minded provided an antidote to the societal and ecclesial atomization that individualism could produce. At the same time its distinction between "nominal" or "formal" and "real" Christianity made it possible to retain the concept of an overarching Christendom that had been fundamental to European identity for centuries.[8] Such a combination of levels of consciousness — the personal relationship with God, the fellowship of "real" Christians, and the larger territorial entity that remained Christian in principle — when equipped with the new instrument of the voluntary society as a "use of means" (as William Carey called it) — made possible the mobilization and deployment of a Protestant missionary force.

At first sight, such a view would seem to coincide with the view that the Protestant missionary awakening begins in the late eighteenth century with such representative figures as Thomas Coke and William Carey. If, however, we view the origins of the Protestant missionary movement in a European context, the picture looks rather different, and the late eighteenth century looks much less like a new beginning. For one thing, the achievement of the Evangelical Revival in combining a renewal of Christian faith and zeal with the Enlightenment values of the individual, and in reconciling the type of ecclesial commitment formerly characteristic of the Anabaptist congregation with the recognition of Christendom and its territorial expressions, had been foreshadowed in Germanic and central European Pietism. Pietism had already provided a Protestant religious dynamic that produced the sort of people who could accept martyrdom, "red" or "green";[9] and that dynamic was backed by a tradition of learning and by commitment to active philanthropy. Halle and Herrnhut are the twin poles of Pietism. The former and its key figure, A. H. Francke, were inevitably associated with the famous university and the equally famous orphan house, the latter with the sort of Protestant-Franciscan spirituality that made people ready to become slaves in order to preach to slaves.

Continental Pietism had a missionary consciousness long before British evangelical consciousness was fully developed. When in 1699 the king of Denmark decided to institute a mission (using, of course, the ready-made base of a Danish colony, Tranquebar), he could find none of his own subjects

---

8. Walls, *The Missionary Movement in Christian History,* pp. 241-54.

9. Adopting the early Celtic identification of the self-offering of the ascetic in a "green" setting with the "red" shedding of blood for Christ's sake, the latter being characteristic of the age of persecution.

suitable and willing to act as missionaries. The needed missionaries were found among Francke's former students in Halle. Bartolomäus Ziegenbalg and Heinrich Plütschau opened a mission that was to operate and expand throughout the eighteenth century and into the nineteenth, establish a significant Christian community, achieve major feats of translation, and survive the vicissitudes of a highly volatile political situation in India. Its membership included such figures as Christian Friedrich Schwarz, who built up a remarkable relationship of trust with the rulers of Thanjavur.[10] Daniel Brunner has explored the labyrinthine procedures by which the king of Denmark's mission came, for logistical reasons arising from the changing political situation, to be linked with London and the Anglican Society for Promoting Christian Knowledge.[11] One of the two key figures in establishing the connection was Heinrich Wilhelm Ludolf, formerly secretary to Prince George of Denmark. The prince, himself deeply influenced by Pietism, became the husband of Princess Anne of England, the future queen, in 1683. Ludolf was a peripatetic promoter of "inner" Christianity and found his ideal in Halle. An even more significant figure was Anton Boehm, a Pietist preacher who became London chaplain to the prince. Of the whole succession of SPCK missionaries in India, all were German, and all were Pietists endorsed by Francke or his successors in Halle. They held Lutheran, not Anglican, ordination and conveyed that ordination to Indian successors. The SPCK seems to have consulted Halle in relation to every missionary appointment. At various times the question of Anglican ordination was broached in SPCK circles but was never forced to an issue. At other times the question arose of the appointment of Englishmen to what was technically a mission related to the Church of England; none were ever identified. It was only in 1825 that this remarkable arrangement came to an end.[12]

Yet Halle was not the sole expression of the growth of a European Protestant missionary consciousness. Equally important, and probably making a heavier impact on a wider public, was the Moravian enterprise associated with Zinzendorf and Herrnhut. The radical nature of the Moravian version of Christian discipleship, the choice of such harsh environments as Greenland and Labrador for mission work, and the eminently practical aspects of their mission activity (exemplified in the new Eden they were held to

10. See Daniel Jeyaraj, *Inkulturation in Tranquebar: der Beitrag der frühen dänisch-halleschen Mission zum Werden einer indisch-einheimischen Kirche (1706-1730)* (Erlangen, 1996).

11. Daniel L. Brunner, *Halle Pietists in England: Anthony William Boehm and the Society for Promoting Christian Knowledge* (Göttingen, 1993).

12. See W. K. Lowther Clarke, *A History of the SPCK* (London, 1959), pp. 59-76.

have planted at the Cape of Good Hope)[13] all made an impression on a range of Christian readers. Recent scholarship has illuminated the variety of groupings within Pietism: Professor W. R. Ward distinguishes Spener-Halle, Moravian-Zinzendorf, Württemberg, Reformed, and Radical; and he has highlighted the conflicts between them, notably between Halle and Herrnhut.[14] To a growing British audience with interest and concern for missions, such conflicts mattered little. What they could see was that pious continental brethren were preaching the gospel among the heathen, and they wanted to emulate them.

If we read William Carey's famous *Enquiry*,[15] so often seen as heralding the new era of missions, against the setting of Baptist thought of the time (as laid out for us by G. F. Nuttall[16] and others), there is little sense of a new beginning. Carey is clearly conscious that missionary work is already and has long been in progress, and he wants his own constituency to become involved in it. The objections to missions that he demolishes are merely such as he met within his own circle, and he deals with them *ad hominem*. In response to the demand for a specific scriptural warrant for preaching the gospel to heathens in any period following the apostolic age, he points out to his Baptist audience that post-apostolic baptism is subject to the same deficiency.[17] His review (section II of the *Enquiry*) of "former undertakings for the conversion of the heathen" is presented as a continuing story from New Testament times to the present day. The story reaches a high point in the establishment and growth of gospel churches in America, evidence that "the Redeemer has fixed his throne in that country, where but a little time ago, Satan had a universal

13. See Bernhard Krüger, *The Pear Tree Blossoms: A History of Moravian Mission Stations in South Africa, 1737-1869* (Genadendal, 1967). The title alludes to the horticultural emphasis of the early Moravian mission to the Cape, seen at the time as reinforcing the association of Christianity with civilization, and in fact affording the few Khoi ("Hottentot") converts a means of subsistence and source of dignity in a white-dominated society. The pear tree outlasted the early mission.

14. W. R. Ward, *The Protestant Evangelical Awakening* (Cambridge, 1992).

15. William Carey, *An Enquiry into the Obligations of Christians to Use Means for the Conversion of the Heathens, in which the Religious State of the Different Nations of the World, and the Success of Former Undertakings, and the Practicality of Further Undertakings Are Considered* (Leicester, 1792). There are several facsimile reprints of this tract; that of 1961 (London: Carey Kingsgate Press) has a useful introductory essay by Ernest A. Payne. Payne also wrote a book with the eloquent title *The Church Awakes: The Story of the Modern Missionary Movement* (London, 1942) that begins with the Napoleonic Wars and the early British societies.

16. Geoffrey F. Nuttall, "Northamptonshire and the Modern Question: A Turning-point in Eighteenth-century Dissent," *Journal of Theological Studies* n.s. 16 (1965): 101-23.

17. Carey, *Enquiry*, pp. 8-9.

dominion."[18] His last words on America are to record that Mr. Kirkland and Mr. Sergeant are employed in the same good work (i.e., with regard to the Native Americans, taking up Brainerd's mantle).

For the rest of the world he had only the resources of the Leicester Philosophical Institute and a small circle of modest dissenting ministerial libraries to draw on, so he knows little about the Halle missionaries in India. He has heard, however, of the king of Denmark's mission in Tranquebar, and of conversions there, though his information comes down no later than Ziegenbalg's time. On the Dutch missions in southeast Asia he is still more out of date, and unduly optimistic, since he seems to assume that though "the work has decayed in some places," the general conditions applying in the late seventeenth century were still in force.

Then comes a salute to the Moravians:

> But none of the moderns have equalled the Moravian Brethren in this
> good work; they have sent missions to Greenland, Labrador, and several
> of the West-Indian Islands, which have been blessed for good. They have
> likewise sent to Abyssinia, in Africa, but what success they have had I
> cannot tell.[19]

The last words in the review are for the efforts of "the late Mr. Wesley" in the West Indies (Wesley had died only the year before) and pleasing accounts of Methodist successes there.

It is clear, then, that Carey saw himself and those whom he was stirring to action as entering into a process already in motion, not as initiating that process. Furthermore, the leading elements in that process in his own time, and for some time past, had their roots in continental Europe.

A similar outlook is reflected in the early volumes of the *Missionary Register,* which appeared from 1813: the *Register* was published by the Church Missionary Society as an ecumenical adjunct to its more "in-house" publications. Its second and third monthly issues reproduced a large part of *A Brief Historic View of the Progress of the Gospel in Different Nations since its First Promulgation* by Hugh Pearson — an essay that was awarded an Oxford University prize endowed by Claudius Buchanan for publication on missions.[20] The ear-

---

18. Carey, *Enquiry,* pp. 35-36.

19. Carey, *Enquiry,* p. 37.

20. Pearson's work was originally published as *A Dissertation on the Propagation of Christianity in Asia. In Two Parts. To which Is Prefixed, A Brief Historic View of the Progress of the Gospel in Different Nations since Its First Promulgation; Illustrated by a Chronological Chart* (Oxford, 1808).

lier part of the essay was heavily dependent on the pioneer work by Robert Millar, minister of Paisley Abbey, which had appeared as long before as 1723.[21]

Of the modern chapter of the story of the propagation of the faith, Pearson identifies the foundation of the Danish Missionary College in 1706 as a landmark.[22] He describes the Tranquebar mission from much better sources than Carey's and enthuses over the work and devotion of the Moravians. They are entitled to hold "a very high rank" in the roll of missionary enterprise, never surpassed by any denomination.[23] Later that year the *Missionary Register* published a lengthy life in five monthly parts of "the eminent missionary Schwarz," the outstanding name among the Halle missionaries in India.[24] Schwarz had died in 1798, but his career as an Indian missionary had begun back in 1750.

There are even examples of missionaries who personally link the British movement that began in the late eighteenth century with the continental precursor. The notable, if eccentric, Wilhelm Ringeltaube, who was involved in one of the first mass movements to the Christian faith in India in the Protestant period, studied in Halle, was converted there, came under Moravian influence, and worked in India in connection with the SPCK. He left it in 1799 and in 1804 was appointed elsewhere in India by the London Missionary Society. He served with that society until 1816 shortly before his mysterious disappearance.[25] Another SPCK missionary was Josef Jänicke, who was the younger brother of Johannes Jänicke, founder of the Berlin Missionary Seminary, which provided the Church Missionary Society with most of its early candidates.[26]

In short, the Protestant missionary awakening did not begin in 1792 or anywhere near that date. What happened in that period was British entry into a well-established continental tradition. This was, indeed, no insignificant event. The evangelical movement as it had developed in Britain made possi-

---

21. Robert Millar, *The History of the Propagation of Christianity and the Overthrow of Paganism Wherein the Christian Religion Is Confirmed. The Rise and Progress of Heathenish Idolatry Is Considered. The Overthrow of Paganism, and the Spreading of Christianity in the Several Ages of the Church Is Explained. The Present State of Heathens Is Inquired into; and Methods for their Conversion Proposed*, 2 vols. (Edinburgh, 1723).

22. *Missionary Register* 1.3 (March 1813): 93.

23. *Missionary Register* 1.3 (March 1813): 95.

24. *Missionary Register* 1 (1813): 193-213, 241-49, 273-82, 305-17, 337-50.

25. On Ringeltaube, see the article by R. V. Pierard in *Blackwell Dictionary of Evangelical Biography*, edited by D. M. Lewis (Oxford, 1995), 2:940.

26. On the Jänicke brothers, see the articles by David Bundy and E. M. Jackson in *Blackwell Dictionary of Evangelical Biography*, 1:603-4.

ble a larger supply of committed mission personnel than had been available previously; though, as we shall see, the supply took some time to build up. The organizational capacity for mission was given new scope by the voluntary society, for development of which, especially given the conditions of a major continental war, Britain offered the fullest possibilities. On the logistical side, British maritime access allowed for a considerable extension of the geographical scope of missions. All these are substantial matters, involving a major enlargement of the missionary movement; but it is an enlargement, a new phase rather than a new beginning.

The entry into the missionary movement of British societal organization and British logistical capability was important not only because it established the missionary contributions of English and Scottish personnel, significant as that was. It also provided a new framework in which the continental missionary consciousness could operate. It is commonly pointed out that the emergence of the new British missionary societies (the Particular Baptist Society in 1792; the Missionary Society, soon after known as the London Missionary Society, in 1795, with the Edinburgh and Glasgow societies soon after; the Church Missionary Society in 1799; and the British and Foreign Bible Society and other agencies in the new century) was followed by the establishment of a succession of missionary societies and agencies on the European continent — Berlin, Basel, St. Chrischona, Leipzig, and the others. This picture furthers the idea of British primogeniture in the movement. It also obscures much of the importance of continental Europe to the British missionary movement, and the extent to which the new British societies depended, especially in their early years, on continental missionary candidates. In fact, the British societies provided a new outlet for a continental missionary movement already in being and to a remarkable extent continued to do so after the new continental agencies had been formed. We may approach the matter with crude statistics. Over the period from its inception in 1799 up to 1850, more than one in five of the missionaries sent out by the Church Missionary Society, a society that had come into being for the very reason that the special concerns and ethos of evangelical churchmen of the Church of England could not be safeguarded by the mission agencies then available, came from continental Europe. If we take the period up to 1830, the tally is higher still — 49 out of 166, well over a quarter, and not far short of a third. If we close the count with the Napoleonic Wars in 1815, the proportion is 17 out of 24, more than two-thirds. Nor does the connection close even in 1850; throughout the nineteenth century, and long afterwards, continental recruits came to the CMS,[27] even after the special

27. The principal source is the CMS *Register of Missionaries (Clerical, Lay and Fe-*

arrangements with the Berlin and Basel seminaries, so important in the early years, came to an end.

Of those serving with the CMS before 1850, the great majority were German, but there were a good number of Swiss, a few Dutch and Danes, and at least one Swede. Among the Germans, the largest single constituency is Württemberg, but many of the earliest were from Prussia, and there are others from all over — from Alsace to Saxony and from Hamburg to Bavaria. There is even one name, Gustavus Nylander, from Livonia.[28]

If we turn to the London Missionary Society, the principal missionary vehicle for evangelical dissenters in the first half of the nineteenth century, the picture, while not as impressive as for the CMS, is striking enough. One remarkable aspect for a London-based society is the size of its Scottish component, and this despite the fact that the foundation of the society immediately produced emulation north of the border.[29] The LMS received a disproportionately large number of Scottish candidates, and its secretariat in its early days was sometimes dominated by expatriate Scottish ministers living in London. Leaving the question of the Scots' presence aside, however, there appear to be not less than 57, and perhaps as many as 63, missionaries of the LMS before 1850 whose origins are in the European continent, out of a total of 506.[30] If we add a further 5 missionaries born in South Africa but of Dutch origin, then something like 13.5 percent of the missionaries of the main agency of the English dissenters before 1850 had their roots in continental Europe. While not so crucial to the society's existence as to the CMS, the continental mission personnel were none the less significant, especially in the period of the Napoleonic Wars. In 1811 5 of the society's 13 new missionaries were German; in 1814 the new men consisted of 2 Germans, 1 Dutchman, 1 Swiss, and 1 Englishman. The Netherlands was the main continental source of supply for the broadly Calvinistic LMS; but their register indicates recruits from several parts of Germany, and from Switzerland, Sweden, Denmark, Bo-

---

male), and Native Clergy from 1804 to 1904, first printed for private circulation in 1896, with a supplement published ca. 1905.

28. CMS, *Register of Missionaries,* no. 3.

29. Cf. A. F. Walls, "Missions," in *Dictionary of Scottish Church History and Theology,* edited by N. M. de S. Cameron et al. (Edinburgh, 1993), esp. pp. 568-70. See William Brown, *The History of the Propagation of Christianity among the Heathen, since the Reformation,* 3 vols. (Edinburgh, 1854). Brown was secretary of the Scottish Missionary Society.

30. The calculation is based on the information given in James Sibree, *London Missionary Society: A Register of Missionaries, Deputations, etc. from 1796 to 1923,* 4th ed. (London, 1923). The information provided in the *Register* varies in extent from entry to entry; many of the early entries in particular do not record place of birth or origin.

hemia, and other parts of the Austrian Empire, with an important group of French Reformed missionaries.

It is clear, then, that the two largest English missionary societies continued to draw heavily on continental sources for their mission personnel well into the period when continental societies were active on their own account. Such arrangements, sometimes formal, sometimes informal, suited both sides. The British societies gained much needed candidates to fill vacancies in the field; the continental agencies received effective outlets for missionary energies. The relationship continued even when the price for continentals was high: not only Anglican ordination (which had not been required in the eighteenth century for the Halle missionaries of the SPCK in India) but reordination for those already in Lutheran or Reformed orders.[31]

For the CMS, the continental supply was not only advantageous, but vital. As is well known, for several years after its foundation (which itself had been the focus of a good deal of theological and ecclesiastical angst) the society had no missionaries at all. Its successive reports had little to report except hopes. The society was rescued from this absurd situation by a continental contact. This was the seminary for the training of missionaries, organized in Berlin by Johannes Jänicke, a missionary enthusiast already linked with Halle and the India mission. The connection was forged by a man whose name appears constantly in evangelical and philanthropic circles in England: Carl F. A. Steinkopf, the German minister of the Savoy Chapel.[32]

The first seven names covering 1804 to 1809 in the register of CMS missionaries are all of Germans. Then follow two English artisans whom the society would like to have called catechists but had to designate as "lay settlers" for New Zealand.

Between 1811 and 1814 there follow seven more Germans, with only one further Englishman, the lay schoolteacher Thomas Kendall. Not until 1815 was this society, set up sixteen years earlier to channel the missionary concern of English evangelical churchmen anxious to preserve Anglican church order,[33] able to send any English clergymen to the mission field. Long after 1815 it continued to rely on German mission staff for its oldest, and in terms of mortality its most dangerous, field, West Africa; thus even in the middle of

31. See J. Pinnington, "Church Principles in the Early Years of the Church Missionary Society: The Problem of the 'German' Missionaries," *Journal of Theological Studies* n.s. 20.2 (1969): 523-32.

32. Eugene Stock, *The History of the Church Missionary Society: Its Environment, Its Men and Its Work* (London, 1899, 1916), 1:82-83.

33. The issue is dealt with at length in M. M. Hennell, *John Venn and the Clapham Sect* (London, 1958), ch. 5.

the century it was possible for the supercilious to describe the lingua franca growing up in Sierra Leone as "German English."[34]

If the continental missionaries stood in the breach where the dead fell into the trench,[35] they also supplied materials often lacking in the British missionary commissariat. One of these was scholarship. English missionary recruits were often of modest educational attainments, and the Church Missionary College at Islington was set up to give such people basic education. Many of the Germans, too, came from a humble background, but their academic potential was often evident. This was especially important in West Africa, since the practice of the CMS was long to send its better educated English and Irish personnel to India. Germans soon took the leadership in African linguistics. The first major figure in this area was J. F. Schön, who came to the CMS from Baden via the Basel Missionary Seminary. He served the society for twenty years but continued long afterwards as linguistic adviser, publishing works on Hausa, Igbo, and Mende and receiving scholarly recognition.[36] Still more significant was the Württemberger, Sigismund Wilhelm Koelle. He, too, came from the Basel seminary, was brought, as the Germans often were, to Islington for orientation and English, and then studied Arabic at Tübingen under Ewald. For most of his career he worked in Muslim contexts in the Middle East, but for a brief, fruitful period he worked in Sierra Leone, producing *Polyglotta Africana,* the pioneer work in the science of comparative African linguistics, based on specimens of a hundred African languages. The CMS often looked to Germany for its linguists, of whom Koelle was perhaps the most distinguished of many.[37] Henry Venn,

34. See Walls, *Missionary Movement,* p. 103, and contemporary descriptions such as R. Clarke, *Sketches of the Colony of Sierra Leone and its Inhabitants* (London, 1863).

35. David Hinderer, the distinguished German CMS missionary in Yorubaland, is said to have used this metaphor in response to his English bride's dismay at the short periods of service and high mortality reflected in the CMS roll of missionaries. The Christian siege of Africa would triumph when missionaries were able to step over the bodies of their fallen comrades into the trench that had so far prevented access to its citadel. Stock, *History of the Church Missionary Society,* 2:116.

36. Schön (CMS, *Register of Missionaries,* no. 181) received the Volney prize from Paris and an honorary D.D. from Oxford for his linguistic work. On the CMS connection with the Basel mission, see Paul Jenkins, "The Church Missionary Society and the Basel Mission: An Early Experiment in Inter-European Cooperation," in *The Church Mission Society and World Christianity, 1799-1999,* edited by Kevin Ward and Brian Stanley (Grand Rapids, 1999), pp. 43-65.

37. On S. W. Koelle see CMS, *Register of Missionaries,* no. 379. *Polyglotta Africana; or a Comparative Vocabulary of Three Hundred Words and Phrases in more than One Hundred Distinct African Languages* (London, 1854). On the background of all these translations see

its ever-busy secretary, got his commercial advice from Manchester but his linguistic counsel from Germany.[38]

The London Missionary Society also received continental recruits of considerable stature. It was indebted to continental Europe for at least one candidate whose coming marked for the society a turning point in its affairs. Johannes Theodorus Van der Kemp entered LMS service in 1798, when he was already fifty years of age. Even apart from his age, he was a new type of missionary. For one thing, while most LMS candidates lamented their early sins and mis-improved talents and opportunities, this ex-dragoon officer really had been a sinner on a fairly spectacular scale. He had also been a deist and a rationalist author. At that time the LMS was not expecting well-endowed candidates and had been conditioned to recruiting missionaries of artisan background. Moravian advice even indicated that these made the best and toughest missionaries. The appointment of Van der Kemp to open the new field at the Cape of Good Hope revolutionized the concept of a missionary as it stood in 1798. It is safe to say that no English equivalent of Van der Kemp, whether from Anglican or dissenting circles, would have been a potential missionary candidate at that date.[39]

The appointment of people of such stature did not always make for easy relationships. Van der Kemp had been brought to South Africa as a Dutchman to talk to Dutchmen, at a time when Britain had newly acquired the colony only through the fortunes of war and was not committed to staying there. His uncompromising behavior brought the question of race relations on to the missionary agenda and kept it there. Notwithstanding the importance of the later activity of John Philip,[40] it is doubtful whether the mission would or could have maintained so firm a stand in a hostile environment without the initial confrontations with Van der Kemp, a man who could not be ignored. Missionaries of stature could also prove uncomfortable for the committee, as the CMS early found out in the matter of C. T. E. Rhenius. This young Prus-

P. E. H. Hair, *The Early Study of Nigerian Languages: Essays and Bibliographies* (Cambridge, 1967).

38. Venn called in the assistance of Professor Carl Lepsius of Berlin, as well as of scholars resident in Britain (such as Max Müller of Oxford), for questions related to the Yoruba Bible, one of the landmark mission translations, and this orthography was used in later translations. Cf. J. F. Ade Ajayi, *Christian Missions in Nigeria, 1841-1891: The Making of a New Elite* (London, 1965), p. 127.

39. On Van der Kemp (Sibree, *London Missionary Society*, no. 34), see Ido Hendricus Enklaar, *Life and Work of Dr. J. Th. Van Der Kemp, 1749-1811: Missionary, Pioneer and Protagonist of Racial Equality in South Africa* (Cape Town, 1988).

40. See Andrew Ross, *John Philip (1775-1851): Missions, Race and Politics in South Africa* (Aberdeen, 1986).

sian was one of the first two missionaries appointed by the society to India in
1814. Besides being a major Tamil linguist, he proved remarkably effective in
building up the church. He can now be seen as far ahead of his time in his vision of what an indigenous church should and could be. At that time, however, the society could see only that its carefully preserved ecclesiastical principles were being jeopardized by Rhenius's proposals for ordination of local
ministers. Rhenius was disconnected; the test of his work is the extent to
which the Indian congregations continued with him.[41]

This chapter has considered the European setting of the missionary
movement very much in terms of situating the British missionary movement
in the context of the continental. The justification for this is the common assumption that the Protestant missionary movement was essentially a British
product that received eventual reinforcement from the European continent.
It is argued here that its origins are continental and that continental Protestantism helped to sustain the British movement through its fledgling period,
while the organizational and logistical features of the British movement,
products of peculiarly British conditions, gave impetus and new outlets to the
continental movement. Other important aspects of the context have been neglected; some of these are highlighted by the relationship between the British
and continental movements.

One such issue is the extent to which Pietist and evangelical religion created a sense of common understanding and purpose between groups separated by geography, nationality, and confession. The expressions of Pietist
and evangelical faith could be very diverse; Halle, Herrnhut, and Württemberg produced manifestations that were not only divergent from one another
but conflicting; and the Evangelical Revival as it operated in the British Isles
and North America, and the *Réveil* in Switzerland and France, produced an
equally diverse array. It is a perplexing feature of Pietist and evangelical religion that it could be grafted onto practically any of the existing theological,
confessional, or ecclesiastical traditions, sincerely affirm loyalty to the "true"
nature of any historic church, and adapt itself to any national or local cultural
ethos. Yet all forms acknowledged the primacy of personal religion; all sought
to express "real" Christianity within a society whose symbols, confessions,
and sense of historic identity were already Christian. This distinction between "real" or "inward" and "nominal" or "formal" Christianity in Pietist
and evangelical religion posed an implicit challenge to the idea of Christen-

41. On Rhenius (1790-1838), see C. J. Rhenius, *Memoir of the Rev. C. T. E. Rhenius*
(London, 1841) and the article by R. E. Frykenberg and R. V. Pierard in *Blackwell Dictionary of Evangelical Biography*, 2:926-28.

dom, that territorial expression of Christianity, the idea of the comprehensive Christian realm, which had been a constituent of the European experience since the conversion period that accompanied the collapse of the Western Roman Empire. The challenge was implicit, not explicit; far from desiring to overthrow the Christendom model, with its communal acknowledgment of the lordship of Christ in the national sphere, Pietists and evangelicals frequently sought to bolster it and deepen communal Christian allegiance by the infusion of "real" Christianity. This could produce alliances that at first sight seem unlikely, such as that we have already noticed between Halle Pietists, whose theology could react sympathetically to English Puritanism, and the High Church Anglicans of the SPCK, who were eager to encourage the practice of a devout and holy life but reacted to the Puritan tradition with revulsion. Perhaps neither Pietism nor evangelicalism ever fully resolved the tension between the desire to retain a Christian society and the recognition of personal responsibility in response to God's initiative for human salvation. Perhaps too, the missionary movement was to reveal this tension in a particularly significant way, especially as it entered the colonial era.

Moreover, this tension brought the Pietist and evangelical movements into currents of their times that had quite different origins. The underlying principle of Christendom was initially breached by the Protestant Reformation itself, which replaced the thought of a universal territorial church by mutual recognition of national churches, and Pietists and evangelicals of all descriptions found their identity in the Reformation. A further breach was opened in the original idea of Christendom whenever political realities forced some degree of religious toleration in place of national religious uniformity. Such developments, even though they left the national symbolic apparatus intact, had the effect of moving religion from the sphere of the public and communal to the sphere of the private and personal, and thus to the sphere of group and family, and ultimately to individual responsibility and choice. Such developments in turn were fertile soil for the intellectual movements arising in the various expressions of the Enlightenment in different parts of Europe. These emphasized the responsibility and even the autonomy of the individual and developed the principles of contract and association as the modes by which this responsibility could be collectively expressed. These emphases and processes posed a direct threat to the idea of the territorial Christian realm that lay at the heart of European Christianity. Such a further impetus to the movement of religion from the sphere of public requirement to that of private choice could easily be seen as an attack on Christianity as it had hitherto been understood in European history. In this paradoxical way, such thoroughly Christian developments as Pietism and evangelicalism, by radically adopting the principle of personal responsibility in religion and by developing with marked success the principles of contract and association to give that religion communal form, did not simply help Protestantism to adapt to the Enlightenment but perhaps even enabled this strand of Christianity to survive its impact. Whether this constituted a rescue or a temporary reprieve lies outside the scope of this inquiry; but it is clear that the missionary movement played its part in developing the sense of personal responsibility in religion, and the use of contract and association to give it communal expression.

We have seen how a sense of common purpose could link groups in different countries who stood for "real" Christianity, the Pietist and evangelical islands, some large, some tiny, in the sea of Christendom. There have been illuminating studies of the networks developed among evangelicals in Britain and how those networks crossed the Atlantic;[42] it is also clear that the networks crossed Europe. The significance for the missionary movement of two German ministers living in London, Anton Boehm (or Böhme) and Carl Steinkopf, has already been mentioned. Boehm has been well served by Dr. Brunner,[43] but Steinkopf, who forged the link between the CMS and the institution that blossomed into the Berliner Missionsgesellschaft, and whose name appears in connection with so many evangelical agencies and activities, deserves more attention. Evangelicals from all over Europe visited the American businessman S. V. S. Wilder, who later became American minister in Paris. (He had other visitors too; he was party to a plot to spring Napoleon from St. Helena.) He provided the safe house in which the Paris Evangelical Missionary Society could be born in the heart of Bourbon France.[44] The radical evangelicals — Scottish, English, French, and Swiss — who gathered in Geneva had their visitors, too, and were the source of some important minority movements in mission theory and practice.[45]

With varying degrees of formality, links were established between missionary societies in different countries. The association between the Netherlands Missionary Society and the LMS was first realized in Van der Kemp and

42. See Susan O'Brien, "Eighteenth-century Publishing Networks in the First Years of Transatlantic Evangelicalism," in *Evangelicalism: Comparative Studies of Popular Protestantism in North America, the British Isles, and Beyond, 1700-1990*, edited by M. A. Noll, D. W. Bebbington, and G. A. Rawlyk (New York, 1994).

43. See above, n. 11.

44. On Wilder, see *Records from the Life of S. V. S. Wilder* (New York, 1865). On the foundation of the Paris Evangelical Missionary Society, see J. Bianquis, *Les Origines de la Société des Missions Évangéliques de Paris, 1822-1929* (Paris, 1930).

45. See T. C. F. Stunt, *From Awakening to Secession: Radical Evangelicals in Switzerland and Britain, 1815-1835* (Edinburgh, 2000).

his colleague Johannes Kicherer;[46] and Van der Kemp was screened for the LMS by an elder of the Scots Kirk at Rotterdam. Peter Fjellstedt, who worked with the CMS in India and Syria between 1831 and 1840, left to become the pioneer architect of Swedish missions and the founder of the Lund Missionary Society. He did not forget the CMS; he was responsible for recruiting to its ranks Johann Ludwig Krapf, the pioneer and prophet of East African missions.[47] One of the most unusual developments of the missionary movement was the emergence of a Roman Catholic priest, Johann Evangelista Gossner (1773-1858), first as revivalist preacher, then as Lutheran pastor, and eventually as founder of a major missionary society. At one point Gossner tried to hand his mission, which had some rather radical features, to the CMS.[48] The transfer failed, but Gossner's successor was Johann Detloff Prochnow, a Prussian in the service of the CMS in India.[49]

All the springs for the Protestant missionary movement lay in the movement for "real Christianity" within Christendom. Overseas missions were not a separate growth from home missions or European missions; they arose in the same soil and were rarely rivals. Enthusiasts for one were frequently enthusiastic for the other, and their histories overlapped. In 1801, at a time when the six-year-old LMS was engaged in strengthening its missions in the Pacific and in South Africa, it appointed a French prisoner of war, Louis Cadoret, as a missionary to other prisoners of war in England. During the Peace of Amiens the society assisted his removal to France, where he worked as a minister.[50] Gossner, before founding the mission that was to bear his name, traveled widely with his revival message, including to Finland and Russia. Ebenezer Henderson and John Paterson were originally designated by the Scottish evangelical Robert Haldane as missionaries to India. Finding themselves in Copenhagen in transit to their appointment there, they became impressed with the spiritual needs of northern Protestantism. Henderson's remarkable career as preacher, translator, and Bible distributor led him from Denmark to Sweden, thence to Iceland, and, above all, to Rus-

---

46. On Kicherer, see Sibree, *London Missionary Society,* no. 35.

47. On Fjellstedt (CMS, *Register of Missionaries,* no. 169), see Olaus Bränström, *Peter Fjellstedt: Mångsidig Men Entydig Kyrkoman* (Uppsala, 1994); and the article by Eric J. Sharpe in *Biographical Dictionary of Christian Missions,* edited by G. H. Anderson (New York, 1998), p. 214.

48. On Gossner see Johannes Aagaard, *Mission, Konfession, Kirche: Die Problematik ihrer Integration,* Bd. 2 (Lund, 1967); W. Holsten, *Johannes Evangelista Gossner: Glaube und Gemeinde* (Göttingen, 1949).

49. See CMS, *Register of Missionaries,* no. 333.

50. See Sibree, *London Missionary Society,* no. 84.

sia.[51] In the Russian Empire the mission to Christendom and the mission to the non-Christian world met. Tsar Alexander I had for a time such a zeal for the Bible, and such favor for the Bible Society, as to give rise to a belief that he had undergone evangelical conversion. He was also ready to allow evangelical missionaries to the Tatars and other non-Christian peoples of his empire. No chapter of Protestant missionary activity raised higher hopes, or induced bleaker despair, than that associated with the Russian Empire. Within that story are different layers of the movement's early vision: the evangelization of unknown peoples, the renewal through the Scripture of ancient churches, and the spiritual revival of Protestantism and its return to the Reformation roots. The missionary movement in its European context had the whole world in its sights. Those sights had as their prism the Pietist-evangelical understanding of "real Christianity," but there were to be strange events in the movement's itinerary. The very success of the Pietist-evangelical project brought almost every section of the Western Church into the missionary movement. The advance of Western hegemony and the colonial era raised the issue of territorial Christendom in a new form. New Christian communities came into being as a result of missionary activity without the clear distinction between "nominal" and "real" Christianity so formative in Europe. Christianity independent of Christendom appeared. Some of those new communities, though emerging from the work of missions that were in so many ways products of the Christian encounter with Enlightenment, produced in due time versions of Christianity that were independent of the Enlightenment. These are not topics that can be pursued within the scope of this chapter or volume, but they suggest something of the range of investigation that the study of the Protestant missionary movement opens up, not least when viewed in its European context.

51. On Henderson see Thulia Susannah Henderson, *Memoir of the Rev. Ebenezer Henderson, Including his Labours in Denmark, Iceland, Russia, etc. etc.* (London, 1859); and the article by Nancy Stevenson in *Biographical Dictionary of Christian Missions*, p. 288.

CHAPTER THREE

The British Raj and the Awakening of the Evangelical Conscience: The Ambiguities of Religious Establishment and Toleration, 1698-1833

PENNY CARSON

"A Christian governor could not have done less . . . a British governor ought not to do more."[1]

I ndia was the stage on which a number of the most important battles of the early nineteenth-century Protestant missionary movement were fought. Not least of these was the question of how far Britain, as a Christian country, should go towards propagating the faith in her overseas territories. Richard, first Marquis Wellesley and governor-general of India from 1798 to 1805, made the above comment during the 1813 parliamentary debates at the renewal of the East India Company's charter. In his speech he was echoing Lord Cornwallis, governor-general from 1786 to 1793, in setting out what he regarded as the limits to the relationship between church and state in the context of company rule in India. On the one hand, Britain had a religious establishment (in both England and Scotland), and Wellesley followed the determination of his predecessor, Sir John Shore (later Lord Teignmouth), "to make it be seen that the christian religion was the religion of the state."[2] Although not religiously minded himself, Wellesley took care to attend church

---

1. Lord Wellesley in *Parliamentary Debates* 25 (9 April 1813): col. 698.
2. Charles Simeon, ed., *Memorial Sketches of the Rev. David Brown* (London, 1816), p. 303.

regularly and supported regulations that were aimed at ensuring that Sundays were properly observed and that "pernicious habits" such as gaming were stopped. His new college for the instruction of company servants in Bengal was set up on Christian principles, and he appointed two evangelical company chaplains (David Brown and Claudius Buchanan) as provost and vice-provost. His avowed aim was to "cherish in the minds of the servants of the Company a sense of moral duty."[3] He also supported the Serampore Baptist missionaries in their translations of the Scriptures into Indian languages. However, he would not order their dissemination, nor would he give official sanction to any other form of missionary activity. He argued in 1813 that, as a British governor, he "knew" he ought not to do more because this might infringe the company's "compact" with its Indian subjects to allow them the free exercise of their religions. As governor-general, he had declared that he would not allow "the slightest interference or even encouragement to be given by the Government to the conversion of the natives to the Christian religion."[4]

The arguments of both supporters and opponents of missionary activity in India used the language of the Enlightenment with its emphasis on rationality, freedom, natural rights, religious toleration, and the "happiness" of the people. Thus Wellesley maintained that

> it would not only be impolitic but highly immoral to suppose that Providence has admitted of the establishment of British power over the finest provinces of India, with any other view than of its being conducive to the happiness of the people, as well as to our national advantage.[5]

Evangelicals would not have disagreed with this statement. They saw no inconsistency between their conviction that Providence had given India to Britain for a higher purpose (an assumption that by this time underlay most arguments about India) and their belief that possession of India should also contribute to the national wealth. However, they were also increasingly concerned about the state of Indian society and its spiritual and moral welfare. Evangelicals argued that only through the inculcation of Christianity could Britain improve not only the spiritual but also the moral and material condition of the people. It was also the only way to bind rulers and ruled. They

3. A. Berriedale Keith, ed., *Speeches and Documents on Indian Policy, 1750-1921* (Oxford, 1922), 1:197.

4. BL Add Ms. 37281, Wellesley Papers, Series II, correspondence of Sir George Barlow with Wellesley, unsigned and undated note (ca. 1807).

5. Keith, *Speeches and Documents on Indian Policy,* 1:197.

therefore demanded free access to India for their missionaries. The company, on the other hand, argued that Indians would be happiest if left to worship in their traditional ways. One of Wellesley's first acts as governor-general was to confirm the ancient Hindu and Muslim laws in all matters connected with "religious prejudices." Far from considering that the propagation of Christianity would bind India to Britain, he considered that "the respect shown by Government to the Religious ceremonies of the Natives was one of the primary causes of the confidence of the Natives in the Government & that if the time ever arrive when a different system of policy should be pursued that in his opinion we should lose India."[6] In this he was acting consistently with the company's long-established caution about permitting any European to enter its domains who might unsettle the native population.[7] While he tolerated the presence of unlicensed missionaries in British India, he would not allow them to proceed exactly as they wished if he felt their actions to be a danger to the security of British territory.

In contrast to many earlier Christian endeavors, the British missionary activity initiated by evangelicals in the late eighteenth century was carried out by voluntary societies that were wholly independent of the state. This reflected the gradual severance of religion from the state that was intrinsic to the European Enlightenment. The Catholic empires of Spain and Portugal had imposed Catholicism on their conquered territories, asserting the state's duty to further the progress of the *Corpus Christianum*. The idea of a unitary Christendom did not, however, die with the Reformation, and the interdependence of church and state continued. The colonial expansion of England was thus taken to imply the expansion of *Ecclesia Anglicana* — the church of English Christians. The Society for Promoting Christian Knowledge (SPCK) came into formal existence by 1699,[8] and was followed in 1701 by the foundation of the Society for the Propagation of the Gospel in Foreign Parts (SPG). Whereas the SPG was set up by royal charter and its work in the British colonies was supported by parliamentary grants, the SPCK was a voluntary society on which the bishops smiled. Although both societies enjoyed the approval of the Anglican authorities, the SPCK, by its newly established connection to the Pietism of Halle in the person of Anton Boehm, was able from 1710 to tap into

6. BL, Wellesley Papers, undated note from Sir George Barlow.

7. The 1698 charter granted the company the right to exclude persons from its domains. Hence all those who were not company servants — whether missionaries or not — required a license to enter its territories.

8. Evidence from banking and subscription records suggests that the SPCK was in existence by 1696, though the earliest extant committee minutes of the society date from 8 March 1699.

the European continental reservoir of overseas mission enthusiasm described by Professor Walls in chapter two.[9] By its decision that year to give financial support to the Danish Lutheran mission at Tranquebar, the society became the first British body to take an interest in India as a field of missionary endeavor. In 1726-27, on the initiative of Benjamin Schultze, the mission extended its sphere of operations to company jurisdiction in the Madras presidency, and Schultze was adopted as a missionary of the SPCK. Nevertheless, the Lutheran missionaries whom the SPCK took under its wing from 1727 until 1825 had little more than a nominal relationship to the Anglican authorities. The mission thus set an essentially independent pattern for missionary activity in India that later evangelical societies expected to follow: the Halle missionaries in practice functioned in substantial autonomy of Anglican control.[10]

Moreover, in England itself the concept of ecclesiastical conformity had started to break down in the face of political realities and Enlightenment ideals. By 1689 toleration of conscience had become the only way forward in England because of the increasing numbers of Dissenters. The established church had to accept the existence of religious nonconformity. Extension of this toleration to the sphere of full political and civic rights was, however, to take another century and a half. The bishops were not distinguished by a passion for the dissemination of Christianity among the indigenous population of the colonial territories and were certainly no more keen to see Dissenters propagating their particular brand of Protestantism abroad than they were at home.

The question of what precisely the role of Christianity should be in India raised many ambiguities. Much of the argument hinged on differing interpretations of the words "toleration" and "neutrality." Are religious neutrality and toleration the same thing? The Company argued that indeed they were, whereas many in the missionary lobby professed to uphold toleration but abhor neutrality. Did toleration for one group mean intolerance or even persecution for another? Anglican evangelicals were quick to perceive inconsistencies in the company's position but less ready to perceive the anomalies in their own thinking. A related question at issue was whether there should be an established church in India. The logic of the Enlightenment implied the separation of religion from the state. Similarly, the logic of evangelicalism, with its strongly individualistic understanding of Christian conversion, might be thought to be antithetical to the principle of an established church.

9. See above, pp. 30-31.

10. See James Hough, *The History of Christianity in India from the Commencement of the Christian Era* (London, 1839-60), 3:376-474; Stephen Neill, *A History of Christianity in India, 1707-1858* (Cambridge, 1985), p. 48.

Anglican evangelicals were, however, as strong supporters of an ecclesiastical establishment in India as they were in England; they accordingly believed that missionary activity in British India should be subject to the control of the Anglican authorities. Evangelical Dissenters, however, wanted official toleration for their own brand of Christianity and were determined not to be controlled by the Church of England. They thus invoked the aid of the principal bodies concerned with the defense of Dissenting interests: the Protestant Dissenting Deputies (founded in 1732) and the Protestant Society for the Protection of Religious Liberty (founded in 1811). In this way the campaign to "open" British India to missions became part of the wider campaign by Dissenters, both evangelical and nonevangelical, to obtain religious toleration.

High Anglicans were drawn into the controversy by their desire to force the company to set up a full ecclesiastical establishment in India. This led some to support the missionary cause, although most High Churchmen before the Oxford Movement held aloof from missions. They did not, however, remain aloof from the nondenominational British and Foreign Bible Society (founded in 1804). Many were active in it and supported its local associations in India. Lord Castlereagh expressed the feelings of many conscientious High Churchmen when he told the inaugural meeting of the Westminster Auxiliary Bible Society:

> I trust that I feel as strongly attached as any man to the particular merits of that religious system, which, as an individual, I profess — to the established religion of the government under which we live: but I hope that I shall not be suspected of indifference to that religion, when I reflect, with gratitude and self-satisfaction, that, amidst those shades of difference which divide Christians among themselves at home, we are all united under the same standard, which it is now our object to plant to a still wider extent. . . . No religious difference or controversial points should impede the great principle upon which this Institution is founded; namely that of delivering the unsophisticated word of God . . . to all mankind, of every persuasion.[11]

The role of religious and political developments in England in shaping both the missionary movement itself and government and Company policy towards it is crucial. Dissenters, Anglican evangelicals, the British government, and the Company all pursued their respective aims. However, India was not a

---

11. J. Owen, *The History of the Origin and First Ten Years of the British and Foreign Bible Society* (London, 1816-20), 3:334-35.

tabula rasa, and the specific Indian context had a great impact on attitudes towards how she should best be governed. Missionaries faced years of almost fruitless toil in the face of Indian hostility and the caution of company officials. India and Britain were two separate but interlinked spheres, and the progress of missions in India cannot be understood without reference to both.

The East India Company and Missions

The East India Company's attitude towards the propagation of Christianity throughout its domains was essentially and inescapably pragmatic. It accepted the principle that Christian ministry should be made available to Company servants, and its 1698 charter accordingly made provision for the appointment of Anglican chaplains to the principal stations.[12] Anglican ministry was therefore brought to India very early on. What is more interesting in the light of subsequent history is that the 1698 Act further recommended that these ministers should "learn the Portugueze and Hindoo languages" so that they could "instruct the Gentoos . . . in the Christian religion."[13] This involved the chaplains in work that was missionary in nature, though it was restricted to company "servants or slaves."

Not surprisingly in the wake of the 1689 Toleration Act and with the influence of the Enlightenment beginning to make itself felt, a key word in the India debates was "toleration." Englishmen liked to contrast their own "tolerance" with the "persecution" of the Portuguese. "Tolerance" was first of all directed towards the many Catholics resident in company territories in the form of practical encouragement and financial help for Roman Catholic missionaries.[14] The 1661 cession of Bombay from Portugal to the English crown had been carried out on the assurance that its Roman Catholics would have the free exercise of their religion.[15] Although the Company directors in England regretted the necessity of making concessions to Catholicism, its ser-

12. Anglican chaplains had, however, been stationed in the presidency of Madras even before the 1698 charter; see Frank Penny, *The Church in Madras* (London, 1904-22), vol. 1, chs. I-V, and pp. 661-68.

13. Cited in P. J. Marshall, ed., *Problems of Empire: Britain and India, 1757-1813* (London, 1968), p. 194.

14. See Kenneth Ballhatchet, "The East India Company and Roman Catholic Missionaries," *Journal of Ecclesiastical History* 44.2 (April 1993): 273-88; and *Caste, Class, and Catholicism in India, 1789-1914* (London, 1998).

15. E. R. Hull, *Bombay Mission History: The Padraodo Question* (Bombay, 1927), 1:20.

vants in India felt that it would be counterproductive to alienate the large numbers of mixed Portuguese Catholics working in its territories, whose knowledge of Indian languages and customs was very useful and whom they did not want to be seduced by France. Other "inducements" included land for houses and the services of a priest. Toleration, however, only went so far, and the activities of Roman Catholic priests and missionaries did not go entirely unrestricted. Various officials tried to prevent priests from making new converts among the European population. Missionaries had to have the permission of the Company to reside in its territory and to take an oath swearing "implicit obedience to his Britannic Majesty."[16] In 1715 the Company decided that Portuguese *padroado* priests (those under the ecclesiastical jurisdiction of the Portuguese crown) were politically suspect and expelled them, replacing them with more politically acceptable Carmelites from Surat who were subject to the jurisdiction of the Vatican's *Propaganda Fide*.[17] The Company's position on religious matters was clearly stated in 1744 when the Court of Directors informed the Madras government that "the Church must never be independent [of] the state, nor the French suffered to intermeddle in our affairs."[18] The French priests were expelled and the Portuguese once again became *personae gratae*.

How did the Company regard the Lutheran missionaries who operated at first beyond, and later within, its territorial jurisdiction from the early eighteenth century? Some of its chaplains certainly viewed them with favor. In 1712 George Lewis, the Company chaplain at Fort St. George, encouraged the SPCK to support the work of the Danish missionaries, saying,

> The missionaries at Tranquebar ought to be and must be encouraged. It is the first attempt the Protestants ever have made in that kind. We must not put out the smoaking [*sic*] flax. It would give our adversaries, the papists . . . too much cause to triumph over us.[19]

Dislike of Catholicism and a desire to limit its influence in the Company's settlements was at the root of this recommendation. In 1716 Lewis's successor

16. See Hull, *Bombay Mission History*, 1:31, for an example of an oath administered. Hull gives numerous examples of the tension between the company and Roman Catholic priests of different nationalities. See IOR, E/3/113, Court to Madras, 25 January 1716, para. 82, for the expulsion of the *padroado* priests and their replacement with Capuchins "who will not secretly try to do mischief."

17. Hull, *Bombay Mission History*, 1:27.

18. IOR, E/3/109, Court to Madras, 7 February 1744, para. 42.

19. Penny, *The Church in Madras*, 1:184.

at Fort St. George, William Stevenson, recommended far more than encouragement or toleration. He told the SPCK that if "the itinerant missionaries, catechists &c" were not to be "molested nor interrupted in their work, they must be powerfully recommended to the favour and protection of the governors at Fort St. George and Tranquebar."[20]

In its response to Stevenson, the Court of Directors agreed that missionary work was a "noble enterprise," and they told the governor of Madras to "do whatever you think proper for the strengthening their [the Tranquebar missionaries'] hands in this difficult but honourable work of spreading the Gospel among the heathens." The official reply of the governor-in-council to the court's exhortations said that it was happy to give pecuniary support and was sure that others would do the same, provided any missionaries dispatched to its own territory were of "tempers and qualifications fit for the undertaking."[21] As with the Roman Catholic missionaries mentioned above, the Company was not prepared to allow the Lutheran missionaries *carte blanche*. The request from the SPCK in 1727 that Benjamin Schultze be permitted to reside within its domains in Madras was granted, on condition that any missionaries so admitted "behave respectfully and suitably to the Rules of the place."[22] "Toleration" was dependent on good behavior. This caveat remained Company policy throughout its rule. The Company zealously protected its right, granted by Parliament, to expel *any* person, whether of a religious or secular character, whom it considered unfit.

The SPCK at the time made no comment on this, and the matter was never put to the test since none of their adopted missionaries was ever asked to leave its domains by the Company. Indeed, by 1740 their work was well established, and replacement of deceased or retired individuals had become routine. The position of the Lutheran missionaries in India was not wholly dependent on Company favor, since many operated outside its domains. However, the Company granted them free passages, a free mail service, and allowances for performing divine service and running charity schools and asylums. It also helped with land and buildings. This was more than toleration. Nevertheless, it was not a blank check but subject to the good behavior of the missionaries in the eyes of their local officials.

As a private trading corporation, the East India Company had from the outset no option but to "tolerate" Indian religions. Yet the Company went

---

20. Cited in *An Abstract of the Annual Reports and Correspondence of the SPCK from the Commencement of Its Connexion with the East India Missions, AD 1709 to the Present Day* (London, 1814), p. 22; see Hough, *History of Christianity in India*, 3:378-79.

21. Cited in Penny, *The Church in Madras*, 1:185-86.

22. IOR, E/3/104, Court to Madras, 14 February 1728, para. 93.

further than mere toleration. As part of its consolidation of control, the Company extended the existing process of the absorption of religion into state structures whereby local governments had begun to take over the management of the often massive landed endowments of temples (as well as mosques, and even some synagogues and churches). The Company cemented local loyalties by confirming the tax-exempt status of such endowments, collecting pilgrim taxes, and giving police support at the major festivals associated with many of the temples. The growing Company involvement in the management of Hindu religious activity played a crucial part in the construction of "Hinduism" as a recognizable official entity. It also provoked a growing campaign of protest in Britain against such official connection with "idolatry." By the 1830s it seemed to many British evangelicals as if the Company were running British India as a Hindu-Muslim state in which there were three "established" religions: Christianity for Europeans, and "Hinduism" and Islam for Indians. The perception that professedly Christian governors were treating "Hinduism" and Islam as established religions was anathema to evangelicals.[23]

The 1790s: Toleration in Retreat?

By the 1790s, the company's policy of strict religious neutrality was increasingly contested. By this time the situation in India had changed dramatically. The East India Company had been transformed from a purely commercial organization to a company of merchants with imperial responsibility for vast areas of the Indian subcontinent. In Britain, Parliament had assumed considerable control over the Company's management of its affairs. The itinerant lay preaching encouraged by the Evangelical Revival posed an increasing threat to ecclesiastical order and even Anglican supremacy.[24] The 1689 Toleration Act notwithstanding, Dissenters were regarded with renewed suspicion and dislike, and by the 1790s had replaced Catholics as the scapegoat of the "mob" in "Church and King" riots. The French Revolution, the subsequent Terror, and the upsurge of political radicalism at home, sent a *frisson* through the establishment. Evangelicals took note of the expanded scale of British re-

23. See R. E. Frykenberg, "Constructions of Hinduism at the Nexus of History and Religion," *Journal of Interdisciplinary History* 23.3 (Winter 1993): 536-37, 545; also Jörg Fisch, "A Pamphlet War on Christian Missions in India, 1807-1809," *Journal of Asian History* 19.1 (1985): 22-70.

24. See Deryck W. Lovegrove, *Established Church: Sectarian People: Itinerancy and the Transformation of English Dissent, 1780-1830* (Cambridge, 1988).

sponsibilities in India and argued that providence had given India to Great Britain in order to create a Christian nation there. Behind this lay the implicit warning that if Britain did not perform her Christian duty, divine vengeance would be wreaked upon her.

Charles Grant, a leading Company servant in India and a director of the East India Company from 1794, was peculiarly instrumental in turning evangelical attention to India.[25] In his opinion the Company had done far too little to encourage the growth of Christianity. Like William Stevenson before him,[26] he came to the conclusion that the support of the English government was crucial. The evangelical Company chaplain, David Brown, similarly believed that anything undertaken without the permission of the governor-general would "wither and die."[27] In 1787 Grant, in association with Brown, William Chambers, and George Udny, sent to leading churchmen in England *A Proposal for Establishing a Protestant Mission in Bengal and Behar.*[28] Lord Cornwallis's reaction to Grant's proposal foreshadowed all future government pronouncements on the subject: as governor-general he could not actively support such a scheme, but he would not oppose it either.[29] Both in theory and because of the pragmatic difficulties of governing such a vast territory, he wanted imperial rule to cause as little upheaval as possible in India by limiting its impact on the population. This was the guiding principle behind his Permanent Settlement of 1793. Extended to Britain's policy towards Indian religions, the principle meant that Indians should be left free to worship as they wished. Under Cornwallis, this policy became enshrined in Section 1 of Bengal Regulation III of 1793 and became known as the Company "compact" with the Indian people. However, while the rhetoric claimed that Britain continued to govern India by Hindu and Muslim law and traditions, the reality was that much was changed, both because the Company did not fully understand these traditions and because of the needs of the Company itself. The inconsistencies arising from the Company's effective manipulation of Hindu and Muslim customs and traditions were later exploited by evangelicals. Ironically, evangelicals themselves, by the concentration of their rheto-

25. See Allan K. Davidson, "The Development and Influence of the British Missionary Movement's Attitudes to India, 1786-1830," Ph.D. thesis, University of Aberdeen, 1973, ch. 2; A. T. Embree, *Charles Grant and British Rule in India* (London, 1962); Henry Morris, *The Life of Charles Grant* (London, 1904).

26. See above, p. 52.

27. Simeon, *Memorial Sketches of the Rev. David Brown*, p. 243.

28. Morris, *Life of Charles Grant*, pp. 105-14. See also Lambeth Palace MS 2100, Bishop Porteous's "Memoranda and Recollections."

29. Morris, *Life of Charles Grant*, p. 122.

ric on the Hindu to the exclusion of the Muslim, were reinforcing the idea of India as a Hindu state.

Grant's 1787 proposal came to grief, not because it was refused, but because he could get no enthusiasm for it. However, apathy would later stiffen into resistance. The new scheme was not originated by an official body of the Church of England. Its proposers were evangelicals, whose strict loyalty to the church could be questioned and whose "enthusiasm" for the propagation of Christianity could be regarded as subversive of social order. This lack of support for a missionary scheme put forward by members of the established church and respected servants of the Company was a forerunner of trouble to come, and events took on a worse complexion in the aftermath of the French Revolution.

At this inauspicious point, Charles Grant and William Wilberforce decided to bring the question of missionary activity in India into the public arena at the 1793 renewal of the Company's charter, and William Carey and John Thomas, the first missionaries of the newly founded Baptist Missionary Society (BMS), decided to set sail for India without licenses. The progress of the missionary proposal through Parliament set the terms of the debate that would follow over the next twenty years. What Wilberforce and Grant were aiming for was some form of Anglican ecclesiastical establishment in India, financed by the Company, whereby the Church of England would propagate the "purest" form of Christianity to both the "dissolute" Europeans and the "depraved" Indians. After consultation with the Speaker of the House of Commons and the Archbishop of Canterbury, Wilberforce moved the following resolution:

> That it is the peculiar and bounden Duty of the Legislature to promote, by all just and prudent Means, the Interests and Happiness of the Inhabitants of the *British* Dominions in *India;* and that, for these Ends, such Measures ought to be adopted as may gradually tend to their Advancement in useful Knowledge, and to their Religious and Moral Improvement.[30]

This has become known as the "pious clause." The clause passed the House without division, as did a second clause, introduced three days later, empowering and requiring the Company to send out "schoolmasters, and Persons approved by the Archbishop of Canterbury . . . for the Religious and Moral Improvement of the Native Inhabitants of the British Dominions in India."[31] The passing of this clause in the House of Commons, almost without com-

---

30. *Journals of the House of Commons* 48 (14 May 1793): 778.
31. *Journals of the House of Commons* 48 (14 May 1793): 792; see also J. C. Marshman, *The Life and Times of Carey, Marshman, and Ward* (London, 1859), 1:37-38.

ment, seems surprising in the light of the subsequent history of opposition to missionary activity in India. It is very similar to the course of events in the campaign for the abolition of the slave trade, where a resolution recommending the abolition of the trade passed the Commons in 1792 but was defeated in the Lords when the "West India interest" had marshaled forces against it. Indeed, the parallels and overlapping of personnel between the two campaigns are considerable.[32]

A special meeting of the Court of Proprietors was immediately convened in order to discuss this new clause, and virtually every speech made opposed it. Lord Lushington, in the chair, was strongly against this "very dangerous and expensive measure." Furthermore, he foretold the end of British rule in India if missionaries proved to be successful. Even the evangelical director, Samuel Thornton, found it necessary to state that the missionaries were not to go out to make proselytes but merely to instill the "virtuous and moral principles of the religion of the Church of England" into the minds of the natives.[33] Opposition was not limited to the East India Company. Charles James Fox considered "all systems of proselytisation as wrong in themselves, and as productive, in most cases, of abuse and of political mischief."[34] During the debate in the House of Lords there was little disagreement that more chaplains should be provided for the main settlements, but great reservations were expressed about the desirability of a specific measure for the conversion of India. The prime concern of prelates in England remained the still tiny European population of India.[35]

For a commercial company in dire financial straits to have the discretion to permit missionaries to enter India was one thing. To have to pay for their upkeep was quite another. Grant felt that another reason for opposition, unstated in the debates, was that the Company's main fear was not so much disturbing the religious susceptibilities of the people but the political impact the egalitarian effects of Christianity might have on a subject race.[36] The Company's two overriding fears were for the political stability of its possessions and the considerable increase in expense that the "pious clause" implied.

---

32. The petitioning campaign to open India to missionaries also has considerable links with other contemporary petitioning movements, particularly the campaigns by Dissenters for the Repeal of the Test and Corporation Acts, and in 1811 against Lord Sidmouth's Protestant Dissenting Ministers' Bill.

33. *The Diary or Woodfall's Register,* 24 May 1793.

34. *The Parliamentary Register* 35 (24 May 1793): 584.

35. See, e.g., *The Senator* 7 (5 June 1793): 896-97; *The Gazeteer and Daily Advertiser,* 6 June 1793.

36. Embree, *Charles Grant and British Rule in India,* p. 154.

The debate about missions in India conducted from 1793 centered on three issues, all of which in some measure involved the established church. First, should there be an increase in the ecclesiastical establishment for the benefit of the growing numbers of Europeans in India? There was no dissent from the premise that a Christian nation should provide Christianity for its own people. However, exactly how this should be achieved was contested. Not all Christians wanted to see an Anglican ecclesiastical establishment dominant in India. While most Company servants did not object to such an establishment, some believed that its official position would cause Indians to believe that it was the intention of government to convert them. A second and more contentious issue, however, was the question of whether Christianity should be propagated to the Indian people, and, if so, what methods of propagation were acceptable. Henry Dundas perhaps made a fair comment when he argued during the parliamentary debates that the question as far as he could see was not whether the government "wished well to the establishment of Christianity in India," but whether such an object "could be best attained by the means he [Wilberforce] was anxious to suggest."[37]

The debate that followed over the next twenty years was very much a child of the Enlightenment.[38] This was most obviously so in terms of the explicit appeal made by both parties to the values of humanity, happiness, and reason. According to evangelicals of all denominations, humanity and Christianity called with one voice for missionary action whenever such evils as the slave trade, the "barbarism" of the South Sea islanders, or the "degradation" of the Hindu became known. In the case of the Hindus, action was doubly urgent in the light of the fact that they were now fellow British subjects. The distinctively evangelical belief that known wrong could not be tolerated was hitched to the Enlightenment ideal that government should aim at the happiness of the people. Whereas both opponents and supporters of missionaries maintained that they had the happiness of the Indian people at heart, evangelicals claimed that such happiness could be achieved only if India became Christian. Once the spiritual and moral condition of India improved through the inculcation of Christian principles, the material position of its inhabitants would improve also. Moreover, as the Protestant Dissenting Deputies pointed out in their petition to Parliament on 9 April 1813,

37. *The Senator* 7 (24 May 1793): 858-59.

38. The issues were set out in the petitions sent to Parliament in 1813 at the renewal of the company's charter. See P. S. E. Carson, "Soldiers of Christ: Evangelicals and India, 1784-1833," Ph.D. thesis, University of London, 1988, pp. 197-304, for a fuller discussion of the popular support for India missions at this time.

the encouragement of Christianity was the only rational position to take. They maintained that

> to represent a system of idolatry and superstitions as equally tending to produce moral virtue and human happiness was no less contrary to the dictates of sound reason and philosophy than irreconcilable with the first principles on which our faith is built.[39]

The anti-missionary lobby argued, however, that it stood to reason that the people of India would be unhappy if missionaries were allowed to attack their gods and deeply felt beliefs and traditions. If Britain bowed to pressure from the missionary lobby, this would be to abandon the "natural right" of India to worship in freedom. This would lead to unrest and ultimately the loss of India. It is important to note, however, that most opponents of missionary activity took care to state that their ultimate wish was to see India become a Christian country. The ensuing debate (which in essential outline has continued throughout the history of modern missions to the present day) hinged on varying perceptions of what are morally acceptable and practically effective methods of spreading Christianity. For this reason, some who were strongly anti-missionary supported the British and Foreign Bible Society.[40] Circulating the Bible "without note or comment" was not necessarily regarded as missionary activity.

Rivalry between Church and Dissent

A third and equally contentious issue was raised by the arrival of Dissenting missionaries in India from 1793 onwards: namely, the question of what kind of Christianity should be propagated. It was the presence in Bengal of the first BMS missionaries, followed shortly thereafter by the LMS, which brought this additional dimension to the question at the very point when Wilberforce and Grant had just inserted the subject of missions in India into the debate over the renewal of the Company charter. The introduction of Dissent to British India contributed to a polarization of views. Dissenters regarded the opening of Company territory to unrestricted access for missionaries as part of their wider campaign for religious toleration in Britain. They saw the freedom to worship without hindrance from government as their "natural right." The admission of missionaries into British India was but one of a number of

---

39. *Parliamentary Debates* 25 (9 April 1813): cols. 764-65.
40. See below, p. 64.

political issues in the late eighteenth and early nineteenth centuries that were at least partly concerned with the relationship of religious dissent to the existing constitution of church and state. By 1812 Dissenters were suffering almost continuous harassment. The attempts of Anglican magistrates and others to restrict the preaching activities of Methodists and Dissenters in the early years of the century pulled these groups together, with some measure of support from Anglican evangelicals, to fight to ensure that their civil liberties were secured. The commencement of British evangelical foreign missions extended this issue to the imperial scene. It raised the question of not only whether Christianity should be preached but of what form of Christianity should be preached. The Tranquebar missionaries adopted by the SPCK, which had the patronage of the crown and the full support of the Anglican bishops, had encountered no problems in working as they wished, despite the fact that they propagated a Lutheran form of Christianity with the Book of Common Prayer superimposed. Roman Catholic missionaries were also given countenance and support. However, Dissenting missionaries in India experienced difficulties that were paralleled by their colleagues elsewhere in the British empire, notably in Jamaica.[41]

The association of missionary activity in many minds with Methodism and Dissent made it very difficult for the missionary leaders to promote their cause. Their democratic organization and their appeal in areas of political radicalism seemed to prove that their churches were becoming, to quote John Walsh, "the unconscious tools of a popular democracy that sought to destroy the existing order in church and state."[42] As he points out, distrust of Methodism developed into a suspicion that on occasion bordered on hysteria. Such suspicion was not limited to England. In 1799, the same year that the government prohibited corresponding societies, a clergyman at the General Assembly of the Church of Scotland made explicit the association of missionary activity with political radicalism. He accused the members of missionary societies of meeting "under the pretext of spreading abroad Christianity among the heathen." In proof of this he pointed out how

> they are *affiliated,* they have a *common object,* they correspond *with each other,* they *look for assistance from foreign countries,* in the very language of many of the seditious societies. Above all it is to be marked, they have

41. See E. Daniel Potts, *British Baptist Missionaries in India, 1793-1837* (Cambridge, 1967), pp. 177-82.
42. J. D. Walsh, "The Yorkshire Evangelicals in the Eighteenth Century with Special Reference to Methodism," Ph.D. thesis, University of Cambridge, 1956, p. 327.

a *common fund* . . . [which] . . . certainly will be, turned against the constitution.[43]

He could also have mentioned that they distributed cheap tracts and pamphlets, another radical activity. The overthrow of established authority in France and its chaotic and bloody aftermath gave a powerful weapon to those who were hostile to missionary activity carried out by Dissenters. The support some evangelical Dissenters had initially given the Revolution, their membership of radical societies, and their subsequent opposition to the war with France enabled churchmen to raise the cry of "Church and State in danger."[44] Their cause was not helped by the attempt of Dissenters in 1789 to have the Test and Corporation Acts repealed, during which they set up a nationwide network to demand their "rights." Instead of the hoped-for mass demonstration of support for Dissenting claims, there was widespread and violent reaction against them.

It was but one step further to connect fanaticism at home with fanaticism abroad. Sidney Smith, in his famous diatribe against the "anabaptist" missionaries in India in the *Edinburgh Review* of 1808, provides the most colorful example of this. He deprecated the fact that the task of conversion, which he admitted to be important, had devolved upon the lowest of persons because no one else could be found to go out. These men, in Smith's opinion, were unlikely to carry out their task with discretion and would be dangerous. Such "madness," in his view, was

disgusting and dangerous enough at home: — Why are we to send out little detachments of maniacs to spread over the fine regions of the world the most unjust and contemptible opinion of the gospel?

He warned that

even for missionary purposes . . . the utmost discretion is necessary; and if we wish to teach the natives a better religion, we must take care to do it in a manner which will not inspire them with a passion for political change, or we shall inevitably lose our disciples altogether. . . .[45]

43. EUL, Laing Ms. II, p. 500, Extract of the proceedings and debate in the General Assembly of the Church of Scotland, 27 May 1796.

44. Hough, *History of Christianity in India*, 4:103-4; Deryck Lovegrove, "English Evangelical Dissent and the European Conflict, 1789-1815," in *The Church and War*, edited by W. J. Sheils, Studies in Church History 20 (Oxford, 1983), pp. 263-64.

45. *Edinburgh Review* 12 (1808): 179 & 171.

How did these developments in Britain affect the course of events in India? The Baptist and LMS missionaries were advised not to put the matter of licenses to the test and entered India clandestinely.[46] Once there, contrary to popular mythology, they were accepted and not expelled. Nevertheless they were not happy with the clandestine nature of their arrival, which must be seen against the background of the routine admission of SPCK-sponsored missionaries that continued throughout the period 1793-1813. In 1796 Robert Haldane, a wealthy Scottish landowner, David Bogue, a Congregational minister, and William Innes and Greville Ewing, at that time both ministers of the Church of Scotland, put forward to the Court of Directors an extensive mission proposal for Benares.[47] The plan was refused for several reasons. First of all, relatively large numbers of missionaries were envisaged. Second, at least two of the proposers had known democratic leanings and had spoken of their dislike of religious establishments. Haldane and Bogue had welcomed the French Revolution, believing that it heralded the prospect of a better order of things. Haldane had also spoken out against the war with France and the raising of volunteers for it. Bogue in a 1791 sermon had presaged that "this generation shall not pass away before the expiring groans of arbitrary power are heard through every country in Europe."[48] Even William Wilberforce found them "all perfect democrats, believing that a new order of things is dawning."[49] Military commanders in India did not want democratic notions being spread among their troops, European or otherwise.

Haldane felt that he was being unreasonably excluded from India because he had become a Dissenter. He told Henry Dundas,

> We think we have an equal right with the missionary sent from the English Society for propagating the Gospel [the SPCK]. . . . We think our claim is not inferior to theirs. If no bad effects have arisen from their efforts to propagate the Gospel, why should they be feared from ours?[50]

Arguments were based on perceptions of the relationship of the British government to Indian religions. The missionary lobby vehemently argued that a

---

46. See, for instance, Mitchell Library Ms., Haweis letters, A3024, fol. 235, Ambrose Searle, Transport Office, to T. Haweis, 23 December 1796.

47. Both Innes and Ewing subsequently left the Church of Scotland ministry, Innes becoming a Baptist and Ewing a Congregationalist.

48. EUL, Laing Ms. II, p. 500, Porteous to Dundas, 20 February 1797.

49. R. I. and S. Wilberforce, *The Life of William Wilberforce* (London, 1838), 2:176.

50. EUL, Laing Ms. II, p. 500, Haldane to Dundas, 28 September 1796. The SPCK missionary referred to was probably W. T. Ringeltaube.

Christian government had a positive duty not only to protect Christianity but also to do all in its power to facilitate the peaceful conversion of the population. Without exception, governors-general believed that government must be kept separate from the actions of missionaries. Even the evangelical, John Shore, shared this belief; he found it difficult to reconcile his duty to promote Christianity with his responsibilities as governor-general. The fact that India had to be defended by a sepoy army reinforced the Company's belief that it had to be extremely cautious in any interference with matters affecting Indian religious practices. Shore had expressed the belief before any Dissenting missionaries had entered India that if the sepoys' religion was ridiculed or forbidden, "the bond of attachment would soon be dissolved, and disaffection and aversion be substituted for subordination."[51] Subsequent events such as the Vellore Mutiny of 1806, in which over two hundred Europeans were killed or wounded, made the Company even more cautious.

Although individual officials differed in their treatment of missionaries and responded to specific circumstances in a pragmatic way as time went on, certain principles can be discerned. Company servants were instructed not to support missionary activity in their official capacity, although the Company was prepared to protect missionaries from persecution and to give them nonmissionary employment. Thus, Dissenting missionaries were not granted licenses to enter British India but were permitted to operate in Company domains once they reached the country. As has been pointed out, this was inconsistent with the routine granting of licenses to the missionaries adopted by the SPCK. The continuance of all missionaries in Company territory was dependent on their good behavior. The use of the Scriptures was not permitted in government-funded schools, nor would government give financial help to charitable societies that were suspected of having any intention to proselytize. Religious tracts were not to include anything that might be considered offensive to Hindu or Muslim sensibilities. Missionaries were not usually permitted to work in unsettled border areas where Company control was fragile, nor to proselytize among sepoys. Commanding officers had discretion over the dismissal of sepoys who converted to Christianity. The Company argued that these steps were necessary in order to protect the "toleration" promised to Indians in the Company "compact." The Company's prime consideration was political and not religious: the tranquillity of its own domains.

Evangelicals did not regard this policy as being one of neutrality or tolera-

---

51. *Memoir of the Life and Correspondence of John Lord Teignmouth. By his son*, Lord Teignmouth (London, 1843), 1:281; see also J. W. Kaye, *Christianity in India: An Historical Narrative* (London, 1859), pp. 140-47.

tion towards Christianity. In 1808 Andrew Fuller, the secretary of the BMS, asked Robert Dundas, president of the Board of Control, for an "express permission, or what perhaps wd. be called a toleration, allowing us to itinerate and settle missionary stations in the country that we might not be interrupted by magistrates."[52] Fuller's use of the word "toleration" is significant; the term appears again and again in pamphlets, letters and petitions. Both supporters and opponents of missionary activity claimed that toleration was what they sought. Supporters of missionary activity wanted toleration for Christianity in India. By this they meant no restrictions on the peaceful propagation of the faith and protection for their converts. They regarded the restrictions placed on them by the Company government not merely as intolerance of Christianity but as persecution. Their opponents, however, believed that preaching, itinerating, and distributing tracts was intolerant of Indian religions. Lord Minto, governor-general from 1807 to 1812, in a letter to Edward Parry, the evangelical chairman of the Company, urged him to peruse some of the missionary publications himself:

> especially the miserable stuff addressed to the gentoos, in which without one word to convince, or to satisfy the mind of the heathen reader, without proof or argument of any kind the pages are filled with Hell fire, and Hell fire & still hotter fire, denounced against a whole race of men for believing in the religion which they were taught by their fathers and mothers, and the truth of which is simply impossible that it should have entered into their imagination to doubt. Is this the doctrine of our faith? ... I am of the sect which believes that a just god will condemn no being without individual guilt.[53]

Minto was particularly concerned at the Baptist demand for the total abolition of caste, and he referred to the Vellore Mutiny in which the simple proposal "to efface a mark of cast from the forehead of soldiers on parade, has had its share in a massacre of Christians." Minto feared that "your government" would next "be required to countenance public exhortations addressed to a gentoo nation, to efface, at once, not [merely] a little spot in yellow paste from the forehead, but the whole institution of cast itself, that is to say, the whole scheme of their civil polity as well as their fondest and most rooted religious tenets." Minto went on to give his own opinion of how missionaries should operate:

52. BMS Ms. H1/1, Fuller to Ward, 6 February 1809.
53. NLS Ms. 11339, 29ff., draft despatch Minto to Parry, 19 September 1807.

> In my opinion the missionaries would advance better by mixing with the people, by habituating them individually to the more amiable points of their doctrine, and attracting them rather by its beneficent influences than by the mysteries and dogmas of faith. Let their minds be prepared by the former for the reception of the latter. I have some reason the think that the press and the pulpit have not work'd well. . . . *Generally,* those who have not been made angry have been made merry by both these engines of conversion. The Mahometan frowns, the Gentoo is apt to laugh. . . . [T]he assertion that his religion is false is an absurd proposition to him.

The progress of Christianity in India, Minto believed, would necessarily be slow, "not carried by storm" but by "long, cautious, and pacific negotiation."[54]

While not everyone agreed that missionaries were the most effective means of propagating Christianity among the Hindus, many people favored distribution of the Bible, without note or comment, as the only acceptable means of conversion. By far the most successful society in attracting support from a wide spectrum of the British public for the propagation of Christianity was the British and Foreign Bible Society. It was nondenominational but the founders of the society deliberately aimed at attracting the aristocracy and episcopate to its ranks. For this reason they stressed that distributing the Bible was *not* missionary activity. It provided a largely acceptable way for Dissenters and High Churchmen to cooperate in the task of propagating Christianity. The society's work was important for India because it supported the Baptist translations at Serampore, and the work in India was reported to its members. In 1813, in line with its policy of remaining as uncontentious as possible, it did not officially take part in the campaign to open India to missionaries. It provided a transitional phase for those reluctant to support overt missionary activity and helped many to make the intellectual link between the two. Both Warren Hastings and Lord Liverpool were members. However, there was tension because many members of the establishment regarded the society as a way in which to keep Dissenters under control, or as Nicholas Vansittart put it, "lessening both the political and religious evils of dissent."[55]

The difficulties experienced by Dissenting missionaries in India should be put in the context of the treatment of their colleagues elsewhere. In the West

---

54. NLS Ms. 11378, 53ff, Minto to Parry, 11 December 1807.
55. Owen, *History of the Bible Society,* 2:147-48. See also BL Add Ms. 38287, 272-78, Liverpool to Wilberforce, 26 September 1820.

Indies matters were even worse. In 1802 the Jamaica Assembly passed an "Act to Prevent Preaching by Persons not Duly Qualified by Law." In justification, it maintained that there existed an evil,

> which is daily increasing, and threatens much danger to the peace and safety therefore, by reason of the preaching of ill-disposed, illiterate, or ignorant enthusiasts, to meetings of negroes and persons of colour . . . whereby the minds of the hearers are perverted with fanatical notions, but opportunity is afforded them of concerting schemes of much private and public mischief.[56]

As a result of the Act, Dissenting places of worship were closed and several Dissenting preachers were thrown into prison. The Methodists and Dissenters in England immediately reacted to this trespass of their "legal toleration" and asked Wilberforce to help in lobbying the government. The British government duly disallowed the Act, though in 1807 the Jamaica Assembly made a further attempt to prohibit missionary work among the slaves. Similar difficulties were encountered in other parts of the British Caribbean. In 1811 John Wray, an LMS missionary in Demerara, was informed that the Demerara "Court of Policy" was determined to expel him from the country, and the governor issued a proclamation forbidding Negroes from assembling for worship between the hours of sunrise and sunset.[57]

Rivalry between High Churchmen and Dissenters was also an important component of the religious scene in mainland North America. The SPG had been set up as much to counter Dissenting influence among the colonists as it had been to propagate the gospel among the Indians. The creation of the first colonial Anglican episcopate in Nova Scotia in 1787 was due at least in part to the desire to ensure that the Church of England would make greater headway than Dissenting sects.

In such a fraught ecclesiastical context, the relationship of Anglican evangelicals to their Dissenting partners was inevitably ambiguous. They were loyal to the established church and believed it should be predominant. They were also struggling for acceptability within the Church of England. However, at heart, they were more in tune with Methodists and evangelical Dissenters than with their fellow Churchmen. While evangelical chaplains in India did

---

56. Oxford, Regent's Park College, BMS Ms. H/4, Papers about Persecution Arising from the Act of Assembly 1801; see Mary Turner, *Slaves and Missionaries: The Disintegration of Jamaican Slave Society, 1787-1834* (Urbana, 1982), pp. 14-15.

57. London, School of Oriental and African Studies, CWM Ms. LMS Minute Book 5/6, 12 August 1811.

much to smooth the path to respectability and acceptance of Dissenting missionaries, there is no doubt that they felt superior to their less well educated brethren and tried to control their activities.[58] Buchanan's successor as Presidency chaplain, David Brown, issued a public notice asking the public not to support the free school the Baptists were proposing to set up (the Calcutta Benevolent Institution) because it was to be conducted by Dissenters and this was "improper interference with the education of the parochial poor."[59] They attempted to control the Serampore mission's translations and funds.[60] They felt the necessity to further the interests of the established church and earn the approbation of the Company and their own ecclesiastical authorities. Claudius Buchanan's *Memoir of the Expediency of an Ecclesiastical Establishment for British India* (1805), was an attempt to persuade the Church of England to take the lead in promoting missionary activity in India.[61] Dissenters regarded such proposals to set up an Anglican episcopate in India with great suspicion. Their fears had considerable foundation. Indeed, a common Anglican view was expressed by the acting judge at Dacca in 1816 when he told the BMS missionary, O. Leonard, that "dissenters were like a set of miners rocking the foundations of the church which will soon come tumbling down, and carry the state along with it."[62]

By 1813 many evangelicals had decided that their position in India was untenable. They felt that Christianity was the only religion not being tolerated in British India and were determined to ensure that they achieved a "legal toleration" at the renewal of the Company's charter. Anglican evangelicals and Dissenters cooperated in lobbying politicians and the Company. The Anglicans realized they needed the numerical support of the Dissenting body if they were to make an impact with their case. Dissenters for their part realized the political realities of the situation and that they and Anglican evangelicals were in danger of being like the mouse and the frog in the fable, so busy brandishing their spears at one another that the opposition would be the winners.[63] Their

58. Oxford, Regent's Park College, Angus Library Ms. Copy letter, Fuller to Chamberlain, 18 May 1809.

59. BMS Ms. IN/19, Marshman to Ryland, 24 February 1811.

60. See S. Wilberforce, ed., *Journals and Letters of the Rev. Henry Martyn, B.D.* (London, 1837), 2:79; also Carson, "Soldiers of Christ," pp. 187-92.

61. However, only the first twenty pages of the *Memoir* were explicitly devoted to arguing for an Anglican establishment in India; see Davidson, "Development and Influence," p. 170.

62. BMS Ms. IN/28, Leonard to Marshman, 11 November 1816.

63. BMS Ms. H1/1, Fuller to Ward, 7 October 1811. For a fuller discussion of the 1813 campaign see Carson, "Soldiers of Christ," chs. 7-8.

cooperation climaxed with an enormously successful petitioning campaign in which 895 petitions were sent to Parliament with nearly half a million signatures.[64] Many of the petitions used the language of the "rights of man" and came from the "friends of religious liberty" who demanded "the liberty to transmit our faith to those under our control." Religious liberty was equated with civil liberty, and missionary activity was regarded as an inalienable right, "which must not require licence from any human authority" nor depend for its continuance on "human caprice."[65] A number of petitions also came from the Church of Scotland whose adherents wanted their own ecclesiastical establishment. Only 6 of the 895 petitions came from Anglican sources. This reflects the anxiety of Anglican evangelicals not to upset the bishops by appearing to side with the radical libertarian language of the Dissenting petitions. Dissenters, whose own struggle for religious liberty in Britain inclined them to adopt the terminology and campaigning methods of radical politics, took the lead in the campaign for evangelical liberty in India; Anglican evangelicals, being much more wary of the political vocabulary of the Enlightenment, adopted a lower profile in the alliance.

The evangelical campaign of 1813 was apparently successful in that a "pious clause" was included in the new charter, an Anglican episcopate was set up, and the Church of Scotland was granted an ecclesiastical establishment. The right of a Christian country to propagate Christianity in her colonies had been publicly acknowledged. There is no doubt that the East India Company had had its wings clipped both economically and as regards licenses for missionaries. It lost its monopoly of trade to India, keeping only the lucrative China trade. Henceforth it would not refuse licenses to missionaries, and Dissenters would not be excluded from propagating their own brand of Christianity in India. The campaign of 1813 can be interpreted as a moral victory for Dissenters in England over the vested interests of both the Company and their opponents within the established church. It represented the political influence Dissenters as a body had now obtained: politicians were loathe to alienate such a large body of respectable and economically powerful citizens. The 1813 "victory" demonstrated that a major readjustment in Britain's political and economic priorities had taken place.

Yet had evangelicals — especially Dissenting evangelicals — gained the "legal toleration" they had demanded? In 1821 a Wesleyan missionary evi-

---

64. *Evangelical Magazine and Missionary Chronicle* 21 (1813): 321-23; Carson, "Soldiers of Christ," pp. 218, 412.

65. BL Add Ms. 38410, 242-43, Protestant Society for the Protection of Religious Liberty to Lord Liverpool, 1 April 1813.

dently thought not, when he complained to his society that "on the one hand we are restrained and confined by the political authorities, on the other are libelled and censured by the ecclesiastical authorities . . . in this state what are missionaries to do?"[66] Missionaries in India were still subject to the requirement for licenses, and the only legal improvement in their situation obtained in 1813 was the right of appeal to the Board of Control. The question can be judged only by reference to how the missionaries were treated in India after 1813. While no missionaries were refused licenses to enter British India, the Company continued to use its powers to restrict their activities and movements. In fact missionaries were more restricted after 1813 than before. Furthermore, there was growing concern for the implications of a number of laws and regulations on Christian converts. The Hindu and Muslim laws of inheritance effectively disinherited Christian converts. Madras Regulation VI of 1816, an order strictly forbidding the employment of any except Hindus and Muslims in the native courts as agents or conductors of suits, was regarded by the missionaries as injurious to the progress of Christianity as the loss of caste itself. They felt it was in effect a complete bar to the employment of Christians in public office because "the law operates extensively by implication and unless repealed it will always offer a serious obstacle to the general spread of Christianity."[67] The danger seemed all the greater "when viewed in connection with the prohibition against admitting natives who have embraced the Christian religion into the army, or allowing them to remain there after becoming converts."[68] In 1821 the Marquess of Hastings refused the bishop of Calcutta's request for an ordinance forbidding the employment of native workmen on Sundays. He felt that such a law would do violence to the religious habits of Muslims and Hindus and would be connected in Indian minds with the recent appointment of the bishop.[69] Moreover, the Company's superintendence of Hindu festivals and collection of the pilgrim tax continued. The Company's concern to exercise a benevolent management of Hindu religious practice was regarded by the missionary lobby as tantamount to intolerance or even persecution of Christianity. On occasion, however, the Company bowed to Christian and humanitarian pressures to ban Hindu practices that were regarded as contrary to the dictates of humanity. In 1801 Lord Wellesley banned infanticide in the Saugur area and in 1829 Lord Bentinck abolished *sati*. In both these cases, considerable time and ingenuity

66. WMMS Ms., Box 433, Fletcher to WMMS, 7 April 1821.
67. LMS Ms. S. India Tamil Incoming Letters, Box 4, W. Taylor to LMS, 17 March 1831.
68. LMS Ms. N. India (Bengal), Box 3, G. Gogerley to LMS, 24 February 1831.
69. IOR, E/4/106, Bengal Ecclesiastical Letter, 4 January 1821, para. 24-31.

were spent in "proving" that these practices did not have the support of Hindu scriptures. Missionaries provided much information that Wellesley and Bentinck used to justify their bans (though not as much as that supplied by Ram Mohan Roy and other Hindu reformers).[70]

How did the establishment of an Indian episcopate affect Anglican evangelical and Dissenting missions? The CMS had hoped that the new episcopal establishment would smooth the way for its English missionaries, the first of whom sailed for India in 1815. However, Middleton, the first bishop of Calcutta, would not "acknowledge any relation" to the CMS and refused to license its missionaries to preach in his churches. He was no friend of missionary activity and was especially hostile to Dissenting missionaries. In 1821 he gave a charge to his clergy deprecating the fact that the 1813 charter had enabled "sectarian schismatic sentiments" to be brought into India.[71] In 1821 the SPG began work in Calcutta, and in 1825 the society assumed responsibility for the entire SPCK India mission. Both Lutherans and English Dissenters began to encounter marked antipathy from the High Church missionaries of the SPG. George Gogerley of the LMS wrote in 1823 of "the jealous eye with which the prosperity of dissenters was regarded by Churchmen."[72] Dissenters felt strongly that their situation in India was worse than that of their fellows at home. One missionary expressed his feelings graphically when he wrote that in England "party spirit" was like a "contemptible worm" only crawling out under the concealment of darkness: whereas in India it was a "lurking serpent," "darting upon every passing traveller and mangling what it cannot devour."[73]

By 1833 the Company seemed to be distancing itself still further from any connection with missionary activity. The Indian administration was forbidden from employing missionaries to perform the duties of chaplain unless there was a dire necessity. The Court of Directors, echoing its 1744 statement of the relationship between church and state, maintained that

> interference with non-Christians could never be left to the personal discretion of individual chaplains uncontrolled by any authority . . . it was a temporal matter in which the safety of the Empire was concerned and

70. See K. Ingham, *Reformers in India, 1793-1833* (Cambridge, 1956), ch. 3; Bruce Robertson, *Raja Rammohan Ray: The Father of Modern India* (Delhi, 1995), pp. 41-42.

71. WMMS Ms., Box 433, Fletcher to WMMS, 22 March 1821; see Kaye, *Christianity in India,* pp. 301-14.

72. LMS Ms. N. India (Bengal), Box 1, G. Gogerley to J. B. Warden, 25 September 1823.

73. LMS Ms. N. India (Bengal), Box 1, Calcutta Annual Report, 25 September 1823.

it was necessary that it should be carefully looked to and strictly controuled by the Government which could never divest itself of that imperative duty.[74]

Toleration for one religion can mean persecution for another. At some point there have to be limits. By the 1830s many Britons wished to see India become Christian. In a post-Enlightenment world this could not be achieved by coercion. In addition, India's millions were held by a sepoy army. Religious toleration was the only pragmatic course to take. The real question at issue for Christians was what was meant by mission and how could this best be achieved in a conquered country. The Company's attempts to tolerate all religions, but particularly Hinduism and Islam, were plausibly interpreted by Christians as being in practice discriminatory against their faith. In effect the company ran India as a Hindu state, and it was not religiously neutral. Over a century later, India's 1947 constitution set up a secular state with freedom of worship. However, since then there has been unremitting pressure to wed the Indian state to an explicitly Hindu identity. One of the results has been active discrimination against Christians and Muslims. Once again, this is not religious neutrality.

74. IOR, E/4/147, Bengal Ecclesiastical Letter, 29 September 1834, para. 20.

CHAPTER FOUR

Patterns of Conversion in Early Evangelical History and Overseas Mission Experience

D. BRUCE HINDMARSH

A little more than two and a half centuries ago John Berridge, fellow of Clare Hall (now Clare College) in the University of Cambridge, was known as a witty raconteur, the toast of the senior common rooms. As Vicar of Everton, he later experienced a profound evangelical conversion and became one of the most colorful clergymen of the Evangelical Revival. The epitaph that he composed for his own gravestone is perhaps one of the shortest evangelical conversion narratives on record:

> Here lie the earthly remains of John Berridge
> Late Vicar of Everton,
> And an itinerant servant of Jesus Christ,
> Who loved his master and his work,
> And after running on his errands many years
> Was called up to wait on him above.
> Reader
> Art thou born again?
> No salvation without a new birth!
> I was born in sin, February 1716.
> Remained ignorant of my fallen state till 1730.
> Lived proudly on faith and works for salvation till 1754.
> Was admitted to Everton vicarage, 1755.

Fled to Jesus alone for refuge, 1756.
Fell asleep in Christ, January 22, 1793.[1]

Berridge's epitaph is but one cryptic example of the kind of biographical reconstruction in which countless men and women engaged as they came to identify in one way or another with evangelical faith and practice in eighteenth-century England, and, indeed, across the North Atlantic world. Christian believers have not always found it compelling or important to give an account of their own lives as stories of religious conversion, but two and a half centuries ago large numbers did.

The question to be explored in this chapter has to do with the conditions that are necessary for such a genre to flourish, and the conclusion is that it requires a certain sense of introspective conscience along with a certain sense of individual self-consciousness — both of which come together distinctively in the North Atlantic world in the early modern period. This will become all the more apparent when the rise of the genre of conversion narrative in early modern England is contrasted with the appropriation, substantial modification, or even total absence of such narratives in some of the non-Western contexts of early evangelical mission history in the late eighteenth and early nineteenth centuries.

The Rise of the Evangelical Conversion
Narrative in England, 1650-1790

As a popular genre, the conversion narrative is about a hundred years older than the Evangelical Revival. The genre was established in the seventeenth century, and the theology that supported it was expounded in key works such as Richard Baxter's *Call to the Unconverted* (1658) and Joseph Alleine's *Alarm to the Unconverted* (1672). The spiritual autobiography, organized around the *leitmotif* of personal conversion, persisted among English Nonconformists well into the eighteenth century, especially through the oral church relation required for membership in many churches. Then, with the series of remarkable conversions in the late 1730s and early 1740s that signaled the beginning of the Evangelical Revival, conversion narratives again multiplied.[2]

1. L. E. Elliott-Binns, *The Early Evangelicals: A Religious and Social Study* (London, 1953), p. 279.
2. For the Puritan genre see further Patricia Caldwell, *The Puritan Conversion Narrative: The Beginnings of American Expression* (Cambridge, 1983); Charles E. Hambrick-

From the earliest examples in the seventeenth century, such as John Bunyan's *Grace Abounding to the Chief of Sinners* (1666), it is possible to identify a common U-shaped pattern that begins with serious religious impressions in childhood, followed by a descent into "worldliness" and hardness of heart, followed by an awakening or pricking of religious conscience, and a period of self-exertion and attempted moral rectitude, which only aggravates the conscience and ends in self-despair. This self-despair, paradoxically, leads to the possibility of experiencing a divinely wrought repentance and the free gift of justification in Christ. Forgiveness of sins comes thus as a climax and a psychological release from guilt and introduces ideally a life of service to God predicated on gratitude for undeserved mercy. This idealized pattern could be developed in various ways, but, on the whole, it emerges with remarkable consistency as the generic element in manifold spiritual autobiographies in the early modern period from August Hermann Francke in seventeenth-century Germany to Henry Alline in late eighteenth-century Nova Scotia.[3]

The turning point was the moment when guilt was finally removed and the soul was filled with "joy unspeakable and full of glory."[4] While there were evangelicals such as William Jay and Charles Simeon who allowed that conversion could be gradual, more often it was a sudden, datable crisis. This was certainly the case for Sampson Staniforth, one of Wesley's lay preachers. He remembered his conversion as a twenty-five-year-old soldier in the English army, while stationed in the Low Countries at the height of the War of the Austrian Succession:

> From twelve at night till two it was my turn to stand sentinel at a dangerous post. . . . As soon as I was alone, I kneeled down, and determined

---

Stowe, *The Practice of Piety: Puritan Devotional Disciplines in Seventeenth-Century New England* (Chapel Hill, N.C., 1982); William K. B. Stoever, *"A Faire and Easie Way to Heaven": Covenant Theology and Antinomianism in Early Massachusetts* (Middletown, Conn., 1978); Owen Watkins, *The Puritan Experience: Studies in Spiritual Autobiography* (London, 1972); Daniel B. Shea, Jr., *Spiritual Autobiography in Early America* (Princeton, 1968); Norman Pettit, *The Heart Prepared: Grace and Conversion in Puritan Spiritual Life* (New Haven, Conn., 1966). For the evangelical conversion narrative among English Nonconformists in the early eighteenth century see Geoffrey F. Nuttall, "Methodism and the Older Dissent: Some Perspectives," *United Reformed Church History Society Journal* 2 (1981): 259-74.

3. My focus is, however, chiefly English spiritual autobiography. The important role of England in the popularization of modern autobiography is discussed in Michael Mascuch, *Origins of the Individualist Self: Autobiography and Self-Identity in England, 1591-1791* (Cambridge, 1997), pp. 23-24.

4. This key text of the Revival (1 Peter 1:8) was the motto for Jonathan Edwards's classic analysis of religious psychology in his *Religious Affections*, vol. 2: *The Works of Jonathan Edwards*, edited by John E. Smith (1st ed., 1746; new ed., New Haven, 1959).

not to rise, but to continue crying and wrestling with God, till He had mercy on me. How long I was in that agony I cannot tell; but as I looked up to heaven I saw the clouds open exceeding bright, and I saw Jesus hanging on the cross. At the same moment these words were applied to my heart: "thy sins are forgiven thee." My chains fell off; my heart was free. All guilt was gone, and my soul was filled with unutterable peace. I loved God and all mankind, and the fear of death and hell was vanished away. I was filled with wonder and astonishment.[5]

In Staniforth's case conversion might even be described as V-shaped, rather than U-shaped, but the pattern is still unmistakable.

As one more example of this pattern of guilt under the law and comfort under the gospel, consider the following account from a barely literate woman named Elizabeth Hinsom, who recorded her conversion in the very early days of Methodism. This is from a letter she wrote to Charles Wesley in 1740:

I was a Pharisee but god was pleast to convince me by heareing mr Witfeald sermon. . . . I know my self a damd sinner. I came home and I thought I was then sinking into hell. This was in march I think but it did not pleas god to reveal him self in me till last september the 4 day. . . . Satan raged within and I have reson to bles my god for he iustifyd the un godly in me. Your brother [John Wesley] expounded the 12 chap of sant John and the lord work mytelly in me and I felt a strong conviction and wold have hid it but my lord huw loves sinners still carrid on his work and brought all my sins to my rememberance and then I trembeld an should have fell done but the people heald me up and I was out of my senses but the lord a wakened me with peace be unto you your sins are for giveing you. I went home full of ioye not knowing ware to bestow my self. So I continued all next day. . . . I am lost in wonder when I see what god has done for my soul I have now peace with god and I know that my redemer liveeth to make intersestion for me. I can now look up and say christ is ful of grace for me. I have grasuse vissits from god and I trust I shal not reast till I find christ the hope of glory formd within me.[6]

---

5. John Telford, ed., *Wesley's Veterans: Lives of Early Methodist Preachers Told by Themselves* (London, 1912), 1:74-75.

6. Manchester, John Rylands Library, Methodist Archives, Early Methodist Volume, folio of MS letters, Accounts of Religious Experience of Early Methodists in Letters to Charles Wesley, ca. 1740–ca. 1786 [with a few later additions, 1806, 1827, 1828].

Together with the accounts of Staniforth and Berridge, this letter bears witness to the popularity of conversion narrative as a genre during the Evangelical Revival. It was the preserve not only of the literate, but also of the uneducated and even illiterate, for it was an oral genre as well. Even the three examples given here comprehend a wide range within English society: a university educated clergyman, a baker's apprentice who later enlists in the army, and a poor young woman.

There are indeed distinctions that can be made within the genre. Different kinds of plot lines and themes appear among different denominations, theological partisans, and classes or groups of people. For example, the unpublished narratives by lay people, especially by women — as in this case — include more bodily and psychic phenomena than the more clerical published sources.[7] Or again, Arminian autobiography reads more as a peregrination, with multiple peaks and valleys, than the more tightly scripted Calvinist narratives.[8] In political and ecclesiastical terms, some Nonconformist narratives express dissent from prevailing norms, and others by members of the Established Church express, albeit usually in *apologia* form, a desire to be seen as conforming to establishment ideals.[9] On the whole, however, the basic U-shaped pattern, described above, remains consistent in all the evangelical autobiographies, whatever their differences and variations at other levels.

We could say that the narrative pattern that unifies this early modern conversion literature functioned as the formal equivalent of the conventions of, say, an Elizabethan sonnet. An Elizabethan sonnet has fourteen lines of iambic pentameter, divided into three quatrains and a concluding couplet (rhyming *abab, cdcd, efef, gg*). Yet these limitations are full of potential for introducing diverse problems, bringing them to a crisis, and resolving them in the

7. One could contrast here the lives of the early Methodist preachers in Telford, *Wesley's Veterans*, 7 vols. (1912-14) with Accounts of Religious Experience, ca. 1740–ca. 1786, in the Methodist Archives, Manchester.

8. The pilgrimage motif in Wesleyan autobiography is examined in Isabel Rivers, "'Strangers and Pilgrims': Sources and Patterns of Methodist Narrative," in *Augustan Worlds*, edited by J. D. Hilson, M. M. B. Jones, and J. R. Watson (Leicester, 1978), pp. 189-203. On Calvinist narratives see Bruce Hindmarsh, "The Olney Autobiographers: Evangelical Conversion Narrative in the Mid-eighteenth Century," *Journal of Ecclesiastical History* 49 (1998): 61-84.

9. This point is illustrated in the American context by Jerald C. Brauer, "Conversion: From Puritanism to Revivalism," *Journal of Religion* 58 (1978): 227-43. Cf. Mark A. Noll, "Revolution and the Rise of Evangelical Social Influence in North Atlantic Societies," in *Evangelicalism: Comparative Studies of Popular Protestantism in North America, the British Isles, and Beyond, 1700-1990*, edited by Mark A. Noll, David W. Bebbington, and George A. Rawlyk (New York, 1994), p. 131.

final couplet. Likewise the evangelical pattern of conversion was a narrative structure that could be exploited as a creative means of literary (or oral) self-discovery. Furthermore, just as there are good and bad sonnets, so there are interesting and uninteresting spiritual autobiographies. Still, the pattern offered an opportunity for the subjects to orient themselves personally to Reformation doctrines, to take their stand, in a kind of spiritual and moral space, and to explore how their story uniquely reflected common themes, even at times by negating or crossing the expected patterns.

Thus, the first section of Jonathan Edwards's *Faithful Narrative* explores the diversity of the experience of conversion in the Connecticut Valley revival of 1735-36, but the second section goes on to explain the profound continuity in the midst of all this variety, how there was a "great analogy" in all.[10] Moreover, Edwards recognized the important dialectic between content and form, religious experience and its written counterpart:

> A scheme of what is necessary, and according to a rule already received and established by common opinion, has a vast (though to many a very insensible) influence in forming persons' notions of the steps and method of their own experiences. I know very well what their way is, for I have had much opportunity to observe it. Very much, at first, their experiences appear like a confused chaos. . . . [B]ut then those passages of their experience are picked out, that have most of the appearance of such particular steps that are insisted on; and these are dwelt upon in the thoughts, and these are told of from time to time in the relation they give: these parts grow brighter and brighter in their view; and others, being neglected, grow more and more obscure: and what they have experienced is insensibly strained to bring all into an exact conformity to the scheme that is established.[11]

What Edwards refers to as a rule "received and established by common opinion" that "insensibly strained" the experience of his parishioners is the interpretative culture and tradition that stands behind evangelical conversion narrative. It is that which supplied the principles by which one selected, arranged, and explained the events of one's life.

Above all, it was the dialectic of law and gospel, the problems of conscience and their resolution, which was central to all these narratives. Evan-

---

10. C. C. Goen, ed., *The Great Awakening,* vol. 4: *The Works of Jonathan Edwards* (New Haven, 1972), p. 160.

11. Edwards, *Religious Affections*, 2:160.

gelical homiletic stimulated and expressed this pattern. Thus, for example, John Berridge wrote to Charles Simeon when Simeon was a young man, and urged him to preach in precisely such terms: "When you open your commission, begin with ripping up the Audience, and Moses will lend you a Carving Knife, which may be often whetted at his Grind-Stone. Lay open the universal sinfulness of nature." Berridge went on, "When your Hearers have been well harrowed, and the clumps begin to fall . . . let them know that all the Treasures of Grace are lodged in Jesus Christ, for the use of poor needy sinners."[12]

Such preaching tapped into a rich vein of assumptions left behind as a kind of theological deposit in the cracks and crevices of society as Christendom receded in the early modern period.[13] The revived Augustinianism of the Reformation, diffused widely through Protestant preaching, casuistry, and catechism, did much to spread certain ideals of Christian faith and life in the North Atlantic world. This occurred even as the territorial ideal of united Christian societies under Christian princes, sharing a sacred language and serving a single church under a single apostolic bishop — even as that Christendom ideal — was supplanted by ideals of limited religious toleration after the exhaustion of seventeenth-century religious warfare. In seventeenth- and eighteenth-century Protestant lands, the vestigial framework of Christendom assumptions, augmented by Reformation catechesis, was the tinder to which vivid preaching, which did not shrink from proclaiming all the sanctions of traditional eschatology, set the spark. The evangelical Anglican leader, Henry Venn, even in his preconversion days, used to walk around the cloisters of Trinity College, Cambridge, while the great bell of St. Mary's tolled nine o'clock, and brood on the awful facts of death and judgment, heaven and hell.[14] As Thomas Scott put it (and as he found for himself), "Hell is an awakening reflection, God's sword in the conscience."[15]

---

12. *Arminian Magazine* 17 (September 1794): 496-98; cf. Richard Whittingham, ed., *The Works of the Rev. John Berridge . . . with an Enlarged Memoir of his Life* (London, 1838), pp. 476-77.

13. I use the term "Christendom" here to refer not principally to the receding territory of Christian Europe that was under threat from the Ottoman Turks in the East, but rather to the receding *ideal* of a united Christian society with a ubiquitous and distinctively Christian culture, an ideal that was more or less realized at different times and in different places, but that was supremely the product of the high Middle Ages. The ideal of Christendom in this sense is captured in the title of Peter Berger's study on the social reality of religion, *The Sacred Canopy* (New York, 1967).

14. John Venn, *Life and . . . Letters of the Late Rev. Henry Venn,* 2nd ed. (London, 1835), pp. 14-15.

15. Thomas Scott, *The Force of Truth: An Authentic Narrative* (London, 1779; reprint, Edinburgh, 1984), p. 25.

Andrew Walls has commented on how important this Christendom back-drop was to the Evangelical Revival. As he writes, "The evangelicalism of the period takes its identity from protest, and in effect from nominal Christianity. Evangelical religion presupposes Christendom, Christian civil society."[16] A telling and ironic example of this comes from John Wesley's observations after touring Wales with Howell Harris in 1739. Wesley reflected on what he had witnessed:

> Most of the inhabitants are indeed ripe for the gospel. I mean (if the expression appear strange) they are earnestly desirous of being instructed in it; and as utterly ignorant of it they are as any Creek or Cherokee. I do not mean they are ignorant of the name of Christ. Many of them can say both the Lord's Prayer and the Belief. Nay, and some, all the Catechism; but take them out of the road of what they have learned by rote, and they know no more (nine in ten of those with whom I conversed) either of gospel salvation or of that faith whereby alone we can be saved, than Chicali or Tomo-chachi.[17]

Chicali and Tomo-chachi were Creek Native Americans whom Wesley had met in Georgia. Yet for Wesley to dismiss the fact that his Welsh hearers knew only the Lord's Prayer, the Apostles' Creed, and the Catechism underestimates the importance of the Christendom heritage to evangelical revival and probably rather overstates the paganism of Wales. Wesley's hyperbolic observations should be taken instead as an indication of the extent to which real, as opposed to merely nominal, faith was valued by the preachers of the Revival.[18]

Indeed, nominal Christianity provided many of the assumptions about

16. Andrew Walls, "The Evangelical Revival, the Missionary Movement, and Africa," in *Evangelicalism*, p. 312.

17. *Journal of the Rev. John Wesley,* edited by Nehemiah Curnock (London, 1911), 2:296.

18. Upon arriving in West Africa in the nineteenth century, Henry Hughes Dobinson sounded remarkably like Wesley: "We feel the absence of spiritual life out here in the Church. Conversion is practically unknown, and has certainly not been required as essential for admission to baptism. A mere knowledge of the Creed, Lord's Prayer and the Ten Commandments has always been reckoned as sufficient ground for baptizing anyone who offers himself. Can anyone be surprised if under such circumstances the Church is impure and rotten through and through?" *Letters of Henry Hughes Dobinson* (London, 1899), pp. 49-50, quoted in Andrew F. Walls, "Black Europeans — White Africans," in *The Missionary Movement in Christian History: Studies in the Transmission of Faith* (Edinburgh and Maryknoll, N.Y., 1996), p. 107.

creation, providence, moral order, eschatology, and much else, which the evangelical preachers used to urge their hearers to take faith more seriously and to make their Christianity more personal. These assumptions were, as it were, at the fingertips of the preachers and their hearers. The work of the orthodox apologists in the earlier part of the century in natural theology and evidential argument helped to reinforce these assumptions.[19] In his much-quoted Hulsean Prize Essay, Haddon Willmer put it this way: "Evangelicalism, then, was the answer to the religious problem of Eighteenth Century man. . . . [T]he common background of thought was, humanly speaking, evangelicalism's most powerful instrument of evangelism. It created the need for the Evangel."[20]

The most important legacy of Christendom for the eighteenth-century man or woman was what Krister Stendahl has called the "introspective conscience of the West." In a landmark essay in 1961 Stendahl critiqued the view that St. Paul's conversion stands as archetype of the evangelical pattern of conversion in which relief for a plagued conscience is found through the message of justification by faith. Stendahl argued that the plagued conscience is instead the product of centuries of Christianization in the West, and should not be read back into the apostle's experience on the Damascus road — an experience that is better understood in its context as something like the calling of a Hebrew prophet through a vision at noonday prayer.[21] Of the development of the plagued conscience, Stendahl writes,

> When the period of the European mission had come to an end, the theological and practical centre of Penance shifted from Baptism, administered once and for all, to the ever repeated Mass, and already this subtle

19. Charles J. Abbey and John H. Overton, *The English Church in the Eighteenth Century* (London, 1878), 1:6-7; John Walsh, Colin Haydon, and Stephen Taylor, eds., *The Church of England, c. 1689–c. 1833: From Toleration to Tractarianism* (Cambridge, 1993), p. 43. John Gascoigne, *Cambridge in the Age of the Enlightenment* (Cambridge, 1989), p. 262, argues differently that the evangelical insistence on revelation and grace actually posed more of a threat to the natural theology of the earlier period, and that evangelicalism should be seen more in terms of discontinuity with "the 'holy alliance' between Newtonian natural philosophy and latitudinarian theology." Even so, the evangelicals made much use of the work of the apologists, even while arguing that reason must ultimately be supernaturally "enlightened."

20. Haddon Willmer, "Evangelicalism, 1785-1835," Hulsean Prize Essay (University of Cambridge, 1962), p. 66.

21. Debate about the conversion of Paul is helpfully reviewed in Larry W. Hurtado, "Convert, Apostate or Apostle to the Nations: The 'Conversion' of Paul in Recent Scholarship," *Studies in Religion* 22 (1993): 273-84.

change in the architecture of the Christian life contributed to more acute introspection. The manuals for self-examination among the Irish monks and missionaries became a treasured legacy in wide circles of Western Christianity. The Black Death may have been significant in the development of the climate of faith and life. Penetrating self-examination reached a hitherto unknown intensity.[22]

Thus Stendahl traces a line from Augustine, through the Middle Ages, to the climax of the development of the introspective conscience in the penitential struggle of Luther. We could extend Stendahl's line further by tracing a process of Protestant catechesis through pulpit and press during the course of the seventeenth and eighteenth centuries, as Puritans, Pietists, and evangelicals sought to reform popular culture through an extension and application of Reformation doctrine into personal life and domestic piety.[23]

While Stendahl emphasizes Luther's crisis as a high point in the development of the introspective conscience, it is important to note that the *autobiographical* moment, as such, did not come with the Reformers in the sixteenth century but with the Puritans and Pietists in the seventeenth.[24] The magisterial reformers wrote tracts, treatises, and catechisms, but they did not on the whole write spiritual autobiographies. We have to go to Luther's 1545 autobiographical fragment in the introduction to his *Works* to find his famous "tower experience." Moreover, many scholars now argue that Luther, looking back as an old man, telescoped a much longer process of growing insight into that alleged breakthrough some twenty years earlier, and that it may be problematic in any case to construe it as his "conversion."[25] Calvin likewise reflects back after some twenty-five years upon his own "sudden conversion" *(subita conversio)* to teachableness, but again, to find this reference you have to look hard through his works and run your finger down the preface to his *Psalms*

22. Krister Stendahl, "The Apostle Paul and the Introspective Conscience of the West," in *Paul Among the Jews and Gentiles and Other Essays,* edited by Krister Stendahl (London, 1976), pp. 82-83.

23. J. I. Packer, "Puritanism as a Movement of Revival," in *Among God's Giants: The Puritan Vision of the Christian Life* (Eastbourne, 1991), pp. 41-63. Cf. William Haller, *The Rise of Puritanism* (1st ed., 1938; reprint, New York, 1957), pp. 3-82; F. Ernst Stoeffler, *The Rise of Evangelical Pietism,* Studies in the History of Religions 9 (Leiden, 1971), pp. 23, 26-27; Walsh, Haydon, and Taylor, *Church of England,* p. 14.

24. Cf. Mascuch, *Origins of the Individualist Self,* p. 19.

25. See further Marilyn J. Harran, *Luther on Conversion* (Ithaca, N.Y., 1983), who reviews the primary sources and the range of interpretations of Luther's conversion. Harran's own view was that Luther's conversion was a "culminating insight" (p. 185).

Commentary (1557) to find the cryptic, passing reference.[26] There is no genre of sixteenth-century Reformation conversion narrative.[27]

To sum up thus far, we have seen the way in which the introspective conscience is central to the genre of evangelical conversion narrative, and how there was an important Reformation and Christendom background that fed into this. So what changed to make the mid-seventeenth century *the* autobiographical moment for Protestantism? This is where we need to consider the importance of a heightened sense of self-consciousness and individuality in early modern society. This is the crux upon which Reformation catechism turns into evangelical piety. Certainly, once models such as Bunyan and Francke are available, the genre takes off.

Before returning to this theme, we shall consider the fate of the conversion narrative in early evangelical mission experience. If the genre of conversion narrative originates in mid-seventeenth-century England, there is a sense in which it terminates in early nineteenth-century Polynesia, for it was precisely this narratable experience of personal conversion that many early evangelical missionaries found so difficult to replicate among their converts in certain non-Christian, non-Western societies (such as in Polynesia). The evangelical missionary experience in the late eighteenth and early nineteenth centuries demonstrates how many beliefs and attitudes, which could be assumed for the most part in Britain, needed to be taught afresh in the new setting before the missionaries could expect to see evangelical conversion of the kind they had themselves experienced. To illustrate, the nature of conversion to Christianity may be observed in three episodes in early evangelical mission history from America, Africa, and the South Pacific. In each of these settings we see an alternative cultural backdrop to the Christendom context of the Evangelical Revival in which most of the missionaries were themselves brought to conversion and thence to a missionary vocation.

26. On Calvin's conversion see Peter Wilcox, "Restoration, Reformation and the Progress of the Kingdom of Christ: Evangelisation in the Thought and Practice of John Calvin, 1555-1564," D.Phil. thesis, University of Oxford, 1993, pp. 177-209.

27. Cf. the comments of W. R. Ward, *The Protestant Evangelical Awakening* (Cambridge, 1992), p. 2: "The movements of renewal and revival of the eighteenth century sought their legitimation in the hand of God in history; their characteristic achievement was not, like the Reformers of the sixteenth century, to offer a confession of faith for public discussion, but to accumulate archives which would support their understanding of history."

David Brainerd's Mission to the Delaware
Native Americans in New Jersey, 1744-46

While there had been earlier efforts to evangelize Native Americans, including, for example, the work of Thomas Mayhew, Jr. (ca. 1620-57) on Martha's Vineyard in 1642, or the ministry of John Eliot (1604-90) among the Massachusetts Native Americans from 1646, it was the mission of David Brainerd (1718-47) among a small band of Delaware Native Americans in New Jersey during the Great Awakening that especially captured the imagination of evangelicals across the North Atlantic world when his diary was published by Jonathan Edwards in 1749. Brainerd's *Life* became a runaway best-seller and went through multiple editions.

Brainerd's life was held up by Edwards as a specimen of the ideals expounded in his *Treatise on the Religious Affections*, much as Sarah Edwards had been earlier in *Some Thoughts Concerning the Revival*.[28] Furthermore, Brainerd's piety was indeed inspirational for many evangelicals, not least for John Wesley, who abridged his *Life* for his Christian Library and exhorted his preachers to read it as the most effective possible means of reviving the Methodist work where it had decayed.[29] If Brainerd's own conversion and example of self-dedication was inspirational, his success among the Delaware Native Americans was equally so, for Brainerd's *Life* recounts a religious awakening in 1744-46 that seemed to show all the Edwardsean signs of evangelical conversion and revival. During his first year among the Delaware band, he claimed to have baptized thirty-eight adults and thirty-nine children, including Moses Tinda Tautamy, his interpreter. The several cases of Native American conversion narrated by Brainerd very much follow the evangelical pattern of conversion, and, indeed, he appears to have judged these cases by the rules that he found in Edwards's *Distinguishing Marks*.[30]

Brainerd's interpretation of Native American conversion needs to be qualified, however. For instance, Brainerd describes the conversion of one elderly Native American who had been a murderer, drunkard, and conjurer. In Brainerd's narrative, recounted in terms of awakening, soul-travail, relief, and so on, one can still hear a note of something foreign to the typical evangelical conversion in the European context. When Brainerd provides indirect quotation or paraphrase, the language of the Native American convert emphasizes

---

28. Norman Pettit, "Editor's Introduction," in *The Life of David Brainerd*, edited by Norman Pettit, The Works of Jonathan Edwards 7 (New Haven, 1985), p. 5.

29. Rivers, "Strangers and Pilgrims," pp. 195-96.

30. Pettit, "Editor's Introduction," p. 23.

the kind of contest of the gods, or power encounter, we are familiar with from other missiological settings, or indeed, from the conversion of Europe in the early Middle Ages. Brainerd reports at one point: "And then, [the Native American convert] says, upon his feeling the Word of God in his heart (as he expresses it), his spirit of conjuration left him entirely, that he has had no more power of that nature since than any other man living; and declares that he don't now so much as know how he used to charm and conjure. . . ."[31] Again later, when challenged by an elderly Native American at the Forks of Delaware who threatened to bewitch Brainerd and his people, this new convert "challenged him to do his worst, telling him that himself [*sic*] had been as great a conjurer as he, and that notwithstanding as soon as he felt that Word in his heart which these people loved (meaning the Word of God), his power of conjuring immediately left him. 'And So it would you,' said he, 'if you did but once feel it in your heart; and you have no power to hurt them, nor so much as to touch one of them,' etc."[32] These elements bracket what is otherwise a carefully crafted account of conscience, travail, self-despair and resignation, divine illumination, and moral transformation. However, we can see that there is also something indigenous taking place in terms of a contest and confrontation of spiritual powers.

Now, although it is hard to be sure given the evidence we have, it seems that what Brainerd was seeing primarily in terms of "the problems of conscience and their resolution" was seen by the Native American converts rather more in terms of Elijah on Mount Carmel. Moreover, if we look at the revival under Brainerd's ministry in terms of the stage of acculturation of the Native American band with whom he worked, we find that whites had occupied much of the surrounding territory for over a century, and that his displaced group of Native Americans were leading a marginal existence, decimated by disease, reduced to poverty by whiskey traders, and peddling homemade wares to their white neighbors.[33] Brainerd's ministry among them lasted only sixteen months. His younger brother, John, took over the work after his death and held it together over the next thirty years. Yet faced with the encroachment of the land-hungry white population, these Delawares were eventually forced onto reservations. By John's death in 1781 even this reservation had been seriously reduced by deaths and departures, and John was never replaced at the mission. In 1801 the last New Jersey Delawares sold their reservation and joined other refugee Native Americans at New Stockbridge, New

31. *Life of Brainerd*, p. 392.

32. *Life of Brainerd*, p. 395.

33. Henry Warner Bowden, *American Indians and Christian Missions: Studies in Cultural Conflict*, edited by Martin E. Marty, Chicago History of American Religion (Chicago, 1981), p. 153; cf. Pettit, "Editor's Introduction," pp. 26-28.

York. Thus, in the longer term history of this particular group of Native Americans, their accession to evangelical Christian belief came at a point of advanced contact with a dominant white civilization. In this respect, it is significant that the band was located in the heartland of the Great Awakening in the Middle Colonies. Indeed, on one occasion, when Brainerd was absent on one of his many trips, the Delawares went a few miles up the road to attend the ministry of the famous revival preacher William Tennent ("whose house they frequented much while I was gone").[34] The Delawares were clearly not in some distant, pristine wilderness.[35]

This wider contextualizing of Brainerd's mission is not intended to discredit his interpretation of the Native American response to Christianity as an evangelical awakening. However, it does suggest that from the perspective of the Native Americans themselves, hard as this perspective is to reconstruct from our sources, they were responding to Christianity against the background of a massive social change in which traditional religious patterns failed to satisfy or were powerless to cope with the new realities of their lives. In terms of conversion and conversion narrative, Brainerd's *Life* did much to spread the message that the pagan world could be expected to respond to the simple preaching of the law and gospel, much as men and women responded in the Evangelical Revival and the Great Awakening. However, conversion was not quite so straightforward among Brainerd's Native American hearers, and many missionaries in other contexts would be disheartened to find it even less so.

The Sierra Leone Colony, 1792–ca. 1830

Granville Sharp's foundering Province of Freedom in Sierra Leone in West Africa was taken over by the Sierra Leone Company in 1791, and the few old

---

34. *Life of Brainerd*, p. 305.

35. Robert Berkhofer has outlined several possible sequences of acculturation among Native Americans between 1760 and 1860 as they encountered Protestant missionaries. The situation of Brainerd's Delaware tribe seems most closely to approximate to his second sequence, the "Fragmented Community Sequence," in which the Native American social system, as well as its cultural system, is divided by response to Christianity. Instead of the original pagan society reintegrating in some sort of manner, two new societies form, and in each culture and society and political authority can be coterminous. So, for example, a new all-Christian village may be formed, as was done under Brainerd's ministry. Berkhofer observes that this process often occurs at about the time political autonomy is lost, just before reservation life commences, and, again, this seems to fit the chronological pattern of Brainerd's Delaware band. Robert F. Berkhofer, Jr., "Protestants, Pagans, and Sequences among the North American Indians, 1760-1860," *Ethnohistory* 10 (1963): 201-32.

settlers that remained were integrated into the new immigrant community of black Nova Scotians. Sierra Leone offers a unique case study in evangelical conversion, for if we cannot exactly say that the settler community of Nova Scotians, with the later recaptives, represented a non-Western society, neither can we say that they had a traditional European framework of Christian beliefs and practices.[36]

The black Baptist pastor David George (1743-1810) was one of those who migrated to Sierra Leone as part of the Clapham-inspired repatriation of former slaves after the American Revolutionary War. His spiritual autobiography was transcribed from spoken conversation and reported in John Rippon's *Baptist Annual Register* (1790-93). It provides the best specimen of the kind of background the first Nova Scotian settlers brought to Sierra Leone.[37] George's experience is also a case study of social dislocation if ever there was one. He was a second-generation African-American slave, born in Virginia, but he escaped his master to live for a time among the Creek Native Americans. Resold into slavery in South Carolina, he had only vague apprehensions of Christianity (he knew the Lord's Prayer); but after being confronted about his bad life by a passing slave, he came under conviction for sin, cast himself upon the mercy of God, and found relief from his distress. Soon afterward, George heard a sermon by the pioneer black Baptist pastor George Liele (1750-1828) and found himself confirmed in his conversion experience. He began to exhort and then to preach, but with the onset of the Revolutionary War he fled to Savannah, Georgia, and then to Charleston, South Carolina, before being evacuated by the British to Nova Scotia, where he founded several black churches and became one of the key leaders in the black community. All of this preceded his emigration, with many of his church members, to Sierra Leone in 1792.

It is because the Nova Scotia settlers brought this kind of background to Sierra Leone, and because the colony was itself inspired by the Clapham Sect, that Andrew Walls can describe Sierra Leone as the "stepchild of the Evangelical Revival."[38] Walls has also recounted the way in which these Nova Scotian settlers set the tone for the colony in religion as in other matters as Sierra Le-

---

36. The standard history of Sierra Leone is Christopher Fyfe, *A History of Sierra Leone* (Oxford, 1962; reprint, Aldershot, 1993).

37. George's narrative is given in full in Grant Gordon, *From Slavery to Freedom: The Life of David George, Pioneer Black Baptist Minister* (Hansport, Nova Scotia, 1992), pp. 168-83.

38. Andrew F. Walls, "A Christian Experiment: The Early Sierra Leone Colony," in *The Mission of the Church and the Propagation of the Faith,* edited by G. J. Cuming, Studies in Church History 6 (Cambridge, 1970), p. 107.

one's population was enlarged by an increasing number of recaptives (slaves recaptured from ships intercepted along the West African coast).[39] These recaptives, having been uprooted from their own traditions, became in Sierra Leone "the first mass movement to Christianity in modern Africa."[40]

If America has been described as a melting pot of immigrant groups, then Sierra Leone was by the second decade of the nineteenth century a cauldron — with all its diverse African peoples, languages, and cultures. The only possibility for the recaptives in Sierra Leone was to take on a new identity, and what developed was a distinctively and self-consciously Christian and Europeanized Krio culture.[41] The Nova Scotian settlers' Christianity, along with the influence of governors and English missionaries, contributed to this identity.

What kind of evangelical piety did the recaptives encounter, then, when they integrated with the earlier settlers? David George and the Nova Scotian Baptists and Methodists brought to Sierra Leone a particularly radical tradition of evangelicalism, which George Rawlyk has described as "a peculiar antinomian blend of American Southern and Nova Scotian New Light popular evangelicalism."[42] This can be seen with particular clarity when George's piety is viewed as a kind of foil to Zachary Macaulay's much more staid and stolid evangelicalism. Macaulay was governor of Sierra Leone (1793-99) and an intimate of the Wilberforce circle at Clapham. In Macaulay's journal, he recorded his observations after an interview with David George, saying:

Ask either one or the other [Methodists] how he knows himself to be a child of God, and the answer from both will be pretty much in the stile of David George, "I know it," not because of this or the other proof drawn from the word of God but because (perhaps) twenty years ago I saw a certain sight or heard certain words or passed thro a certain train of impressions varying from solicitude to deep concern & terror & despair & thence again thro fluctuations of fear & hope to peace & joy & assured confidence.[43]

39. Walls, "A Christian Experiment," p. 116.
40. Walls, "A Christian Experiment," p. 128. See also Andrew F. Walls, "A Colonial Concordat: Two Views of Christianity and Civilisation," in *Church Society and Politics*, edited by Derek Baker, Studies in Church History 12 (Oxford, 1975), p. 301.
41. Wells, "Black Europeans — White Africans," pp. 102-4.
42. G. A. Rawlyk, *The Canada Fire: Radical Evangelicalism in British North America, 1775-1812* (Kingston, Ontario, 1994), p. 33.
43. Rawlyk, *The Canada Fire*, p. 39; Gordon, *Slavery to Freedom*, p. 149.

Because the Nova Scotians had been so often disappointed by white American and European elites — through slavery in the south, through mistreatment and racism in Nova Scotia, and through mismanagement in Sierra Leone — their radical evangelicalism was, as often as not, also part of an expression of distinctive, and even dissenting, piety. Here the genre of conversion narrative was appropriated to the Nova Scotians' own context in at least two significant ways.

First, there is a telling phrase in David George's conversion narrative. When George began to exhort and to preach after his conversion, he realized he needed to learn to read. His comment after learning a little was: "I can now read the Bible, so that what I have in my heart, I can see again in the Scriptures."[44] That is to say, the oral and the personal was anterior to the written and the discursive element in his experience. Indeed, George's phrase for many of his meetings with his people emphasized the oral context: they met "to hear experiences."[45] This spoken context of evangelical conversion narrative gave such testimonies a keen sense of immediacy. Whether in Bristol in 1741, in New Jersey among the Delawares in 1744, or in South Carolina in the 1770s, such "live performances" called forth a less scripted and more impassioned expression of conversion. In talking about what he had "in his heart," David George was not talking about a strict Edwardsean piety in which the Calvinist *ordo* is carefully teased out from Scripture and rationalized in terms of intellectually grounded affective dispositions; he was talking about his *feelings*. Once he learned to read, there it was in the printed text too, but only *ex post facto*. The heart strangely warmed by the spoken word came first.

Second, the spiritual autobiographies of ex-slaves such as George were often constructed not only around a theme of evangelical conversion but also around the entirely sympathetic and biblical theme of emancipation and freedom from bondage. The key Scripture text in George's conversion — the one that resonated most deeply for him — was Matthew 11:28: "Come to me all ye that labour, and are heavy laden, and I will give you rest." After he had heard Liele preach on this text, he went and told him that he was such a one, "that I was weary and heavy laden, and that the grace of God had given me rest."[46] In Sierra Leone itself, the Nova Scotian settlers were reputed to have sung the song of Miriam as they marched ashore, celebrating their arrival and crossing of the Atlantic in terms of the Israelite exodus and crossing of the Red Sea. The exodus theme became a powerful organizing motif for slave

44. Gordon, *Slavery to Freedom,* p. 173.
45. Gordon, *Slavery to Freedom,* pp. 176, 179, 180.
46. Gordon, *Slavery to Freedom,* p. 172.

narratives of spiritual conversion.[47] An unidentified European recorded a message preached by a black minister in Sierra Leone — very possibly David George himself — in which the Israelite exodus typology was made explicit: "We all mind since it was so with us; we was in slavery not many years ago! Some maybe worse oppressed dan oders, but we was all under de yoke; and what den? God saw our afflictions, and heard our cry, and showed his salvation, in delivering us, and bringing us over de mighty waters to dis place."[48]

One can the more easily appreciate that a piety revolving around evangelical conversion, so construed, would be sympathetic to the recaptive Africans whose identity-giving past had been so entirely obliterated. In forging a new identity, evangelical conversion came to play a key role, as the revivals of 1816 in Regent town under William Johnson, and afterward, bore witness.

Did the recaptives have what we have described in the English context as a "Christendom" inheritance? What of the "introspective conscience of the West" developed through centuries of penitential discipline, and the assumptions writ large in early modern European culture about creation, providence, moral order, and eschatology? No, they did not have this inheritance, but what is particularly fascinating is how quickly they were given something like it through Governor Charles MacCarthy's program of Europeanization, with virtual squire-parsons ("squarsons") set up in an organized pattern of parish administration including stone churches, parsonages, storehouses, schools, high-walled government buildings, European-style dress, houses, furniture, and crockery. MacCarthy ordered bells, clocks, and weathercocks from England for the church towers, scales and weights for the local markets, forges for village blacksmiths, quill-pens, copy-books, prayer books and arithmetic books for the schools, hats for the men, bonnets for the women, and so on.[49] This program of Europeanization was so successful that these Sierra Leoneans have been rightly described as "Black Europeans" and even contrasted ironically with the holiness-inspired missionaries of a slightly later period in Nigeria whose ideals of indigenization — bringing of the gospel into the day-to-day realities of African life — led them to dress as natives and

---

47. Albert J. Raboteau, "The Black Experience in American Evangelicalism: The Meaning of Slavery," in *The Evangelical Tradition in America,* edited by Leonard I. Sweet (Macon, Ga., 1984), p. 194; Albert J. Raboteau, *Slave Religion: The "Invisible Institution" in the Antebellum South* (New York, 1978), pp. 3, 11-12.

48. Gordon, *Slavery to Freedom,* pp. 131-32, quoting an "Extract of a letter from Sierra Leone, containing part of a sermon, by a black preacher at Freetown," *Missionary Magazine* 1 (1796): 77.

49. Fyfe, *History of Sierra Leone,* pp. 129-31.

hence to appear as "White Africans."[50] These missionaries would be quick to lament the prevalence of nominal faith among West Africans, much as evangelical preachers scorned the Christianity of nominal churchgoers in Britain.

Evangelical Missions to the South Pacific, 1797–ca. 1830

The closest situation we have to cultural contact with a pure and undiluted non-Western society, where missionaries were in the vanguard of cross-cultural encounter, is in the evangelical mission enterprises in the South Pacific from roughly the end of the eighteenth century to the third decade of the nineteenth century. The story of Western contact with the peoples of Australasia has been told elsewhere, along with the missionary history from the sailing of the LMS ship, the *Duff,* and the landing of ill-prepared missionaries on Tahiti and other islands in the Marquesas and Tonga, to the revivals throughout Polynesia from 1830 to 1850.[51] What we may note here in particular is the early missionary reflection on the islanders' experience of conversion.

Missionaries to the South Seas, many of whom had been inspired by Brainerd's diary, were often perplexed that islanders experienced so little abject misery in the first stages of conversion, when made aware of their past wrongdoing — even when this included infanticide, cannibalism, or human sacrifice. There was often a complete lack of emotion in conversion. One missionary to the Society Islands, William Ellis (1794-1872), wrote:

> Under declarations of the nature and dreadful consequences of sin . . . the denunciation of the penalties of the law of God, and even under the awakenings of their own consciences to a conviction of sin, we seldom perceive that deep and acute distress of mind, which in circumstances of a similar kind we should have expected.[52]

Likewise, upon being made to understand the doctrine of the cross, the islanders did not frequently express "that sudden relief, and that exstatic [*sic*] joy, which is often manifested in other parts of the world, by individuals in corresponding circumstances." Again, Ellis reflects,

50. Walls, "Black Europeans — White Africans," pp. 102-10.
51. See Niel Gunson, *Messengers of Grace: Evangelical Missionaries in the South Seas, 1797-1860* (Melbourne, 1978); K. R. Howe, *Where the Waves Fall: A New South Sea Islands History from First Settlement to Colonial Rule* (Sydney, 1984).
52. Gunson, *Messengers of Grace*, p. 223.

the varied representations of the punishment and sufferings of the wicked, and the corresponding views of heaven, as the state of the great-est blessedness, being to them partial and new, the impressions were probably vague and indistinct; while with us, from long familiarity, they are at once vivid and powerful.[53]

Ellis, then, would appear to confirm the hypothesis of the need for a certain level of Christianization of conscience as a condition of evangelical conver-sion narrative. In any case, the missionaries worked hard to change this atti-tude of indifference into real contrition through both civil and ecclesiastical discipline, and through the preaching of sin and hell, since as Neil Gunson comments, "they wished their converts really to feel their guilt."[54]

Ellis's consternation at the absence of typical patterns of response to the evangelical message was apparent from the comments of other missionaries as well. Sometimes this came out in correspondence between the field and mission authorities back in England. There was a tendency for home authori-ties to regard the success of mission work according to standards derived from their own experience. "I often wish," wrote one LMS missionary to the directors, "that our joy on the shores of Tahiti were in some measure propor-tionate to yours on the platform in Exeter Hall." It was difficult for those at home to realize that change in the islands was a very gradual process, and that mass conversion to Christianity was more often the beginning than the cli-max of mission work.[55]

The usual pattern after the arrival of the first missionaries was initial re-sistance, next perhaps a few conversions of marginal members of an island society, then the conversion of the chief, followed by a mass conversion of the island, and the beginnings of long-term process instruction to make the nominal faith of the group more personally meaningful for its members.[56]

53. Gunson, *Messengers of Grace*, p. 223.
54. Gunson, *Messengers of Grace*, p. 223.
55. Gunson, *Messengers of Grace*, p. 131.
56. Cf. Berkhofer's first sequence of community reintegration in "Protestants, Pa-gans, and Sequences among Indians," pp. 206-8. Note, however, the large-scale conversion of the Maoris in New Zealand, where the native population was more decentralized into small groups and often at war with each other; conversion followed more of a bottom-up pattern and came to be associated with reconciliation and peace making rather than with the victory of a warrior patron such as Pomare II. Extensive debate about the reasons and conditions of Maori conversion may be followed in Harrison M. Wright, *New Zealand, 1769-1840: Early Years of Western Contact* (Cambridge, Mass., 1959); Judith Binney, *The Legacy of Guilt: A Life of Thomas Kendall* (Christchurch, New Zealand, 1968); J. M. R. Owens, "Christianity and the Maoris to 1840," *New Zealand Journal of History* 2 (1968):

One recent historian of the South Seas describes this phenomenon of mass conversion under the influence of the chief by analogy with the conversion of the Germanic peoples of early medieval Europe. The way in which Tahitians acceded to Christianity after Pomare II went to war in the name of Jehovah and united the island under his rule in 1815 is thus the Polynesian equivalent of the Christianization of Spain by Charlemagne. K. R. Howe's concluding observation on Tahiti is that "the doctrine of *cuius regio, eius religio* (as the King, so the religion) has universal, not just European application."[57]

The result of this pattern of conversion was that many of the South Sea islands came to embody more of a "parish" than a "gathered" model of church, and to embrace a "mixed body" (Augustine: *corpus permixtem*) of Christians in which there was a profound distinction between nominal and earnest Christian allegiance. Consequently, the lament of missionaries in this situation was often the same as that of evangelicals in Europe. When George Pritchard complained in 1826 "that nine-tenths, of those who were in Church fellowship [were] strangers to the power of vital Godliness," he could as easily have been John Berridge opening his evangelical ministry at Everton, as an LMS missionary to Tahiti.[58] Because Christianity in the islands was eventually adjusted to the existing tribal structure of society, the most difficult problem for the missionaries was often the role of the chiefs in the religious life of the community. Here too there is an analogy to the long history of church-state tension in Europe from the German investiture controversy in the high Middle Ages to the Scottish Disruption of 1843 over the voluntary principle.

In the South Pacific, Gunson concludes that there were two types of conversion experienced by the islanders:

> There was the experience of heart-acceptance or faith, and there was the outward profession necessitated by a national change of religion. Even this nominal profession, or renunciation of the old gods, was a major break with the past. . . . However, this was only part of the pattern. Old

18-40; Judith Binney, "Christianity and the Maoris to 1840: A Comment," *New Zealand Journal of History* 3 (1969): 143-65; K. R. Howe, "The Maori Response to Christianity in the Thames-Waikato Area, 1833-1840," *New Zealand Journal of History* 7 (1973): 28-46; Robin Fisher, "Henry Williams' Leadership of the CMS Mission to New Zealand," *New Zealand Journal of History* 9 (1975): 142-53; Howe, *Where the Waves Fall*, pp. 224-26.

57. Howe, *Where the Waves Fall*, p. 145. On the Christianization of Europe see Anton Wessels, *Europe: Was It Ever Really Christian?* translated by John Bowden (London, 1994).

58. Gunson, *Messengers of Grace*, p. 303.

superstitions persisted, and it was only the heartfelt conversion in which the missionaries found satisfaction.[59]

Indeed, revivals of the latter sort often came later, as in 1845 on Fiji.

The uniqueness of mission history in the South Pacific, fragmented as the region was into thousands of isolated island communities that preserved their indigenous autonomy as social decision–making units, has attracted the attention of cultural anthropologists. Alan Tippett was one missionary anthropologist who developed a sequential model to illustrate the dominant pattern of conversion among the peoples of Oceania, in particular, over the last century. In the transition of such societies from the old pagan context to the new Christian context, Tippett saw first a period of awareness, which climaxes in a point of realization when the new faith is not just an idea but a meaningful possibility, and which introduces a further period of decision making. This period in turn climaxes in a point of commitment, when, if Christianity is embraced, then this is symbolized by an ocular demonstration of their rejection of paganism (such as fetish burning) and acceptance of Christianity (usually through baptism). After this follows a period of incorporation and catechesis into the new faith. Having developed his model to this point, Tippett later added a further point of consummation or confirmation, followed by a further period of maturity. Tippett acknowledged that he grounds this further stage in his own Wesleyan-holiness theology, but also he commented, "The early mission records in the Wesleyan fields of the south Pacific speak of 'two conversions,' one from heathenism to Christianity as a system, a faith experience or *power encounter* . . . , and the second, a little later, a faith experience leading to a positive *assurance of new birth.* In many cases still further 'manifestations of grace' have been recorded, experiences of *sanctification,* associated with revivals rather than awakenings."[60]

Conclusion: The Conditions for Narratable Evangelical Conversion

In the first two mission contexts we observed a significant history of European contact, although the process of Christianization was perhaps less ad-

59. Gunson, *Messengers of Grace,* p. 220.

60. Alan R. Tippett, "Conversion as a Dynamic Process in Christian Mission," *Missiology* 502 (April 1977): 219. A sequential model similar to Tippett's, but elaborated through extensive cross-disciplinary research, is given in Lewis R. Rambo, *Understanding Religious Conversion* (New Haven, 1993).

vanced among the Delaware Native Americans of New Jersey than among the settlers and recaptives of Sierra Leone. We also saw distinctive forms of recognizable evangelical conversion narrative, such as the unnamed old Native American convert under Brainerd's ministry, who weaves into his testimony a concern with the loss of spiritual power, or David George, who looks back on a remarkable spiritual and geographical migration and integrates an exodus theme into his narrative. Among the Pacific islanders whose national conversions, such as under Pomare II in Tahiti, brought about a change of religion to Christianity without initially disrupting their social system in a significant way, missionary testimony bears witness to the absence of recognizable evangelical conversion until the later revivals of the mid-century. What may we conclude from this, and how can this help us to establish the conditions for narratable evangelical conversion?

It seems that there are two key interrelated conditions: first, the development of a heightened sense of introspective conscience (which was noted above), and, second, the rise of a sense of distinctive self-consciousness. Protestant catechesis and the penitential discipline and contritional framework of Western Christendom did much to supply the first condition among European peoples, and arguably this was true also to some extent in the case of the Delaware Native Americans and the Black African diaspora (in the American South, Nova Scotia, and Sierra Leone), where there was a long history of cultural encounter dominated by white Europeans and Protestant missionaries. Yet what of the second condition — a distinctive sense of the self?

The contemporary moral philosopher Charles Taylor has examined the origins of the modern identity in his study, *Sources of the Self* (1989). He writes, "Along with [modern] forms of narrativity go new understandings of society and forms of living together. Corresponding to the free, disengaged subject is a view of society as made up of and by the consent of free individuals." Taylor argues that we do not have selves the way we have hearts and livers, "as an interpretation-free given," but that the sense of personal identity is shaped by moral topography and a conception of society, or what it is to be a human agent among other agents[61] — in other words, by what makes up the conscience and self-consciousness.

The modern identity or sense of the self goes hand in hand then with societies in which self-determination is given significant scope, for it is in these situations that the individual may construe his or her life not in terms of a traditional role handed down, but rather in terms of a goal-directed narrative, where past and present choices of certain courses of action among many

61. Charles Taylor, *Sources of the Self* (Cambridge, 1992), pp. 105-6.

possibilities are projected into an open-ended future. The kinds of societies in which such a sense of the self may be expected to occur are those societies that comprehend relatively more pluralism, that is, those societies in which responsibility devolves upon the individual to make significant choices among viable alternatives that affect his or her destiny. To the extent that these choices move the individual toward or away from what that person conceives to be good or ideal, to that extent the person also understands him- or herself in narrative terms.[62]

Now the narrative, if it is articulated, may come in many forms. It may be curriculum vitae, apologia, memoir, travelogue, or a rags-to-riches tale, but one of the forms it took, as a matter of record, is a narrative of spiritual conversion. Many recent comparative studies of evangelicalism have highlighted the way in which this evangelical impulse has thrived in situations of social disruption, in the cross-pollination of peoples, and even in political revolution.[63] Indeed, the North Atlantic evangelical revivals of the eighteenth century arose themselves in the midst of unprecedented movements of people and a heightened awareness of other nations through the forced and voluntary migrations and through increasingly efficient means of transportation and communication.[64] That kind of stirring of the international pot is also certainly what we witness in Sierra Leone, spectacularly, but also among the Native Americans in New Jersey. So these are situations, it may be argued, in which a narrative form of self-understanding and expression may be expected to flourish. In the South Pacific, where traditional patterns of society are not disrupted, even in national conversions to Christianity, we get a dif-

---

62. Cf. Alasdair MacIntyre, *After Virtue: A Study in Moral Theory,* 2nd ed. (London, 1985), pp. 218-19.

63. "In almost all North Atlantic regions, evangelicalism was already present as a religious impulse before the onset of political revolution. Perhaps with only one or two exceptions, however, evangelicalism did not exert a broad, culture-shaping influence in these societies until after the experience of revolution. . . . [Such a survey indicates] how extraordinarily adaptable the evangelical impulse was in North Atlantic societies during an age of revolution. . . . More than anything else, it was evangelicalism's singular combination of Protestant biblicism and experiential faith that enabled it to flourish in revolutionary settings, precisely because it was able to offer, when other props gave way, meaning for persons, order for society, and hope for the future." Mark A. Noll, "Revolution and the Rise of Evangelical Social Influence in North Atlantic Societies," in *Evangelicalism,* pp. 114-15.

64. Ward, *Protestant Evangelical Awakening,* pp. 1-53; W. R. Ward, *Faith and Faction* (London, 1993), pp. 249-63; Susan O'Brien, "A Transatlantic Community of Saints: The Great Awakening and the First Evangelical Network, 1735-55," *American Historical Review* 91 (1986): 811-32; Susan O'Brien, "Eighteenth-century Publishing Networks in the First Years of Transatlantic Evangelicalism," in *Evangelicalism,* pp. 38-57.

ferent situation in which the kinds of questions that might prompt a personal narrative as an answer do not arise.

To return then to the earlier, related question of why the seventeenth century offers the autobiographical moment in the Western Christian tradition, it should be clear now that in addition to a sense of introspective conscience — which was acute already among the sixteenth-century reformers — evangelical conversion narrative requires the modern conditions of society, in which the individual has greater scope for self-determination. Clearly, there was something distinctive about the conditions of Europe and colonial America in the early modern period that helped to foster the evangelical narrative and to compel countless women and men to resort to confessional diaries, oral testimony, and written autobiographies to interpret their own religious experience as a story of conversion.

It is a commonplace of intellectual history that western Europe did see an increasing involution or individuation of consciousness in the early modern period. From the complex psychology of a character like Lear in Elizabethan drama to the preoccupation with self-portraiture on the part of Rembrandt, from Descartes's *cogito* to Locke's *tabula rasa*, there seems to be a new anthropocentrism and self-reflectiveness in Western society that sets the period apart. The intellectual historian Georges Gusdorf wrote an important essay in 1956, "The Conditions and Limits of Autobiography," which pioneered the critical and theoretical study of autobiography as a genre. He highlights the novelty of this self-consciousness by contrast with what came before:

> The conscious awareness of the singularity of each individual life is the late product of a specific civilization. Throughout most of human history, the individual does not oppose himself to all others; he does not feel himself to exist outside of others, and still less against others, but very much *with* others in an interdependent existence that asserts its rhythms everywhere in the community. No one is rightful possessor of his life or his death; lives are so thoroughly entangled that each of them has its center everywhere and its circumference nowhere. The important unit is thus never the isolated being — or, rather, isolation is impossible in such a scheme of total cohesiveness as this. Community life unfolds like a great drama, with its climactic moments originally fixed by the gods being repeated from age to age. Each man thus appears as the possessor of a role, already performed by the ancestors and to be performed again by descendants.[65]

65. Georges Gusdorf, "The Conditions and Limits of Autobiography," in *Autobiog-*

Gusdorf's picture of premodern consciousness, however idealized, compares well with evangelical missionary experience on Tahiti and elsewhere in the South Pacific and helps to explain one of the missing conditions of evangelical conversion narrative in that context.

In contrast, Gusdorf describes the new consciousness in Western society that autobiography reflects:

> The specific intention of autobiography and its anthropological prerogative as a literary genre is clear: it is one of the means to self-knowledge thanks to the fact that it recomposes and interprets a life in its totality. An examination of consciousness limited to the present moment will give me only a fragmentary cutting from my personal being without the guarantee that it will continue. In recounting my history I take the longest path, but this path that goes round my life leads me the more surely from me to myself. [It] . . . obliges me to situate what I am in the perspective of what I have been. . . . It adds to experience itself consciousness of it.[66]

Or, again, "[autobiography] asserts a kind of tradition between myself and me that establishes an ancient and new fidelity, for the past drawn up into the present is also a pledge and prophecy of the future."[67]

This is precisely what happened in evangelical narratives of conversion, in which the autobiographer places himself personally along the curve of salvation history. In W. R. Ward's words, these narratives expressed a "wish to realize the history of salvation not only as an objective and outward fact but as an event of the soul."[68] The self is projected into a future that follows the Reformation order of salvation — growth in holiness, Christian service, and a pious death with the expectation of eternal felicity hereafter. However, this abstract pattern was read in personal terms from the details of one's own past and present life.

Christians under the conditions that obtained in western Europe in the seventeenth and eighteenth centuries assumed that the narrative self could be a significant theater of revelation and redemption, a location of transcenden-

---

raphy: Essays Theoretical and Critical, edited by James Olney (Princeton, N.J., 1980), pp. 29-30. Gusdorf's account is nuanced and developed in a more detailed way in Mascuch, *Origins of the Individualist Self,* pp. 6-9, 13-24.

66. Gusdorf, "Conditions and Limits," p. 38.

67. Gusdorf, "Conditions and Limits," p. 44.

68. W. R. Ward, "Introduction," in *The Works of John Wesley,* edited by W. R. Ward and Richard P. Heitzenrater (Nashville, 1988), p. 9.

tal significance that was communicable in simple terms. In other words, in talking about myself I can point to something beyond myself. Through my own story I can point to the larger story of God and his saving works. Beyond the relatively uncomplicated question of egotism — Am I drawing undue attention to myself? — these narratives rarely raised the imponderable issues of radical subjectivity that were being considered off and on by philosophers during the century and came finally into clear focus in Immanuel Kant's *Critiques*. The self could be discussed publicly without any real threat that it would dissolve in a kind of hermeneutical solipsism. There was a particular window of time in Western intellectual history from roughly the mid-seventeenth until the late eighteenth century when the self could bear the weight placed upon it by this kind of Christian self-reflection. The didacticism of the Augustan Enlightenment, combined with limited forms of social and political self-determination and other factors, created a situation in which one could speak autobiographically in a way that was difficult to do before or after, or in markedly different cultural contexts.[69] It is no accident that large numbers of these eighteenth-century conversion narratives were written in the form of familiar letters — that most typical of eighteenth-century genres, standing midway between the objectivity of the essay and the subjectivity of the diary, a perfect form for the combination of semipublic argument and self-expression. From our own vantage point at the opening of the twenty-first century, during which the whole notion of the liberal humanist self has become so problematic to moral philosophers and literary theorists, and when the self has been so radically "de-centered" within postmodern and poststructuralist writing, we can better appreciate that this was no mean achievement.

The evangelical conversion narrative flourished, then, whenever and wherever Christendom, or Christian civil society, had eroded far enough to allow for toleration, dissent, experimentation, and the manifestation of nominal and sincere forms of adherence to faith, but not so far as to elide a traditional sense of Christian moral norms and basic cosmological assumptions. It was precisely in the seventeenth and eighteenth centuries that the emerging modern identity could cross paths with the fading Christian moral hegemony in the West. These were the conditions under which large numbers of men

---

69. The evangelical genre of conversion narrative certainly persists into the nineteenth and twentieth centuries — indeed it flourishes — but it may be argued that by the first third of the nineteenth century the genre had come to reflect a much more advanced and englobing sense of the priority of human agency in conversion. See David Bebbington, "Evangelical Conversion, c. 1740-1850," North Atlantic Missiology Project Position Paper No. 21 (Cambridge, 1996), pp. 15, 21.

and women found that the pattern and experience of evangelical conversion expressed their deepest religious aspirations.[70] Where these conditions were absent, as in most of the mission fields to which evangelicals took their message of the transformation of the individual self by redeeming grace, Christian conversion and Christian experience developed according to patterns that profoundly challenged their preconceptions.

70. Walls, "Evangelical Revival," in *Evangelicalism*, pp. 313-14.

CHAPTER FIVE

Ethnology and Theology: Nineteenth-Century Mission Dilemmas in the South Pacific

JANE SAMSON

"The Isles shall wait for his law," said the book of the prophet Isaiah, and in the Second Psalm Jehovah had promised Israel's messianic king: "I shall give you the heathen for your inheritance, and the uttermost parts of the earth for your possession."[1] After reading the narratives of Captain Cook in 1795, it seemed to the founders of the newly formed "Missionary Society" that providence had indeed chosen to reveal the distant Pacific islands to Britain as part of this unfolding of divine purpose for the restoration of lost humanity. There had been earlier British encounters with the islands, and France too was launching explorations in the late eighteenth century. However, it was Cook's voyages that captured the imagination of the British public, and Cook's accounts of human sacrifice, cannibalism, and sexual promiscuity, especially at Tahiti, that prompted the Society, known as the London Missionary Society (LMS) after 1818, to choose the South Pacific as its first field of endeavor. The first LMS missionaries arrived at Tahiti in the Society Islands group in 1797, and from there they extended LMS operations to the Cook Islands and Samoa.

The LMS was only the first of many missions to the South Pacific. In 1814 the Church Missionary Society (CMS) established a mission to New Zealand on the initiative of Samuel Marsden, the evangelical chaplain to the New South Wales colony.[2] The Presbyterian Church in Nova Scotia founded the

---

1. Isaiah 42:4 and Psalm 2:8. These texts, particularly the latter, were much cited in nineteenth-century missionary meetings and periodicals.
2. On Marsden see chapter eight below.

New Hebrides mission at Aneityum in 1848, and the following year Bishop George Selwyn of New Zealand made the first of many voyages to the western Pacific to bring youths to New Zealand for training as mission teachers. The Melanesian mission that he founded became the framework of the new Anglican diocese of Melanesia, established in 1861.

Some missionaries, especially John Williams of the LMS and Bishops Selwyn and Patteson of the Melanesian mission, became well known for their feats of travel and exploration, and the British public devoured their accounts of island voyages and exotic peoples waiting for the gospel. Indeed, British missionaries were the first to provide sustained, detailed, and quasi-scientific observations of Pacific islanders.[3] Their accounts influenced British commercial operations in the islands, especially by stimulating trade in sandalwood, and their publicized dread of French or American incursions prompted discussions about the possibility of British rule in the islands. The economic and political implications of missions have been fairly extensively studied, along with their actual operations in the islands.[4] Less well known are missionary observations and interpretations of island societies, especially with regard to the relationship between empirical observation, theology, and theories of natural history.

During the early and mid-nineteenth century, when South Pacific missions were growing in strength and publicity, anthropology had yet to replace its ancestor, ethnology. Later, anthropologists distanced themselves from ethnology and its religious preoccupations; as historian George Stocking points out, most history of anthropology still avoids ethnology because today's anthropologists share their predecessors' distaste for theology.[5] It is certainly true that the ethnographic writings of British missionaries played a large role in ethnology; indeed, there were as yet no professional distinctions to separate the missionary in the field from the armchair philosopher at home. This invites historians to explore the links between British intellectual history, missions, and imperialism. A recent book by Nicholas Thomas makes the important point that the Enlightenment project gave Europe its first anthropo-

---

3. See Christopher Herbert, *Culture and Anomie: Ethnographic Imagination in the Nineteenth Century* (Chicago and London, 1991), ch. 3; Rod Edmond, *Representing the South Pacific: Colonial Discourse from Cook to Gauguin* (Cambridge, 1997), ch. 4.

4. Niel Gunson, *Messengers of Grace: Evangelical Missionaries in the South Seas, 1797-1860* (Oxford and Melbourne, 1978); John Garrett, *To Live Among the Stars: Christian Origins in Oceania* (Geneva and Suva, 1982); Char Miller, ed., *Missions and Missionaries in the Pacific* (New York and Toronto, 1985).

5. James Cowles Prichard, *Researches into the Physical History of Man,* ed. George W. Stocking (Chicago and London, 1973), p. xxxiii.

logical view of non-Europeans, who were "mapped and ranked . . . in an evolutionary natural history."[6] Yet this is hardly a new insight, as Thomas seems to believe: historians of imperialism have long been interested in the definition of cultural others by European observers; John Elliot's writings on the impact of the discovery of America and *The Great Map of Mankind* by P. J. Marshall and Glyndwr Williams remain invaluable guides to the shift from early modern to Enlightenment constructions of the outside world.[7] The "dominance of the religious frame" that Thomas identifies has also been explored by Doreen M. Rosman, Andrew Porter, Brian Stanley, and others in studies that link Britain's religious history to the expansion of British missions and the wider context of empire.[8]

In the South Pacific, more than almost anywhere else, the first British missions were largely untroubled (except in New Zealand) by British commerce. Their perceptions, then, could not possibly have been driven by the need to justify economic exploitation or atone for earlier "structures of domination and extermination," as one scholar has suggested recently.[9] What mission expansion did complement was the high tide of ethnological speculation about the origin and diversity of humanity, to which missionary observations of Pacific islanders added a great deal. This speculation, based as it was on the empirical observation and classification of non-European peoples, was undoubtedly an Enlightenment project. Even the illustrations of islanders in early mission publications were drawn directly from classical, eighteenth-century treatments: the frontispiece of John Williams's *Narrative of Missionary Enterprises* showed a Rarotongan chief with the approved, statuesque stance and profile, draped in a toga. "Shall Religion refuse to follow, where the love of Science leads?" wondered the author of *The Spirit of Christian Mis-*

6. Nicholas Thomas, *Colonialism's Culture: Anthropology, Travel and Government* (Cambridge, 1994), p. 71.

7. J. H. Elliott, *The Old World and the New, 1492-1650* (Cambridge, 1992; first published, 1970); P. J. Marshall and Glyndwr Williams, *The Great Map of Mankind: British Perceptions of the World in the Age of Enlightenment* (London, 1982). See also Anthony Pagden, *The Fall of Natural Man: The American Indian and the Origins of Comparative Ethnology* (Cambridge, 1982); Anthony Pagden, *European Encounters with the New World* (New Haven and London, 1993).

8. See Doreen M. Rosman, *Evangelicals and Culture* (Aldershot, 1992; first published, 1984); A. N. Porter, "Religion and Empire: British Expansion in the Long Nineteenth Century, 1780-1914," *Journal of Imperial and Commonwealth History* 20.3 (1992): 370-90; Brian Stanley, *The Bible and the Flag: Protestant Missions and British Imperialism in the Nineteenth and Twentieth Centuries* (Leicester, 1990).

9. Mary Louise Pratt, *Imperial Eyes: Travel Writing and Transculturation* (London and New York, 1992), p. 74.

sions.[10] Follow it did, and the relationship between scientific analysis and Christian theology, as communicated by missionaries to their supporters at home, is the theme of this chapter. As Williams himself put it, there was an important difference between generalized beliefs in "the natural depravity of Man," and the fascinating and distinctive features "which arise from the existing state of society and customs of the people."[11]

For missionaries in the South Pacific, theorizing about islanders served a complex purpose. Observations of behavior and institutions that they found immoral, and often repugnant, underscored the need for redemption. However, it was vital to build points of connection with these alien peoples if the gospel was to be preached. The main point, of course, was that all were equal before God and in equal need of salvation. Missionaries went to the islands with faith, but also with preconceived ideas about the task that faced them. They knew from the descriptions of Cook and other explorers that the islands were beautiful, and the romance surrounding their discovery was infectious. Some, like George Vason in Tonga and Thomas Kendall in New Zealand, succumbed to that romance, as interpreted to them by the beauty and sexual freedom of certain island women, and they "went native" — and then recanted — in a blaze of publicity.[12]

Incidents like these remind us that some missionaries found themselves questioning, and even rejecting, their own cultural backgrounds. For most, however, there was strong resistance to the idea of an idealized primitive or "noble savage." Although they believed in a universal human rationality, missionaries also regarded "natural man" as inherently sinful. In his famous sermon to the new Missionary Society in 1795, Thomas Haweis denounced those who saw "the fabled Gardens of the Hesperides" in the South Pacific; Britons should remember instead that "amidst these enchanting scenes, savage nature still feasts on the flesh of its prisoners."[13] Daniel Tyerman and George Bennett also referred to eighteenth-century theories of noble savagery in their account of travels to various mission stations, concluding that "Alas! *Such* a race of 'Indians' never existed anywhere on the face of this fallen world, in a state of nature — or rather, in that state of heathenism in which

10. "A Clergyman," in *The Spirit of Christian Missions* (London, 1815), p. 49.
11. Richard M. Moyle, ed., *The Samoan Journals of John Williams* (Canberra, 1984), p. 282.
12. S. Piggott, ed., *An Authentic Narrative of Four Years' Residence at Tongataboo* (London, 1810); and Judith Binney, *The Legacy of Guilt: A Life of Thomas Kendall* (Christchurch, New Zealand, 1968).
13. [Thomas Haweis], "The Apostolic Commission," in *Sermons Preached in London* (London, 1795), p. 12.

the best feelings of nature are incessantly and universally outraged."[14] Sir George Rose, Conservative M.P. for Christchurch, speaking at the annual general meeting of the Wesleyan Methodist Missionary Society in 1840, noted that British missionaries did not go among those "'children of nature' with such views. They did not venture amongst them because they believed them to be virtuous and good. They knew that the inhabitants of Feejee were monsters in depravity and cruelty."[15]

Rose was contrasting missions with the outlook of the eighteenth-century French explorer La Pérouse and his naturalist Lamanon. However, noble savagery had not always dominated Enlightenment thought about the Pacific islands. Even the most idealistic French explorer could find his idealism challenged by experience; Lamanon lost his life, along with eleven other members of La Pérouse's crew, when Samoans attacked his landing party in 1787. Among Enlightenment philosophers, the idea that "primitive" societies lived by universal laws of nature was challenged by other theories about climatic influence and social evolutionism. For every writer sympathetic to noble savagery, such as the editor of Cook's first voyage, John Hawkesworth, there were scientists like J. R. Forster who used their own observations of the Pacific and other parts of the world to explore the variety and development of human cultures.[16] Tension between these universalizing and particularizing theories is also found in missionary writings about islanders. On the one hand, humanity was sinful, without exception, and redeemable only through the equally universal sacrifice of Christ. On the other hand, many missionaries were fascinated by the similarities and distinctions between island cultures, and by theories about their settlement and development. The point is that their rejection of "noble savagery" did not imply a rejection of all Enlightenment approaches to the study of humanity: in particular it should be noted that their theology did not preclude an interest in empirical observation and classification.

To remind themselves and their readers of the moral imperatives of their mission, many missionaries chose to describe the islands using contrasting biblical imagery of light and darkness. William Ellis, LMS missionary at Tahiti and Hawai'i, and one of the South Pacific's most prominent ethnographers, wrote about the large fires Tahitians lit to mark traditional celebrations

14. Daniel Tyerman and George Bennett, *Journal of Voyages and Travels* (London, 1841), p. 150.

15. WMMS, *Missionary Notices* 18-19 (June-July 1840): 302.

16. Bernard Smith, *European Vision and the South Pacific*, 2nd ed. (New Haven and London 1985), pp. 84-90, 137-44; Marshall and Williams, *Great Map of Mankind*, pp. 263, 266-74.

and was struck by what he called "the contrast between the country, and the inhabitants . . . appearing as if the demons of darkness had lighted up infernal fires, even in the bowers of paradise."[17] As missions moved into the western Pacific, they employed the same language. James Chalmers, the first LMS missionary to New Guinea in the 1870s, appreciated the beauties of this "land of splendid mountains, magnificent forests, and mighty rivers" but noted that it was "to us a land of heathen darkness, cruelty, cannibalism, and death."[18] Even in twentieth-century New Hebrides, missionary Maurice Frater spoke of "the sense of the constant presence of an incarnate evil power" whereby "every beam of sunlight, every vision of tropical splendour, seemed to intensify the degradation of a people living in darkness."[19] The islands seemed to exemplify the passage from Psalm 73, which spoke of the dark places of the earth and the habitations of cruelty.

Within this apparently unified picture of a fallen island world, missionaries perceived differences between various parts of the Pacific. Before discussing this we should note the concern among western islanders today about use of the term "Melanesian," a description that comes from the writings of the French explorer Dumont D'Urville, who divided the South Pacific islands into three groups: *Polynesie,* meaning "many islands"; *Micronesie,* or the "tiny islands" of the central and north-central Pacific; and finally *Melanesie,* the "black islands" of the western area.[20] Only Melanesia was defined so obviously by the skin color of its inhabitants, and its perceived marginalization by the other areas is deeply resented today. It is easy to see why islanders can regard as racist any attempt by outsiders to separate and classify the bewildering web of cultures and physical types in the western Pacific. Yet missionaries were as interested in integration as separation. As William Ellis of the LMS noted: "Without deprecating the pursuits of science, or the advantages of a more enlarged acquaintance with the natural history of our globe" the Christian philanthropist should be more interested in moral issues.[21] After discussing the contribution of Pacific missionaries to ethnography, we will examine the way they integrated their theories and

17. William Ellis, *Polynesian Researches* (London, 1829), 1:62.

18. Cuthbert Lennox, *James Chalmers of New Guinea,* 2nd ed. (London, 1902), p. 42.

19. Maurice Frater, *Midst Volcanic Fires: An Account of Missionary Tours Among the Volcano Islands of the New Hebrides* (London, n.d.), p. 145. Also see [Anon.], *Polynesia, or, Christianity in the Islands of the South Sea* (Dublin, 1828), pp. 6-7.

20. Ben Finney, "James Cook and the European Discovery of Polynesia," in *From Maps to Metaphors: The Pacific World of George Vancouver,* edited by Robin Fisher and Hugh Johnston (Vancouver, 1993), p. 32.

21. Ellis, *Polynesian Researches,* 1:v.

classifications with what, for them, was the overriding imperative of a universal Christian message.

It seemed natural for missionaries to use their pioneering Society Islands mission as a template, from which they made comparisons with other island groups and built a cultural map of the Pacific as their activities expanded. Part of this process was based on the perceived attractiveness of Pacific peoples. Despite their usual aversion to "noble savage" philosophy, missionaries frequently described Tahitian or Samoan islanders as tall, athletic, and attractive. As they moved west, they encountered people who were shorter and darker. John Williams, on an exploratory voyage in 1830, said that the inhabitants of the island of Niue had been rightly named "The Savage Islanders" by Captain Cook, because they had "a more savage appearance than any inhabitants we have seen in the South Seas."[22] At Tanna in the New Hebrides in 1842, Aaron Buzacott found the islanders "civil, but their appearance was very revolting."[23]

We need to note the role played by the Polynesian mission teachers of the LMS in making the observations that the missionaries used in their accounts of the western islands. The Melanesian mission, which brought western island boys back to New Zealand, Norfolk Island, and other bases for education as mission teachers, assumed that what islanders had to say about each other was authentic and accurate. We know relatively little about most of these teachers, and many of the Melanesian mission's boys blended back into their traditional cultures once they returned home. Ta'unga, an LMS teacher from Rarotonga, has left us particularly detailed and revealing responses to his work in the western islands.

Ta'unga was left with another teacher at New Caledonia in the 1840s, where the nakedness and ferocity of the local people appalled him. At Tanna too he disapproved of islanders with a "wild appearance and evil-looking faces. It is a land of people who are black and naked."[24] Amid today's preoccupation with the historical relationship between white and nonwhite peoples, it is important to remember that nonwhites were never a monolithic group. The Tongans despised the "godless" Samoans, who had little publicly organized religion before Christianity, while Tahitians denounced the obsessive warfare of their Tuamotu neighbors. Many islanders accused one another of cannibalism, and about the only thing there seemed to be general agreement about was fear of the New Zealand Maori. When Polynesian teachers encoun-

22. Moyle, *Samoan Journals of John Williams,* p. 43.
23. Aaron Buzacott, *Mission Life in the Islands of the Pacific* (London, 1866), p. 164.
24. Ron and Marjorie Crocombe, eds., *The Works of Ta'unga* (Canberra, 1968), p. 22.

tered western islanders for the first time on a large and organized scale, they brought to their work a complicated mixture of traditional and newly acquired prejudices.

All of this reinforced the impression of both geographical and cultural distance between, on the one hand, Tahiti and other familiar islands of the eastern and central Pacific and, on the other hand, the peoples of the western area. Nowhere was this more apparent than in mission accounts of Melanesian spirituality. Even though missionaries found them depraved, Polynesian religious beliefs were at least recognizable as such. In most places there were hierarchies of priesthood, temples for worship, and sacrificial practices, all of which recalled familiar stories of idolatrous religion in the Old Testament. To the west it was another story. At Port Moresby in New Guinea in the 1870s, W. G. Lawes observed that the inhabitants had no religious system, not even idols, and no concept of a supreme being. "The only religious ideas consist in a belief in evil spirits," he wrote, and although these spirits were feared, they were also considered implacable either by prayer or sacrifice.[25] Disease loomed large in the western islands, where malaria and a range of fevers and skin diseases afflicted islanders and Europeans alike. The prevalence of disease not only made Melanesia seem more forbidding, but it was directly related to Melanesian spirituality in a way that seemed particularly ominous to observers. Both teachers and missionaries described Melanesian religious leaders as magicians or sorcerers, and George Turner reported the way that Tannese sorcerers specialized in different areas such as rain making or fertility. The most powerful men, however, were the disease makers who burned scraps of food in order to induce disease or death in the person who had last touched them. To Turner, this seemed like witchcraft of the most sinister type, and ironically, the Tannese believed the same thing about the missionaries. There was an obvious connection between the arrival of teachers or missionaries and the outbreak of new and often virulent diseases like smallpox and measles. To the Tannese, missionaries were the most powerful disease makers of all, able to launch islandwide epidemics rather than individualized illness.[26]

The problem of disease had a direct and obvious effect on the reception of missions. When Ta'unga was at New Caledonia, the chief Touru drove the teachers away after a plague, and Touru later refused to allow Buzacott to land when he tried to place new teachers in 1842. After a plague in the Loyalty Is-

25. Quoted in Lennox, *James Chalmers*, p. 76.

26. Turner, *Nineteen Years*, p. 24, shows how neighboring villagers killed three Port Resolution people in order to stave off the ill effects of the Port Resolution mission.

lands in the 1840s, the people of Lifu told Ta'unga that "Jehovah is a man-eating god."[27] Western islanders were often suspicious of any travelers, and a belief in omnipresent malign spiritual influences made their outlook on life seem hunted and fearful in comparison with Polynesians. Using the familiar metaphors of light and darkness, Peter Milne summarized New Hebridean religions as born "of terror, of despair, of gloom," adding that "there are no angels of light; the demons of darkness are legion."[28]

Even the sorceries of Melanesia paled into insignificance beside the issue of cannibalism, and it was Fiji that became the symbolic center of this practice in the South Pacific. Cannibalism was found in many island groups, including New Zealand, but the horrified reports of Methodist missionaries made Fiji the "Cannibal Islands" of popular literature. A blend of Polynesian and Melanesian genetic and cultural influences still makes Fiji difficult to classify in terms of physical anthropology, and perhaps that is one reason observers tended to describe its people in terms of sensational cultural practices rather than ambiguous racial designations. Well before the arrival of the first missionaries in 1835, explorers, shipwrecked sailors, and Polynesian mission teachers had given Fijians a reputation for warlike brutality. The mission stations later described Fijian tortures, human sacrifice, and cannibalism in gory detail; missionaries often wrote of their struggle to believe that Fijians were still human beings. For Thomas Williams, such behavior proved "that the heathenism of Fiji has, by its own uninfluenced development, reached the most appalling depth of abomination."[29] Joseph Waterhouse, whose book *The King and People of Fiji* included chapters entitled "Light and Darkness" and "Habitations of Cruelty," said that cannibalism was "Perhaps the most strikingly barbarous and repulsive feature" of Fijian society. Rejecting palliative explanations about cannibalism's development among the protein-starved voyagers who settled Fiji, Waterhouse pointed to Fijian legends about its deliberate introduction and declared that it was now practiced "on the grounds of revenge, religion, pride and appetite."[30]

The complexity and diversity of island societies challenged missionaries in intellectual as well as practical terms. What relationship was there between the different peoples of the Pacific, and how could their settlement of such far-flung islands be explained? Was there proof that islanders were related to

27. Crocombe, *Works of Ta'unga*, p. 81.

28. Alexander Don, *Peter Milne (1834-1924) Missionary to Nguna, New Hebrides* (Dunedin, 1927), p. 29.

29. Thomas Williams, *Fiji and the Fijians*, vol. 1 of *The Islands and Their Inhabitants*, edited by George Stringer Rowe, 2nd ed. (London, 1860), p. 214.

30. Joseph Waterhouse, *The King and People of Fiji* (London, 1866), p. 311.

biblical accounts of the creation and dispersion of the human race? Mission writings about these issues formed only part of a much wider ethnological debate.

By the end of the eighteenth century, European views of the outside world based purely on biblical and classical sources had been supplemented by a variety of theories based on empirical observation.[31] Improved navigational technology combined with Enlightenment philosophy to produce unprecedented speculation about the origin, history, and diversity of the human race. The name associated with such study — ethnology — contained a number of different intellectual traditions. One was the comparative study of human physique, language, and cultural practices for its own sake, proceeding from empirical evidence to conclusions. Such conclusions often involved the judging of different peoples against scales of civilization based on political, technological, and social development. These approaches by no means always glorified European civilization; Rousseau's "noble savage" was more about criticizing European culture than it was a reflection of indigenous living conditions overseas. Other theorists underlined the fluidity of human social development, emphasizing a social evolutionism that saw cultures rise or fall in the scale over time. Still other approaches took the biblical story of human history as its starting point and gathered empirical observations either to support or to challenge it. During the opening of the South Pacific missions, British ethnological debate revolved almost entirely around the question of whether humanity had a single or a multiple point of origin: monogenesis or polygenesis.

In this respect, British evangelicals regarded the Bible "as both revelation and encyclopedia," in Doreen Rosman's phrase, while other ethnologists were more skeptical about the historical and scientific value of Scripture.[32] In Europe especially, biblical literalism was believed to handicap the study of human history, and such ideas found a readier audience in America, where a book of essays on *Indigenous Races of the Earth*, published in Philadelphia in 1857, called for a concerted attack on British scriptural monogenesis and its "medieval credulity."[33] The following discussion focuses on the monogenist approach of missionaries in the Pacific, but it is important to remember that their ideas formed only part of a wide-ranging debate about scriptural literalism, human evolution, and the relationship between theology and science.

31. Marshall and Williams, *The Great Map of Mankind*, pp. 299-303.

32. Rosman, *Evangelicals and Culture*, p. 228.

33. George R. Gliddon, "The Monogenists and the Polygenists," in Alfred Maury et al., *Indigenous Races of the Earth, or, New Chapters of Ethnological Enquiry* (Philadelphia, 1857), p. 446.

Monogenist ethnology during the early and mid-nineteenth century was dominated by James Cowles Prichard and the various editions of his book *Researches into the Physical History of Man,* first published in 1813. Prichard and his colleagues, most of whom were involved with the Anti-Slavery Society or Aborigines Protection Society, sifted through the mass of incoming exploration data to extract physical or cultural evidence of humanity's descent from the family of Noah after the biblical flood. We must be cautious about making simplistic judgments about the race theories of Prichard and his colleagues. It is true that Prichard linked physical appearance to cultural development, placing darker peoples at the lower end of his cultural index. At the same time, he argued passionately against the skull measurement and "missing link" theories about Africans and insisted that racial and cultural categories were volatile. Race was an effect of culture — the consequence of physical and moral distance from the cradle of biblical civilization — but cultures were constantly changing and that change could be accelerated through the activities of missionaries. Moreover, darker peoples had led human cultural development in the Middle East, and it was from them that the ancestors of Europeans had learned to be civilized. In the words of George Stocking, Prichard and his colleagues believed "all men were one in origin, and there was no suggestion that they might not be one in destiny."[34] Mission anthropology was, and still is, about the subversion of determinism; missions are about change. As anthropologist Kenelm Burridge notes, long after anthropology had become the secular study of physical types or social structures, missionaries continued to "address men and women, who but for the cultures that differentiate them, are regarded as universals, enjoying a common human nature."[35]

The monogenist view, so often linked to the antislavery movement, deliberately made the issue of race problematic. In a popular summary of Prichard's work published in 1851, John Kennedy declared that the division of humanity into white, brown, and black was unsustainable because "the intermediate shades of colour are so numerous, and merge so into one another, like the colours of the rainbow, as to render scientific accuracy impossible."[36] Like Prichard, Kennedy was skeptical about the analysis of skull size and shape, a technique popularized by the German ethnologist Blumenbach; to the monogenists, such studies served only to emphasize humanity's differ-

---

34. Prichard, *Researches into the Physical History of Man,* p. lvii.

35. Kenelm Burridge, *In the Way: A Study of Christian Missionary Endeavours* (Vancouver, 1991), p. 215.

36. John Kennedy, *The Natural History of Man, or, Popular Chapters on Ethnography* (London, 1851), 1:15.

ence from other animals rather than pointing to any notable differences between human beings themselves.[37]

Missionary writings had a direct influence on this debate. Philologist Thomas Hodgkin, one of the founders of the Aborigines Protection Society, praised the ethnographic activities of South Pacific missionaries, especially William Ellis, believing that their long-term residence in the islands made their observations more accurate than those of short-term scientific visitors.[38] The growing literature of travel and exploration also drew on missionary accounts.[39] Meanwhile, missionaries themselves pondered the implications of monogenesis and biblical exegesis for the history and prospects of Pacific islanders.

Most missionaries had gone out to the South Pacific ill-prepared for ethnological challenges: the earlier ones in particular carried instructions that contained a wealth of detail about personal and ecclesiastical matters but virtually no guidance about the issues of culture contact.[40] There was much philosophizing about the best way to convert and civilize islanders, but little information about real situations in which certain approaches had succeeded or failed. Missionaries tended to refer to one another's published accounts in the absence of any standardized reference; John Williams, for example, acknowledged his debt to Ellis's *Polynesian Researches,* and his own book, *A Narrative of Missionary Enterprises,* became a reference work in its turn. Most of those who published their own accounts referred to Cook, and often to other British explorers like Bligh and Vancouver. Debate quickly arose about one of the issues that was puzzling explorers and missionaries alike: the mystery of the original settlement of the Pacific.

The Pacific historian Ben Finney reminds us that Captain Cook's charting of "the Polynesian Nation" — inhabitants of the islands stretching from New Zealand to Tahiti and Hawai'i and partly into the western Pacific — had been an unprecedented discovery. Unlike many other observers, Cook credited islanders with substantial navigational skills and listened to their detailed accounts of seasonal wind patterns. He realized that there were people of different physical types in the western islands, but he noted that Polynesian-related languages could be found as far west as Tanna in the New Hebrides. From this evidence he concluded that their ancestors had come from the East Indies.[41]

37. Kennedy, *Natural History of Man,* 1:19.

38. Thomas Hodgkin, *On the Importance of Studying and Preserving the Languages Spoken by Uncivilized Nations* (London, 1835), p. 20.

39. For example, [Anon.], *South Sea Islands,* 2 vols., edited by Frederic Shoberl (London, n.d.).

40. Gunson, *Messengers of Grace,* p. 101.

41. Finney, "James Cook and the European Discovery of Polynesia," p. 29.

William Ellis disagreed. Although he knew little about the islands apart from the Society and Hawai'ian group, he decided in the 1820s that the islanders had come from the Americas.[42] This theory has been finally debunked after Thor Heyerdahl's voyage in the *Kon Tiki* drew attention to it in the 1950s, but in its day it influenced the thinking of ethnographers like John Dunmore Lang, who promoted it in his *View of the Origin and Migrations of the Polynesian Nation,* published in 1834. Ease of travel with the prevailing winds, the presence in the islands of sweet potatoes, and physical similarities between Native Americans and Polynesians all seemed fairly convincing evidence.

We now know that the first migrations from southeast Asia took place in several phases at least 30,000 years ago; time enough to explain the development of such physical and cultural diversity. For those working from a time scale based on a literal interpretation of the Bible, however, matters were more difficult, and the origin of islanders seemed "a dark and mysterious chapter in the history of man."[43] Mission accounts did not describe western islanders as a separate people until the 1860s, when the establishment of the Anglican Melanesian mission brought the word "Melanesian" into popular currency. The question that had confronted pioneers like Williams in the early days was deciding what sort of "Indians" Pacific islanders were. Full of hope, searching for an ever-elusive shortcut to the original "Indies" and their riches, generations of explorers named the peoples they encountered "Indians." Williams and his colleagues added more features to this peculiar human geography, which now stretched from the West Indians of the Caribbean, through two American continents, across the Pacific to Cook's "Indians" in Australia and Williams's "Indians" of the New Hebrides and New Guinea. Far from isolating or marginalizing western islanders, Williams tended to incorporate them into a descriptive pattern that, for all its arrogance, was remarkably flexible with regard to racial difference. In New Guinea, across the narrow Molucca and Banda Seas, the Pacific's newest "Indians" stared the original Indies in the face.

As to the islanders' migrations, Williams, who was a colleague of Ellis's, was at first convinced by the arguments in *Polynesian Researches* about the islanders' American origins. Despite differences in appearance and culture between the inhabitants of the New Hebrides, New Caledonia, and other west-

---

42. Ellis, *Polynesian Researches,* 2:37-63; see also his *Narrative of a Tour Through Hawaii* (London, 1826), pp. 410-12.

43. John Williams, *A Narrative of Missionary Enterprises in the South Sea Islands,* 1st U.S. ed. (New York, 1837), p. 458.

ern islands, there was an even greater difference between all of these and the peoples of southeast Asia. In his journal of 1832, Williams concluded that western islanders — so close to Cook's proposed point of origin in the East Indies — could not possibly have Asian ancestry.[44] He might also have been influenced by encounters with a number of lighter-skinned islanders living in the western Pacific who spoke languages related to Tahitian and Samoan, and by the fact that groups of Polynesians occasionally settled to the west.[45] Later, his own direct experience of island navigational skills prompted Williams to begin to doubt his belief in an American origin. By the time he published his *Narrative of Missionary Enterprises* in 1837 he had changed his mind to side with Cook, but instead of Cook's choice of the East Indies, he preferred Malaysia as the site of origin. He added details, suggesting that in fact the darker western islanders had once been the original population of the whole South Pacific before an invasion of Malaysian peoples wrested the smaller islands and groups away from them.[46] Williams's theories, not Ellis's, were on the winning side, influencing later generations of naval explorers who read his book, and complemented by research in linguistic patterns being conducted by his mission colleagues and others.[47] However, even Williams did not employ the term "Melanesians"; though he identified several physical types in the South Pacific, he maintained a geographical unity by using the term "Polynesia" for all of the area's islands.

The dilemma posed by those physical differences continued to plague mission attempts to describe the history of the islands. Fiji was a particular problem. There were strong Polynesian influences in the eastern part of the group, where Tongans regularly intermarried with Fijians. Thomas Williams noted that western Fijians were closer to what he called the "Papuan Negro" — his phrase for western islanders and Australian aborigines. In their attempts to describe Pacific cultures, missionary ethnography revealed the tensions inherent in the literal scriptural interpretation of human history. On the one hand lay the monogenist emphasis on unity and human potential; on the other was Noah's cursing of his son Ham and, by traditional interpretation, all peoples identified as "Negro." There was also the matter of the Tower of Babel and the subsequent curse of multiple languages. Given their often

44. Moyle, *Samoan Journals of John Williams,* pp. 227-28.

45. Turner, *Nineteen Years,* p. 396.

46. Williams, *Narrative of Missionary Enterprises,* p. 458.

47. M. Russell, *Polynesia: or, an Historical Account of the Principal Islands in the South Sea, including New Zealand,* 3rd ed. (Edinburgh, 1845); J. E. Erskine, *Journal of a Cruise Among the Islands of the Western Pacific* (London, 1853); and Charles Wilkes, *Narrative of the United States Exploring Expedition,* 5 vols. (Philadelphia, 1845), especially vol. 5.

unsympathetic response to western islanders, it is no surprise to find some missionaries leaning further toward the curses than an emphasis on human potential.

From a monogenist perspective, one might expect to find that those people who had dispersed the furthest from the Holy Land, and who lived isolated from other cultures, would best manifest the curse of the fragmentation of language. Nowhere else on earth was there such linguistic diversity as on some of the islands of the western Pacific and in Australia. This invited speculation about how far the peoples of this area must have declined from the antediluvian standard, and observations of extensive stoneworks in the western islands, which the indigenous inhabitants could not explain, seemed to prove a corresponding technological decline. John Geddie of the New Hebrides mission, for example, believed that the islanders' current inability to build in stone indicated "either that the present races have degenerated, or that the islands were previously occupied by a people more advanced in art."[48] References to degeneration were common, particularly in the writings of LMS and New Hebrides missionaries, but too much emphasis on decline worried more sophisticated mission scholars like Bishop Patteson. A contemporary recalled that Patteson "had none of the conventional talk so fatal to all true influence about 'degraded heathen.' They were brethren, ignorant indeed, but capable of acquiring the highest wisdom."[49]

What about Noah's curse? Did western islanders qualify as "black"? During the short-lived LMS mission to Tanna in the 1840s, George Turner referred to darker islanders as "Papuans," a word that would enjoy considerable popularity before it was overtaken by "Melanesians," but he also described them as having "the negro cast."[50] Williams, too, by the time he published his book, had distinguished between the Polynesian whom he regarded as Asiatic and the western islander whom he named the "Polynesian negro."[51] As for Ham, John Inglis wrote that in the New Hebrides "we see this curse lying in all its crushing weight. The Papuans, the poor descendants of Ham, are lying in the lowest state of degradation." In contrast were what Inglis called "the Malay race, descendants of Shem" in Polynesia who "had abandoned heathenism" while most of "the children of Ham, were still lying in heathen darkness."[52] George Brown, who established an Australian Methodist mission at the Duke of York Islands in August 1875, still referred to western islanders

48. George Patterson, *Missionary Life among the Cannibals* (Toronto, 1882), p. 119.
49. Walter G. Ivens, *Hints to Missionaries to Melanesia* (London, 1907), p. 6.
50. Turner, *Nineteen Years*, p. 76.
51. Williams, *Narrative of Missionary Enterprises*, pp. 450-51.
52. Cited in Gunson, *Messengers of Grace*, p. 199.

as "Polynesians" but described them as "of the sub-Papuan or Melanesian family."[53] Brown believed there was one original race in the western Pacific and pointed to tales of "black men" in New Zealand, whom the Maori claimed were there when they arrived. Later migrations from Malaysia produced the societies and physical types of east Polynesia, and thus Melanesian islanders were the most authentic representatives of the ancient, original "Papuan" stock.[54]

The Melanesian mission tended to dwell less on the curse of Ham. Selwyn, during his sermon at the consecration of Bishop Patteson, chose to emphasize that Melanesians revealed "the curse of Babel, and wait for the coming of another Pentecost."[55] Since the Melanesian mission emphasized the recruitment and training of island boys for service as mission teachers, rather than the creation of residential missions at particular islands, the problem of language was paramount. The Melanesian mission also tended to view islanders more benevolently than its New Hebrides mission counterpart, and it deplored some of the negative judgments of its Presbyterian brethren; in his anthropological classic *The Melanesians,* published in 1891, R. H. Codrington, Patteson's immediate successor as head of the mission, reflected that

> when a European has been living for two or three years among savages, he is sure to be fully convinced that he knows all about them; when he has been ten years or so amongst them, if he be an observant man, he finds that he knows very little about them, and so begins to learn.[56]

This might have been a swipe at the Reverend Robert Steel, who published a book in 1880 based on information from the New Hebrides missions. Although he referred to all New Hebrides islanders as "Papuan," he was still anxious to make distinctions between the Eromangans — "lowest in the scale" and "more allied to the negro" — and the inhabitants of Vate, Aniwa, and other places more receptive to the New Hebrides mission, where he diagnosed "a Malay relationship."[57]

At the heart of the debate about human origins, as far as ethnologists and their missionary colleagues were concerned, lay the question of human unity.

53. George Brown, *George Brown, D.D. Pioneer-Missionary and Explorer: An Autobiography* (London, 1908), p. 92.

54. Brown, *George Brown,* p. 102.

55. [Melanesian Mission], *Isles of the Pacific: Account of the Melanesian Mission* (Melbourne, 1861), p. 21.

56. R. H. Codrington, *The Melanesians* (Oxford, 1891), p. vii.

57. Robert Steel, *The New Hebrides and Christian Missions* (London, 1880), p. 20.

Just as the story of Noah's sons gave shape to some missionary descriptions of differences between eastern and western Pacific islanders, and gave their aesthetic and social prejudices an apparent biblical sanction, so the Bible challenged them to view all peoples as equal before God. The crucial scriptural reference was Acts 17:26, where Paul told the Athenians that God "hath made of one blood all nations of men for to dwell on all the face of the earth." Details about migration and racial characteristics were secondary to God's creation of a single pair of humans from whom all others descended, and from whom all inherited both the fall from grace and the need for salvation.

We find references to "one blood" in missionary writings from the earliest days. After Samuel Marsden founded the CMS mission to New Zealand in 1814, he made several journeys on foot into the interior. Horrified by the brutality and cannibalism of Maori warfare, he remarked: "Though God has made of one blood all nations that dwell on the face of the earth, and fixed the bounds of their habitations, yet how widely different are their situations!"[58] In the New Hebrides, amid what he regarded as the mindless barbarities of the Aneituymese islanders, John Geddie noted:

It should be borne in mind, that the Most High "hath made of one blood all nations of men." . . . The condition of these islanders has been most unfavourable to the development of their mental energy. Nevertheless there are indications of a fair amount of intellectual power among them.[59]

Methodist missionaries in Fiji felt uniquely surrounded by horrors, and William Moore had to remind himself that Fijians, too, were the children of Adam and Eve:

Are these the descendants from him who was created in the Image of God? My heart replied. O yes! This is man without the Gospel, "A beast in body, A demon in mind," but there is still hope. . . . My commission extends even to these, for they are still out of Hell, although at its very jaws.[60]

Descriptions of the most shocking aspects of island societies, especially cannibalism, sorcery, polygamy, and homosexuality, were often made with

58. Cited in Garry Hogg, *Pathfinders in New Zealand* (London, 1963), p. 108.
59. Patterson, *Missionary Life*, p. 119.
60. Cited in Gunson, *Messengers of Grace*, p. 199.

reference to scriptural accounts of heathenism. In the first chapter of his epis-
tle to the Romans, Paul had outlined the characteristics of the pagan society
with which his Roman followers were contending.[61] His references to idolatry, deceit, lack of family bonds, murder, and the absence of mercy struck
chords with missionaries in the South Pacific. From Kendall in Polynesian
New Zealand to Geddie on Melanesian Aneityum, this chapter in Romans offered missionaries a way of explaining how such cultural practices could still
fit within God's plan.[62] At Tanna John Paton wrote that "the 'depths of Satan',
outlined in the first chapter of the Romans, were uncovered there before our
eyes in the daily life of the people, without veil and without excuse." Reference
to Paul's remarks allowed missionaries to construct an idea of "heathenism"
that was universal and timeless, and thus to connect their own dislocating
and shocking experiences with those of apostles and saints in the New Testament. History encouraged them to be optimistic: the pagans Paul described
had become part of Christian western Europe; Pacific islanders, so the argument went, were full of the same potential for civilization. Daniel Tyerman
and George Bennett, reeling from the challenges their LMS brethren in Tahiti
were facing in the 1820s, comforted themselves with reference to Sir Walter
Scott's *History of Scotland* and its story of Christian missionary efforts among
the pagan Scots and Picts.[63] Many missionaries took comfort in what they
saw as a continuous history of conversion, from Paul's influence on the
Romans, to Britain's own conversion, and their own present efforts to bring
Christianity to the pagan Pacific. Buzacott likened the efforts of the LMS to
the acts of the apostles, hoping that "the people thus converted become a
great and dominant nation in the earth," with his Pacific islander teachers
themselves becoming like "Augustine, and to the first preachers of Christianity in Britain."[64]

Missionary ethnographers made frequent connections between their new
world and the old by linking island languages and cultures to biblical references. Ellis collected traditional stories at the Society and Hawai'ian Islands
that he believed were accounts of Old Testament events distorted by time and
space. From this he and others concluded that the islanders must ultimately
be of Semitic or Aryan origin; in their customs and mythologies, Ellis wrote,
"the light of truth occasionally gleams through a mass of darkness and er-

61. Romans 1:24-31; see Andrew F. Walls, "Romans One and the Missionary Movement," in Andrew F. Walls, *The Missionary Movement in Christian History: Studies in the
Transmission of Faith* (Edinburgh and Maryknoll, N.Y., 1996), pp. 55-67.

62. Binney, *The Legacy of Guilt*, p. 72; Patterson, *Missionary Life*, pp. 126, 130.

63. Tyerman and Bennett, *Voyages and Travels*, p. vii.

64. Buzacott, *Mission Life in the Islands*, p. x.

ror."[65] Searching for connections between New Zealand Maori culture and the Middle East, Samuel Marsden and Richard Taylor suggested that the Maori were descendants of one of the lost tribes of Israel, perhaps those banished from Egypt. Kendall's more sophisticated work rejected this simplistic connection but argued through linguistic analysis that the ancestors of the Maori must have been in contact with Semitic cultures before migrating to the South Pacific. In an article in the *Evangelical Magazine*, Kendall came to the grand conclusion that the CMS missions in New Zealand were fulfilling Isaiah's prophecy about the conversion of Egypt.[66]

Thomas Williams and Joseph Waterhouse made similar comparisons between Fijian practices and Scripture,[67] as did missionaries in Melanesia. George Turner found stories at Tanna resembling the tales of Jonah and the creation of Eve, believing that the stories' survival at this distance was "a manifest fragment of the Divine doings as recorded in the Mosaic cosmogony."[68] To drive his point home, Turner observed that the Tannese dressed their hair in hundreds of tiny braids, something that reminded him of "the Egyptian Gallery in the British Museum," and the rectangular, curly beards of their religious leaders seemed to him to be Assyrian in origin.[69] A. W. Murray, at Aneityum in the New Hebrides, referred his readers to Kitto's *Daily Bible Illustrations* for an example of hair braiding, which he too was convinced showed the Middle Eastern origins of these islanders.[70] The point, in missionary terms, was that the practices of Pacific islanders revealed the way in which biblical narratives had been "preserved by the most distant tribes of the human family."[71] There was no apparent awareness of the problem of contamination, even in areas like the New Hebrides where the activities of sandalwood traders long preceded the first mission stations. At Nguna, for example, Milne carefully recorded a supposedly indigenous story of the fall, complete with forbidden apple and serpent.[72]

65. Gunson, *Messengers of Grace*, pp. 206-8 and Ellis, *Polynesian Researches*, 1:42-53, and 2:viii.

66. Binney, *The Legacy of Guilt*, pp. 131-33.

67. Williams, *Fiji and the Fijians*, pp. 252-54; Waterhouse, *King and People of Fiji*, p. 359.

68. Turner, *Nineteen Years*, p. 526.

69. Turner, *Nineteen Years*, pp. 78-79.

70. A. W. Murray, *Missions in Western Polynesia* (London, 1863), p. 137. Murray gives an incorrect reference, but the illustration to which he refers is most probably that of an Assyrian head in John Kitto, *Daily Bible Illustrations . . . Evening Series*, vol. 2: *Isaiah and the Prophets* (Edinburgh, 1852), p. 65.

71. Ellis, *Polynesian Researches*, 2:63. Other examples in Patterson, *Missionary Life*, pp. 126, 130.

72. Don, *Peter Milne*, p. 33.

All of this recalled Prichard's argument that race had no deterministic effect on culture; it was Christianity, not skin color, that had given Europe its historic advantages and would bring similar benefits to converted islanders in turn. We have seen the way missionaries contrasted the physical beauty of the islands with the depravity of their inhabitants, but this analogy changed with the spread of Christianity, and descriptions of the western Pacific were no exception. On his 1846 voyage to the New Hebrides, William Gill passed the island of Eromanga, where the people of Dillon's Bay had killed John Williams in 1839. He noted that "thick clouds were resting on [the island's] mountains, and thicker clouds of heathen delusion and degradation enveloped its savage population" in contrast to the nearby island of Vate, where Samoan teachers were laboring, and which he regarded as "a land of hope" where "all nature seemed to animate and encourage us."[73] No one group could be singled out as uniquely fallen; different areas could move from darkness into light. Praising the success of the New Hebrides mission's work at Aneityum in the 1860s, Murray observed that an already beautiful island now featured "beauties more enduring than any that mere natural advantages can confer."[74]

According to missionary prognostications, islanders might even overtake their teachers, just as Britain's empire had overtaken Rome's. To the visiting Quaker missionary Daniel Wheeler, the Maori were "poor miserable natives" in the 1820s, but if Christianized "they would then far outstrip those who have long since made a profession of the Christian religion."[75] Even this belief could find scriptural endorsement, for in the same verse that told of humanity's origin in "one blood" could be found the statement that God had "determined the times before appointed, and the bounds of their habitation" of all nations. Britain seemed "appointed" at the moment to bring Christianity and civilization to the South Pacific, but other nations would take up their own appointments in the future. In this respect, the main distinction between islanders was between Christians and non-Christians. At the Isle of Pines, Aaron Buzacott remarked on the reverence the islanders gave to powerful headmen like Matuku, who "being of great stature, and nearly black, and with a rough voice, . . . seemed a fair specimen of a heathen tyrant."[76] Yet his description of a similar figure, the chief Makea at Rarotonga, was very different. Buzacott tells us that Makea was a vast man, stout as well as tall, extravagantly tattooed, and that he insisted on similar formal obeisance from his

---

73. William W. Gill, *Selections from the Autobiography of the Rev. William Gill* (London, 1880), p. 189.

74. Murray, *Missions in Western Polynesia*, p. 19.

75. Daniel Wheeler, *Extracts* (London, 1839), p. 295.

76. Buzacott, *Life in the Islands*, p. 170.

people. Makea had recently converted, however, and Buzacott described his appearance and behavior by calling him "the ideal of a Homeric hero."[77] Since Britain traced its cultural heritage back, in part, to classical Greece, this was yet another attempt to build connections with islanders across time and space. It was also linked to the belief in human progress that had seen Britain thrive on its classical tutelage, and islanders thriving in their turn on the "Christianity and civilization" brought by British missions.

In this respect, the monogenist position was looking back to Enlightenment ideas about natural law and cultural progress, while anticipating what anthropologists would later call the "psychic unity" of humanity: today's "human nature." Bishop Selwyn, after his first island voyage in 1849, said that he had never seen a "savage"; instead, he had met islanders who were "men of like feelings with ourselves; influenced mainly by the same arguments, guided by a sense of right and wrong."[78] Thomas Williams wrote that "Fijians are greatly wronged by being supposed to be a set of rough untutored brutes. They can feel as keenly, weep as sincerely, love as truly and laugh as heartily as any European."[79] For Bishop Patteson in Melanesia, "the capacity for the Christian life is there, though overlaid with monstrous forms of superstition or ignorance; the conscience can still respond to the voice of the Gospel of Truth."[80] At home in Britain, Kennedy summed up the position by declaring that some ethnologists might

> dwell on the beauty of the Caucasian, and on the deformity of the Negro, but he cannot maintain that the former is more than man, or that the latter is less. . . . The rights of mankind are placed under the protection of this sentiment . . . "TRAMPLE NOT ON MAN, FOR THE IMAGE OF GOD IS THERE."[81]

Whether described as shared conscience, like feelings, or a shared descent from Adam, the "one blood" theory of common humanity played a significant part in shaping missionary attitudes in the South Pacific. Belief in "human nature" underlined mission hopes that preaching the word would not be hindered by cultural barriers. In his *Letters on Missions* of 1830, William Swan exhorted missionaries to "consider that with all the acknowledged variety in

77. Buzacott, *Life in the Islands,* p. 142.
78. Cited in Darrell L. Whiteman, *Melanesians and Missionaries: An Ethnohistorical Study of Social and Religious Change in the Southwest Pacific* (Pasadena, 1983), p. 111.
79. Cited in Gunson, *Messengers of Grace,* p. 212.
80. Cited in Ivens, *Hints to Missionaries,* p. 26.
81. Kennedy, *Natural History of Man,* pp. 139-40.

the intellectual character and external circumstances of men, HUMAN NA-
TURE is universally the same."[82] Murray, at the struggling mission to New
Guinea in 1874, deplored the negative accounts of New Guinea islanders
found in the trade journals and newspapers. Murray himself had never been
attacked, he believed, because "I have found in all my experience that the rule
that holds in dealing with men, whether civilized or savage, is THAT WHAT
WE ARE TO OTHERS, THEY ARE TO US."[83] In the LMS, Tyerman and
Bennett justified the ethnological study of other cultures because it demonstrated how human nature was "essentially the same everywhere though
varying in its aspect according to external contingencies."[84]

The failure of missionaries to recognize the true depth of cultural difference often led to disappointment, and sometimes disaster, especially in the
western island missions. That most famous of missionary "martyrs," John
Williams, was killed with one of his colleagues on Eromanga when he strode
toward a village preparing to hold a religious feast. Failure to take the disease
issue seriously led to the abandonment of the Tannese mission in 1862: John
Paton simply underestimated the extent to which introduced diseases would
affect his mission's reputation.[85] Indigenous politics led to more deaths on
Eromanga, where James Gordon and his wife were killed in 1872. Gordon's
activities had been confined to the coast, where the local people benefited
from his presence at least to the extent of acquiring European goods. The inland people, isolated by language and cultural barriers, experienced the mission's presence only through the transmission of new diseases. Bishop
Patteson, killed on Nukapu (north of the New Hebrides) in 1871, seems to
have become an offering intended to turn away the depredations of labor re-
cruiters. In Fiji, the Methodist missionary Thomas Baker was killed on the island of Viti Levu in 1867 when he ventured into the interior against advice
and snatched a comb from the hair of a chief he was visiting. Before leaving
on his expedition Baker had expressed the belief that his good intentions
would be understood; he would have done better to heed Fijian *tapu* and note
the fact that touching the sacred head of a chief was a capital offense.[86]

This chapter raises questions about the currently prevailing historiography of missions, especially deterministic theories of economic exploitation or

---

82. Cited in Gunson, *Messengers of Grace*, p. 195.

83. A. W. Murray, *Forty Years' Mission Work in Polynesia and New Guinea* (London,
1876), p. 499.

84. Tyerman and Bennett, *Voyages and Travels*, p. v.

85. Murray, *Missions in Western Polynesia*, pp. 403-4.

86. London, SOAS, WMMS archives, FBN 5, fiche 235, Baker to his wife, 17 and 19
July 1867.

totalizing racist discourse. The expression "through European eyes" is commonly used today to describe the categorization of non-Europeans, as though there was a monolithic European way of seeing. Captain Cook found that the Eromangan islanders had "regular features" and "were pretty well made," although he found the women unattractive. Murray, on the other hand, writing after the killing of Williams, compared the islanders unfavorably with others in the New Hebrides, concluding that "they are physically inferior, and, if possible, more deeply sunk and debased."[87] We must acknowledge the contradictions of how islanders appeared "in European eyes" when those eyes could see in so many different ways.

Recent scholarship often seems more concerned with a disapproval of European expansionism than an exploration of its complexities; it is certainly easy to condemn the social Darwinism and biological determinism of later Victorian race theory, and the often questionable alliance between anthropology and empire. However, what about ethnological theories opposing determinism, and their role in the undermining of racist institutions like African slavery? There are other related questions, too, about developing concepts of a universal humanity and the resulting confusion about who defines human rights, and who polices them. Religion, idealism, racial perceptions, and international missions are with us still, still driven by a complex combination of cultural priorities and historical change. To study the ethnology of missions is to begin to grasp the scope of that complexity. As Joseph Mullens, Foreign Secretary of the LMS, declared in 1870:

> Theories of the "true Church," systems of doctrine, theories of civilization, reformation and progress, theories of morals, theories about races, theories of natural and inflexible law, are all affected more or less by the work, the purpose, and the results of Christian missions.[88]

Missionary observations of Pacific islanders reveal all the tensions and contradictions of their times. No one who has read their often anguished diaries can doubt that missionaries experienced a genuine internal struggle between their abhorrence of island cultural practices and their need to retain faith in the universal message of Christianity. They were tempted to classify islanders according to physical appearance and relative attractiveness, and

---

87. Murray, *Missions in Western Polynesia*, p. 175.
88. He uses the South Pacific as his case study in "Modern Missions and Their Results," in *Ecclesia: Church Problems Considered in a Series of Essays*, edited by Henry Robert Reynolds (London, 1870), p. 537.

when the least attractive proved the most resistant to the gospel — as in the western Pacific — missionaries close to despair had to force themselves to remember that divine grace made no exceptions and had no favorites. Although the language and circumstances of their struggle can seem alien now, beneath the surface of missionary writings is a familiar tension between prejudice and idealism; between cultural self-reference and the perceived needs of a universalized humanity. Here there are no easy answers, and more need than ever for research and debate.

CHAPTER SIX

Civilization or Christianity? The Scottish Debate on Mission Methods, 1750-1835

IAN DOUGLAS MAXWELL

For the 1829 edition of *The Life of the Revd. David Brainerd* published by William Collins in Glasgow, James Montgomery, the popular Christian author and hymn writer, provided an introductory essay.[1] In the preface he offered his readers some helpful hermeneutical guidance for a correct reading of Brainerd's *Life*. He insisted that the proper mission method consisted in the simple preaching of the gospel, as exemplified by David Brainerd. Montgomery wrote, "The wisdom of man says, 'First *civilize*, and then *Christianize* barbarians'; but the wisdom of man has proved itself foolishness in every experiment of the kind. . . . The counsel of God is the reverse; 'Go and preach the gospel to the Gentiles . . . you will *civilize them by Christianizing them.*'"[2]

Montgomery's comments about the relative priorities of civilization and Christianity typify a prolonged debate on mission methods that took place in the early nineteenth century, both in Scotland and (as chapter eight shows) in

---

1. I am indebted to Dr. Andrew Ross, Dr. Christopher Smith, and Dr. Brian Stanley for their invaluable comments on the first draft of this chapter, as presented at the NAMP consultation at Westminster College, Cambridge, in September 1996.

2. J. Edwards, *Life of the Revd. David Brainerd revised and abridged with an Introductory Essay by James Montgomery* (Glasgow, 1829), p. xvii. James Montgomery (1771-1854) was born in Irvine, Ayrshire. His father, John Montgomery, was a Moravian missionary in the West Indies, dying there in 1791. James was educated in Moravian settlements in Ireland and Yorkshire. Besides being a prolific hymn-writer, he pursued an active career in journalism as the editor of *The Sheffield Iris*. See A. H. Miles, *The Poets and Poetry of the Century,* vol. 10 (London, n.d.), p. 1.

England. From the very beginning of Scottish interest in missions in the mid-eighteenth century differences in approach had emerged between the two wings of Scottish Presbyterianism, namely, *evangelical* and *rational* Calvinists. In discussions concerning the propagation of the gospel beyond Christendom the question at issue was the relative priority of differing mission methods: whether biblical and apostolic preaching should come first or rather the communication of the civilizing rationality that many assumed to be essential to a full comprehension of Christian faith. By the end of the eighteenth century this debate had entered Presbyterian consciousness to such an extent that any discussion of missions ran the risk of becoming polarized around the two positions. In the popular mind they came to be regarded as mutually exclusive. The aim of this chapter is to provide a brief historical overview of each of these strands within eighteenth- and early nineteenth-century Calvinism, focusing chiefly on the Church of Scotland and the rational Calvinism that was its dominant theology. This will include an examination of the influence of rational Calvinism on the planning of the General Assembly's Institution in Calcutta in the 1820s. The chapter will conclude with an account of the key debate at the General Assembly of 1835 that effectively ensured the triumph of the rational Calvinist paradigm of mission methods. What emerges is that, far from being remote from the concerns of mission policy and method, the theology of the Scottish Enlightenment informed the very basis of the way in which mission in the early nineteenth century was conceived in Scotland.

An unpublished manuscript written by Robert Wallace, minister of New Greyfriars Church in Edinburgh, in the early 1750s provides the earliest documentary evidence of the differences in outlook that would later emerge in the public debate.[3] Wallace was an early leader of what later became the Moderate interest in the General Assembly. He was an acquaintance of David Hume and, indeed, was instrumental in preventing attempts to instigate proceedings against Hume in the General Assembly in 1756. Writing in response to the publication of Jonathan Edwards's *Life of Revd. David Brainerd* (first edition, 1749) Wallace's critical comments anticipate, at least in outline, the objections of later Calvinists to evangelical theories of mission.

In the pages of Brainerd's *Life,* Wallace thought he detected a denial of the efficacy of preaching morally, whereas "preaching the pure doctrine of our Redemption by Jesus Christ" was "much applauded as being accompanied by

---

3. R. Wallace, "Some Thoughts on the Conversion of the Indians, on Whitfield [*sic*] and Irregular Methods of Converting and Reforming the World," Edinburgh University, Laing Ms., La.II 620.23.

a peculiar energy of the Divine Spirit & extraordinary success which has led me to examine what is good sense upon this subject & where the truth lies."[4] He conceded that man was indeed hopelessly corrupted, but the *real* question, he argued, was "in what way . . . God will exert his grace."[5] Wallace envisaged a much wider sphere of divine grace and action than was assumed in Edwards's *Life of Brainerd*. He felt that "a natural and rational foundation of piety and goodness" should be laid by appealing to the natural notions "of superior powers . . . [of] a future life, [of] virtue & vices" that he assumed the Indians already possessed.[6] The unruly influence of the passions was a phenomenon universally present in all natural religions, and Wallace felt that the results of Brainerd's preaching had more to do with the "excitation of passions" than with anything more profound. Representations of hell would have an equal influence on "rude and uncultivated minds" whether one was speaking of "Christ, Mahomet," or for that matter "the Deisticall Scheme."[7]

Wallace suggested that this accounted for the impact of David Brainerd among the Native North American and for George Whitefield's success in England and Scotland. Yet the moral result of such preaching was not, he asserted, a "genuine, naturally pure goodness" but some other spurious, temporary effervescence of the passions. In sum, Wallace laid great emphasis on reason as the basis for the communication and propagation of the gospel. At the same time he was suspicious of any phenomena that were attributed to "the peculiar energy of the Divine Spirit." Wallace's views on preaching and mission anticipated the stance adopted by Scottish theologians in the later eighteenth century.

The leading representative of this theological outlook was Principal George Hill, Professor of Divinity at St. Andrews from 1788 to 1819. Under Hill mainstream Scottish Calvinism had finally broken with the scholastic Calvinism of the Netherlands, a theological discourse that the Scots now regarded as archaic. The chief concern now was to articulate Calvinist theology within the confines of the rationality of the Scottish Enlightenment. As it developed, this theology made an appeal to the English tradition of philosophical theology and drew eclectically on Locke, Cudworth, Tillotson, Clarke, and Butler. Calvinist theologians of this school also depended heavily on the common-sense philosophy of Thomas Reid, though not without some major reservations.

---

4. Wallace, "Some Thoughts on the Conversion," folio 2.
5. Wallace, "Some Thoughts on the Conversion," folio 2.
6. Wallace, "Some Thoughts on the Conversion," folios 2-3.
7. Wallace, "Some Thoughts on the Conversion," folios 3-4.

Like Robert Wallace, Principal George Hill proceeded from the assumption that theological insights were to be judged primarily by the standards of universal rationality. These standards were held to be inherent in the commonly agreed criteria of meaning, truth, and certainty to which all disciplines were required to conform. From the 1780s Scottish theology was subjected, therefore, to a process of "redescription"[8] in order to demonstrate its conformity to the standards of universal rationality. Calvinist theology emerged from this restructuring having gained a second fundamental criterion. To *revelation* it had added the dictates of *reason.* Those theologians who represented this way of thought might best be described as *rational* Calvinists.

While Scottish theology had certainly been influenced by the critical attacks of Hume and Gibbon, a series of internal doctrinal shifts were to take place in the 1780s that clearly reveal the influence of Enlightenment rationality. There was a renewed interest in natural religion, particularly in the rational structures assumed to be universally present in the religious perceptions of humanity. In the doctrinal realm, reason substantially replaced the role traditionally attributed to the work of the Spirit in the doctrines of the means of grace, and faith. Where Calvin had held to a radical notion of sin, George Hill and other rational Calvinists preferred to speak of the "defects" in human reason. Perhaps most importantly, Scottish theology emerged from the Enlightenment with a profound confidence in providence, which was identified with the progress of reason itself. Many of these changes were to be of direct influence upon the way in which the theology of mission was understood in early nineteenth-century Scotland, and they merit, therefore, further examination.

Scottish theologians of the 1780s showed a great interest in the theory of natural religion. The formal and logical framework of the doctrine is a striking feature of George Hill's theology. Christianity was understood to be a *superstructure* founded on a basis of natural religion. Christians, as George Hill told his students at St. Andrews University, were called to make Christianity distinct from the rabble of natural religions by demonstrating its rational superiority and so revealing its superstructural status. Hill assured his students that, having thus impressed their unbelieving hearers, Christians could then attempt to convince them of the importance of Christian faith and the necessity of its adoption. Rational conviction had taken the place of the necessary intervention of the Spirit.[9]

This interest in natural religion, of course, was not unique to the theolo-

---

8. See I. U. Dalferth, *Theology and Philosophy* (Oxford, 1988), pp. 89-93.
9. G. Hill, *Lectures in Divinity,* 6th ed. (Edinburgh, 1854), book II.2, pp. 132-44.

gians. Philosophers such as Thomas Reid and David Hume elaborated common-sense or skeptical theories on the subject; and Dugald Stewart, Professor of Moral Philosophy at Edinburgh University, carried on this tradition into the early years of the nineteenth century. The principles of natural religion, he taught, were also fundamental to the moral, intellectual, and social spheres. Civil religion was vital to the well-being of society and, therefore, the Christian religion was of major social importance. Stewart's views, of course, reflect a consensus in Scottish society at this time. Institutional Christianity was considered to be vital to the viability of civil society. These widely held views on the rational superiority of Christianity and its place in civil society are clearly reflected in later Church of Scotland mission theory. In the 1820s the theologian John Inglis, for example, used a version of Hill's theory of the rational superiority of Christian faith to argue for the establishment of an educational institution in Calcutta.

It was in their understanding of the work of the Spirit that rational Calvinists like George Hill and, later, John Inglis, demonstrated their greater confidence in the powers of human reason. They dismissed the passivity of those hyper-Calvinists who questioned any human action not directly attributable to the divine sovereign will. Instead, they insisted, man could act in complete confidence. There was no absolute distinction between the work of the Spirit and human agency. Human means could be freely employed, as these could often be identified as the very instruments God chose to use.

Evangelical Calvinists, however, defined human means very differently from the rational Calvinist theologians. For an evangelical such as Thomas Chalmers, preaching before the Dundee Missionary Society in 1812, the two main instruments were the *spoken or preached* word and the *written* word of Scripture.[10] In terms of mission method this meant that the preacher or Bible Society agent and Scripture translation were paramount. For Principal Hill, however, advance in the social virtues, economic improvement, and historical progress could all be regarded as essentially instruments of providence.

Among the human means at the disposal of Christian faith it was reason, however, which was paramount. In his lectures between 1788 and 1807 Hill laid out a middle way between the suspicion of reason exhibited by some evangelical Calvinists and the Socinian exaltation of reason. As far as Hill was concerned, practical reason had three aspects. First, reason was a tool for the examination of the Christian evidences. Second, it enabled textual study and the construction of systematic doctrine. Third, one of its most powerful uses

---

10. Thomas Chalmers, *The Two Great Instruments Appointed for the Propagation of the Gospel: A Sermon . . .* , 3rd ed. (Edinburgh, 1812).

was in "repelling the attacks of the adversaries of Christianity."[11] This last aspect of practical reason legitimated the use of rational argument in attempting to convince the unbeliever of the truth of Christian faith. The implications resulting from this were considerable. If rational argument was to be the main form of communication of the gospel, the field of prospective missions should be narrowed accordingly to those cultures whose educated elites could more readily grasp the use of reasoned discourse.

In his lectures to the St. Andrews students, moreover, Principal Hill offered a survey of the massive and often confusing field of the "the Christian evidences" — the arguments used to "repel the attacks of the adversaries of Christianity." These were the rational arguments put forward to defend belief against possible critical objections. Hume's attack on the status of miracles in the 1770s, for example, had had a profound impact on the theology of rational Calvinism, and generations of Scottish theology students were schooled in George Campbell's theologico-philosophical reply to Hume's critique.[12] This attack of Hume's, however, and his skepticism regarding reason, were almost certainly responsible for the peculiarly defensive attachment to rationality that would characterize Scottish Calvinism for decades to come. Hume's skepticism, furthermore, meant that a generation of Scottish Calvinists defined unbelief almost exclusively in terms of skepticism with regard to religion.

Hill's treatment of the doctrine of faith, however, epitomizes the anti-suprarationalism of late eighteenth- and early nineteenth-century Scottish Calvinism. Acknowledging the distinctions made by the Westminster divines between historical, temporary, and saving faith, Hill went on in his lectures to define the essence of faith itself as *a rational act*.[13] Earlier generations were held to have had views of the Spirit's action in which man was regarded as little more than an automaton. Hill's students heard, however, that faith was cumulative. It was "a habit or permanent state of mind, proceeding upon many various acts."[14] The individual's progress in Christian faith came about through the accumulation of these rational acts. Hill taught that coming to faith depended on knowledge of the argumentary evidence and the history of religion just as much as on doctrines and precepts. The use of these "outward means" he averred, was "the ordinary course of [divine] procedure."[15] This only reinforced the view that the communication of the gospel, whether at

11. Hill, *Lectures in Divinity*, book II.5, p. 163.
12. See George Campbell, *Dissertation on Miracles* (Edinburgh, 1762).
13. Hill, *Lectures on Divinity*, book V.1, p. 464.
14. Hill, *Lectures on Divinity*, book V.1, p. 464.
15. Hill, *Lectures on Divinity*, book V.1, p. 463.

home or overseas, involved appeal to accepted standards of rationality through argument and debate.

The influence of Enlightenment rationality, then, can be traced in the theory of natural religion and in the doctrines of conversion and faith of rational Calvinism. Its influence also emerges in certain theological qualifications of the doctrine of original sin. Hill recognized that there were differences among theologians as to "the extent of the corruption of manners" brought about by sin. He argued, however, that there was universal agreement that, due to the effect of sin, "men do not act up to the dictates of right reason."[16] This theological shift enabled rational Calvinists of Hill's stamp to move a problematic doctrine, offensive to some Enlightenment sensibilities, further into the background, leaving the way clear for the expression of much greater confidence in rationality. Once sin was associated with the defects of reason, the stage was set for the identification of the ordered, enlightened progress of rationality with the promotion and propagation of the gospel itself.

Recent research by David Allan has established the existence of a wide consensus in the central scholarly tradition of the Scottish Enlightenment. These scholars drew on an active and rational social theory derived from earlier Renaissance thinkers in Scotland. The social and moral value of learning was upheld in this tradition, and learning itself was regarded as the motor of change in society leading towards "responsible membership of a civilized modern community." The aim was to produce "the rational leader" — an individual endowed with special causal influence. According to Allan, the aim of Scottish scholars was the construction of a "moral apex" of cultivated men within Scottish society.[17] Calvinists like George Hill and, later, John Inglis were very much inheritors of this tradition though, as theologians, they preferred to speak more explicitly of the role of providence in social change.

Hill regarded the history of the progress and propagation of Christianity as a branch of the evidences second only in importance to the evidence for the resurrection of Christ. When, for example, the first volumes of Edward Gibbon's *The History of the Decline and Fall of the Roman Empire* appeared in the 1770s and early 1780s, Hill regarded the purely empirical account of the rise of the Early Church contained in volume 1.15 as "the most uncandid attack which has been made on Christianity in modern times."[18] Gibbon had given a purely secularizing explanation for the progress of the Early Church

---

16. Hill, *Lectures on Divinity,* book IV.1, p. 302.

17. D. Allan, *Virtue, Learning and the Scottish Enlightenment* (Edinburgh, 1993), p. 195.

18. Hill, *Lectures on Divinity,* book I.9, p. 109.

without reference to the doctrine of providence. The response of Scottish theology was to renew its commitment to the doctrine of providence by insisting on the *providential* growth of the Church.

Hill went further. He parted company from Montesquieu and from earlier theologians like George Campbell by directing attention away from the *status* of religion in the structure of civil society. Instead, as Robert Millar had done in the 1720s, he adopted an historical framework to give a dynamic account of the development of the Christian religion.[19] By means of this historical framework, Hill proposed a general model of providence in which gradual development of civil structures and norms culminated in a civilized society. It was a theory that was to be heavily influential in future Church of Scotland missions.

Hill argued that, once the appropriate level of civilization had been reached, the social preconditions were ripe for the appearance of Christianity. He posited the rise of Christianity as a necessary historical moment to be repeated in every civilized society, given the correct conditions.[20]

This providentialism was, furthermore, strongly deterministic. Hill dismissed Reid's philosophical doctrine of the mind's self-determining power as meaningless and in reply reaffirmed a traditional Calvinist determinism.[21] He bolstered this by an appeal to Locke's *Essay on Power* and, more particularly, Jonathan Edwards's *Essay on Free Will*. In his theory of the determination of human nature within the framework of divine providence Hill also called on the theories of continental rationalists such as Leibniz, Canzius, Wyttenbach, and Wolff for additional support.[22]

This theological determinism placed rational Calvinism on the necessitarian wing of the Scottish Enlightenment in the company of such strange bedfellows as Lord Kames and David Hume. However, this determinism was not, of course, that of crude biological necessity or of a purely mechanistic universe. Hill made no attempt to attribute any kind of compulsion to the actions of divine providence. The emphasis was rather on the concurrence or succession of universal *regularities* thought to be observable in man's nature and in his social world. The implications of this doctrine extended far into the social realm. Now the important elements of the gospel were those seen as positively *social* benefits. The gospel was beneficial in "pointing out social ob-

19. See R. Millar, *The History of the Propagation of Christianity . . .* , 2 vols. (Edinburgh, 1723).

20. Hill, *Lectures on Divinity,* book I.9, p. 115.

21. G. E. Davie, "The Scottish Enlightenment," in *The Scottish Enlightenment and other Essays,* edited by G. E. Davie (Edinburgh, 1991), pp. 24, 49.

22. Hill, *Lectures on Divinity,* book IV.10-11, p. 457.

ligation, restraining flagrant transgressions, contributing to the diffusion of religious knowledge, the refinement of manners and the general welfare of society."[23] The associated doctrines of election and predestination were now far less problematic. Once transposed into a rational key, they could now be part of a forceful, dynamic theory of socially determined historical progress.

The implications of this providentialism for missions can be seen very early on. In confident mood, Hill used his moderatorial sermon to the General Assembly in May 1790 to apply the model of the necessary historical development of Christianity to the wider world. The preconditions, he announced, that had evidenced themselves in past centuries prior to the expansion of Christianity in western Europe were now appearing *throughout the world*. Hill assured his hearers that rational Christian modernity was their privileged possession — and the rest of the world would soon join them in sharing its benefits.[24]

As one might expect, many Calvinists in Scotland remained to be convinced by Hill's arguments. Indeed, from the late 1780s, the prolonged debate between the rational and evangelical wings of Scottish Presbyterianism intensified. Those, on the rational side, who argued for the determinist view of history insisted that *historical precedent* demonstrated that civilization was prior to the propagation of Christianity. Evangelical Calvinists, suspicious of the theoretical systematizing of Hill and other rational theologians, argued that *biblically* the proclamation of the gospel always took priority.

By the time of the famous debate on missions at the General Assembly in 1796, Hill's developmental model was matter for common discussion and debate. The assembly's deliberations are clearly framed in terms of Hill's paradigm. Two overtures had been presented by the Popular or evangelical party in the assembly arguing for the church's participation in missions. The Moderates in the assembly, the men, that is, of a more rational persuasion, channeled discussion towards the question of whether, if the appropriate historical moment had arrived in any of the developing societies of the world, the Church of Scotland was at liberty to work for the expansion of Christianity. Principal Hill and his supporters gained majority support for the argument that while the assembly should indeed be attentive to the stage of development of civil societies overseas, the revolutionary 1790s were certainly not an appropriate time for the church to begin missionary engagement.[25] For the

23. Hill, *Lectures on Divinity,* book IV.10-11, p. 445.

24. G. Hill, *Sermons* (London, 1796), p. 352.

25. R. Lundie, *Account of Proceedings and Debate in the General Assembly of the Church of Scotland 27th. May 1796 etc.* (Edinburgh, 1796), p. 23.

next thirty years, as a result, the Scottish contribution to the wider work of missions was to be entirely the preserve of the independent, interdenominational mission societies.

These, furthermore, were mission societies that were supported for the most part by evangelical Calvinists. In consequence, while it was never as systematized as mainstream rational Calvinist theology, evangelical Calvinist opinion regarding mission and mission method became much more articulate from the late 1790s onwards. The question naturally arises as to what these views were.

As regards mission, evangelical Calvinist opinion was consistently *biblicist.* Evangelical Calvinists had remained loyal to an earlier generation of theologians in the Reformed tradition, such as Thomas Halyburton or Thomas Boston. They still held to Calvin's view of the influence of Scripture as entirely dependent on the Holy Spirit. Those in the biblicist tradition regarded the Bible as "the authority . . . the source of all truth."[26] The text of Scripture provided all the models and prescribed the scope and limits for all authentic mission. In the words of William Brown, lecturer at the Scottish Missionary Society seminary in the 1820s and author of *A History of the Propagation of Christianity,* the biblical writers had "furnished most instructive lessons to the Church."[27]

As early as 1777 the theologian George Campbell had commended learning as a possible methodology for future missions.[28] Brown, however, found this view less than congenial, and even when educational missions had become an established pattern, Brown was noting cautiously in the third edition of his *History* that "there is in fact an unhallowed confidence in that magnificent apparatus of means, which is at present in operation, as if it *must* produce a mighty change in the state of the world. . . . [It] may prove an occasion of the influences of the Holy Spirit being withheld from our exertions."[29] Brown's suspicion of the dangers of reliance on "means" was shared by other evangelicals such as Claudius Buchanan, who insisted that "spiritual light" was not given to "a nation or community of men by any system of education, but to individuals."[30]

26. D. W. Bebbington, "Evangelical Christianity in the Enlightenment," *Crux* 25.4 (December 1989): 29.

27. W. Brown, *The History of the Propagation of Christianity among the Heathen, since the Reformation,* 3 vols. (Edinburgh, 1854), 1:ix.

28. George Campbell, *The Success of the First Publishers of the Gospel a Proof of its Truth: A Sermon Preached before the Society in Scotland for Propagating Christian Knowledge* . . . (Edinburgh, 1777), pp. 56-62.

29. Brown, *History,* 1:viii.

30. Cited in Gavin White, "'Highly Preposterous': Origins of Scottish Missions," *Records of the Scottish Church History Society* 19.2 (1976): 112.

Some leading evangelicals also opposed the social emphasis of the rational Calvinist doctrine of providence. In a sermon preached in Glasgow in 1812 the Congregationalist Ralph Wardlaw of Glasgow declared that "the doctrine of a superintending providence cannot consistently be questioned by anyone who is convinced that there is a God, and that the universe owes its existence to his creative power."[31] He and George Hill were agreed on that. They parted company, however, where Wardlaw argued that such providence was "not general only but particular." Placing the emphasis more on the providential care of the individual than on the social aspects of providence, Wardlaw declared that God had not only set the universe in motion but still supervised particular lives.[32] Mention must also be made here of the evangelical theology of the Haldane brothers that was to be such an important influence on later English missions, particularly that of the LMS.

In general, evangelical Calvinists throughout the Presbyterian churches conceived of mission on the apostolic pattern. When the readers of the various evangelical periodicals scanned accounts of the missionary progress of the Scottish Missionary Society in the 1820s, for instance, there was a high expectation of mission reports on the biblical pattern as recorded in the Acts of the Apostles. That is, missionaries were expected to engage in effective, vernacular preaching that bore fruit in conversions immediately following. The paradigm for such work had been supplied for the previous seventy years by Jonathan Edwards's *The Life of the Revd. David Brainerd,* an enormously popular work in Scotland. Brainerd's *Life,* furthermore, was probably also partially responsible for the primitivist turn towards tribal missions in public opinion that made it insist on the priority of Christian preaching over "civilizing" methods.

Within the Church of Scotland Thomas Chalmers had both nurtured and at the same time represented this evangelical opinion. From his earliest missionary society sermons in 1812 to his university lecturing in the 1820s and 1830s Chalmers avoided the radical separation between "Christianity" and "civilization" that so bedeviled popular discussion of mission. He consistently argued, however, against the view that "civilization" was the main object of missions; it was simply an "accompaniment." The primary aim and method was to preach Christ.[33]

Chalmers also promoted this point of view by his insistence on the exem-

---

31. White, "Highly Preposterous," p. 112.

32. White, "Highly Preposterous," p. 112.

33. Thomas Chalmers, *The Utility of Missions Ascertained by Experience: A Sermon Preached before the Society in Scotland . . . for Propagating Christian Knowledge . . .* (Edinburgh, 1815), p. 25.

plary methods of the Moravian missions in Greenland. As Professor of Moral Philosophy at St. Andrews University in the 1820s this was Chalmers's favored topic in addresses given to local mission societies and in a long series of lectures to the University Missionary Society. Lecturing to the students at Glasgow University in the 1830s, Chalmers outlined his broad agreement with Professor George Hill on all the main points of traditional theology. He did, however, make clear his disagreement with Hill on the necessity of a prior civilization before the propagation of the gospel. He found Hill's emphasis on the rational aspects of the work of the Spirit in conversion rather dubious,[34] and he certainly did not accept Hill's developmental approach to Christianity.[35]

To take another example, in 1824 when the General Assembly debated the setting up of a mission committee and the establishment of an educational institution in Calcutta, the Reverend Henry Duncan of Ruthwell, a leading evangelical from the southwest of Scotland, declared his opposition. It had been abundantly demonstrated, he said, that the preaching of *the Scriptures* was the chief instrument of conversion. The assembly should look to the work of the missions among the peoples of the South Sea islands. Their experience confirmed this as the authentic pattern. Another representative of this type of view was the leading missionary of the Scottish Missionary Society in Bombay, Rev. John Wilson. He consistently argued that "the preaching of the gospel is the grand means of propagating the gospel."[36] Within the Church of Scotland itself, however, while evangelical Calvinists continued to oppose anything they regarded as a merely "civilizing" approach to missions, the rational Calvinist tradition came to predominate from 1813 onwards. The man chiefly responsible for this was John Inglis, minister of Greyfriars Kirk in Edinburgh. Inglis was leader of the Moderate interest in the Church of Scotland and a theologian in the rational Calvinist tradition. He claimed George Campbell, Alexander Gerard, and Thomas Reid as his theological and philosophical mentors and shared George Hill's views on the primacy of reason in religious matters.[37] Inglis played a key role in ensuring that the dominant paradigm for the missions of the Church of Scotland would be that of the rational Calvinist tradition.

In a sermon preached before the Society for Promoting Christian Knowl-

34. Thomas Chalmers, *Prelections on Butler's Analogy, Paley's Evidences of Christianity and Hill's Lectures on Divinity* (Edinburgh, 1859), pp. 154-55.

35. Chalmers, *Prelections*, p. 234.

36. George Smith, *The Life of John Wilson, DD, FRS* (London, 1879), p. 56.

37. John Inglis, *An Examination of Mr. Dugald Stewart's Pamphlet etc.* (Edinburgh, 1806), p. 124.

edge in Edinburgh in June 1818, a sermon generally credited with having launched Church of Scotland missions in the nineteenth century, Inglis gave a summation of the by now standard rational Calvinist approach. He argued that the growth of British India, like Rome before it, now offered new opportunities for civil development under imperial patronage.[38] Presbyterian practice in mission, he declared, should give priority to learning and education in order to hasten the civil societies in question towards the historical moment of acceptance of Christianity. From the very beginning of his involvement John Inglis promoted a vision of the social and moral role that established Presbyterianism might play in Indian civil society. It was Inglis, furthermore, who developed the notion of an institution of higher learning in Calcutta that would be related to the Presbyterian establishment there.

In the ten years between 1814 and 1824 the Scottish chaplain in Calcutta, James Bryce, had informed Inglis of local developments. Initially pessimistic about the influence a Scottish mission might have on Hinduism, by the early 1820s Bryce had noted the onset of Westernization. The indications were that this presaged profound social change. He suggested to Inglis that a "Scottish college" might be established under the auspices of the Presbyterian congregation in the city. At that time Inglis was wary of depending too much on Bryce's reports. He was, however, spurred to action by the publication in early 1824 of Charles Lushington's history of charitable institutions in Calcutta. Lushington, in his comprehensive examination of charitable and educational institutions in the city, had observed the same social developments as Bryce and argued that a ready response to the growing enthusiasm of the Bengali elite for instruction in European literature and science was the best way to accelerate the enlightenment and liberation of the Hindu mind from the shackles of idolatry.[39] Using this independent, objective corroboration of Bryce's memoranda, Inglis moved to form a Church of Scotland committee on missions.

In May 1824 the General Assembly debated a motion to set up a Committee for the Propagation of the Gospel in Foreign Parts. John Inglis had been the prime mover in the planning discussion. Once again, the contours of the traditional debate emerged. *The Edinburgh Christian Instructor,* by this time the leading Scottish evangelical journal, informed its readers that the most hotly contested point in the debate had been "about the necessity of civiliza-

---

38. John Inglis, *The Grounds of Christian Hope etc.* (Edinburgh, 1818), p. 136.

39. Charles Lushington, *The History, Design, and Present State of the Religious, Benevolent and Charitable Institutions . . . in Calcutta and its Vicinity* (Calcutta, 1824), pp. 216-28.

tion going before efforts to spread Christianity."[40] Three influential evangelical ministers — Dr. Alexander Brunton, Henry Duncan, and James Paull — contested the project's civil-social emphasis and its elitist aims.[41] The assembly, however, voted to set up the committee. Inglis was its first convener.

From 1824 Inglis labored to develop the idea of an educational institution in Calcutta and to raise the necessary finance for its establishment.[42] Even at this early stage of planning it is clear that the main principles of the project derived from the context of the long debate on the status and development of religion in civil society. From this same debate Inglis derived the notion of institutionally determined social change that was to inform the establishment of the General Assembly's Institution. In a wider context the emphasis on the role of an educated elite in this social change arose directly from earlier Scottish discussions of the importance of a virtuous elite as a motivating force in civil society.

More specifically, John Inglis, like George Hill and most other Calvinist thinkers of the period, was convinced that the development of enlightened ideas and the spread of the British Empire in the late eighteenth and early nineteenth centuries heralded a predetermined "moment" for Indian civil society. East Indian urban society was understood to be entering a process of historical change that would bring it to the threshold of civil and social transformation. Westernization in Bengal seemed to presage such a change. The primary role of the General Assembly's Institution was to provide a propaedeutic for that change. Using Western rationality as its instrument, the institution would play a part in hastening the expected transformation. It would produce "rational leaders" who would take up a leading role in the emergence of Indian civil society, and it would interpolate Christianity into that developed society at its very commencement.

So much for the theoretical perspective that informed John Inglis's thought. Inglis was, however, an administrator and mission theorist. The projected mission still needed a man who could combine practical ability with an

---

40. *The Edinburgh Christian Instructor* 23.7 (July 1824): 484.

41. *The Edinburgh Christian Instructor* 23.7 (July 1824): 484. James Paull (1782-1858) was minister of Tullynessle and Forbes in Aberdeenshire. He was awarded a St. Andrews D.D. in 1844, elected Moderator of the General Assembly of the Church of Scotland in 1846, and appointed H. M. Chaplain in Ordinary in 1852 (Hew Scott, *Fasti Ecclesiae Scoticanae: The Succession of Ministers in the Parish Churches of Scotland, from the Reformation, A.D. 1560, to the Present Time* [Edinburgh, 1867-], 6:145).

42. I. D. Maxwell, "Alexander Duff and the Theological and Philosophical Background to the General Assembly's Mission in Calcutta to 1840," Ph.D. thesis, University of Edinburgh, 1995, pp. 109-45.

overall intellectual grasp of the institution's intended role in East Indian society. The Committee for the Propagation of the Gospel in Foreign Parts, under Inglis's guidance, found just such a man in Alexander Duff. Although the main focus of this chapter is the "Civilization or Christianity" debate in Scotland, the early years of Duff's missionary activity in Calcutta had, in fact, a decisive impact on the discussion of mission method at home and are therefore of interest.

By the early nineteenth century the Faculty of Theology at St. Andrews had developed Hill's *Lectures in Divinity* into a systematic course, establishing St. Mary's College as a leading center of rational Calvinism. While Alexander Duff had been closely involved with the evangelical student missionary association, his theological training was to exercise a profound influence on his future thinking. With a schooling in the theology of rational Calvinism under Principal Haldane, George Hill's successor at St. Andrews University, Duff was the ideal superintendent for the General Assembly's Institution. In 1829 he was appointed to oversee the establishment of the mission in Calcutta. With the help of Ram Mohun Roy, the Hindu reformer, Duff opened the doors of the school in July 1830. The school was soon established on a regular educational basis and by 1831 numbered five hundred pupils.

With the framework of the institution in place, Duff was free to develop the work of the mission in other directions. From the beginning he had taken a keen interest in the long-running student rebellion at Hindu College, the training institute set up to prepare young Bengalis for the civil service. By December 1831 the rebellion had reached a critical stage. A large number of the students had imbibed a form of Hume's skepticism and were less and less willing to accept the demands of the institutional authorities. Duff decided that the rebellion presented an unrivaled strategic opportunity and made plans to confront the student leaders in intellectual debate. In late 1830 he had organized a series of systematic public lectures on the evidences of Christianity. The authorities of Hindu College, however, intervened and, appealing to an archaic law of the East India Company, had the lecture series banned. Now, however, Duff restarted the lectures. His philosophical assaults on Hinduism as a "natural religion," his adept use of evidential theology, and his overpowering rhetoric produced a startling effect on the students. By the end of 1832 four young Brahmin students had become Christians. Duff became convinced that here, in microcosm, was the pattern that would transform the elite of Indian society.

The difficulty now was that if the institution was to be poised to take best advantage of the rapid developments expected to take place, abundant and regular financial support was needed. In turn, the source of that financial backing was for the greater part the evangelical mission–supporting public in Scotland, which had its own opinions as to the proper methods of mission. These opinions, of course, were those of evangelical Calvinism. Biblical, apostolic preaching in the vernacular language was expected to be the norm. If the necessary financial backing were to be forthcoming, the evangelical Calvinist paradigm had to be challenged and the public had to be convinced that the institution was an authentic expression of modern mission compatible with evangelicalism.

For this reason, after Duff was invalided home in late 1834, the General Assembly of 1835 assumed crucial importance as a forum through which the evangelical public could be persuaded to support the institution in Calcutta. The assembly of 1834 had been the first in which the evangelical party had gained the ascendancy, so Duff could expect a keener edge to the interest in missions. Duff, however, whose work in the institution was in an urban rather than classically primitive situation and did not involve vernacular preaching, could also reckon on substantial opposition if he failed to persuade the brethren of the critical importance of the work in Calcutta.

On the day of the debate itself, the 25th of May, the *Scottish Guardian* newspaper confidently informed its readers that "this gentleman is about to introduce a new era in Christian missions."[43] Duff himself, as his close colleague in Calcutta, Thomas Smith, recalled, was much less sanguine, since he was "aware of the existence of a considerable amount of opposition, on the part of his hearers, to the educational character which the mission [had] assumed."[44] At the General Assembly, however, Duff succeeded in bringing about an effective *reinvestment* of evangelical support in the paradigmatic methods of rational Calvinism.

How did he accomplish this? He did not hesitate to use his experience of mission in a non-Western culture effectively to modify notions of mission method and theology in Scotland. After all, evangelical ideas of mission method and theology had been shaped previously by the recorded experiences of missionaries such as David Brainerd or, for that matter, the Moravians. They could, given the proper circumstances, be reshaped once again.

From the moment Duff stood up to address the assembly, consummate rhetorician that he was, his strategy was clear and bold. He put bazaar preaching — the *ideal* of evangelical missionary activity — into question, meeting the evangelical supporters of "prior Christianity" on their own ground. In

---

43. *Scottish Guardian* 4.350 (25 May 1835): 163.
44. Thomas Smith, *Alexander Duff DD, LLD* (London, 1883), p. 58.

starkly pragmatic terms he took bazaar preaching, the epitome of authentic apostolic mission activity, and described its results in Calcutta. Bazaar preaching, Duff declared, foundered in the market place within minutes. Brahmin hearers, for example, made demands for authoritative proof from the missionary. Once the unfortunate preacher made appeal to evidential theology he immediately found it was of no help. Hindu cosmological histories dwarfed biblical historical evidence; Brahmin mythology swamped Scripture miracle. As for the "internal evidences" or "the argument from prophecy," they were simply incomprehensible to a Brahmin audience. What was missing, Duff insisted, was the prior Western rationality, which provided the framework necessary to grasp the significance of "the evidences." Western rationality, Duff continued, had both negative and positive aspects. It had a destructive impact on the sacredness of the Hindu Shasters. If, he announced, "you only impart ordinary useful knowledge, you thereby demolish what by its people is regarded as sacred."[45]

In perhaps the most powerful part of his address Duff went on to argue for the formative influence of Western knowledge. He gave an account of the lectures on the evidences to the students of Hindu College as a particular example, a microcosm, of the kind of revolution in ideas he expected Western rationality to bring about.[46] This, he reminded his hearers, was not mission in an idealized "primitivist" context. On the contrary, it was a debate with students who had read Locke, Reid, Stewart, and Brown. The students of Hindu College, he suggested to his hearers, provided experimental verification of the entire future of the scheme. When the students demanded authoritative proof for Duff's arguments in the public lectures, they "*unlike* the older Hindus . . . were enabled to comprehend the nature of evidence."[47] This was because, Duff insisted, "they had studied our language, our histories, and our science. They were acquainted with the sources and facts of history and chronology. They were initiated into the first principles of inductive reasoning. They knew the laws that regulate the successions of state in the material universe."[48] They were able, therefore, to grasp the evidential arguments from history, miracle, or prophecy. To underline the importance of this situation, Duff then described the progress of the public lectures and their culmination in a Scripture doctrine course for the students and, crowning this, the first conversion of a young Brahmin. This, Duff suggested to the assembly, was

45. Alexander Duff, *The Church of Scotland's India Mission etc.* (Edinburgh, 1835), p. 7.

46. Duff, *The Church of Scotland's India Mission*, pp. 10-11.

47. Duff, *The Church of Scotland's India Mission*, p. 13.

48. Duff, *The Church of Scotland's India Mission*, p. 13.

what Western education would produce — a generation of students capable of understanding the arguments of evidential theology. Duff pressed home his advantage by reminding his hearers that the assembly's institution offered a *Christian* education in the tradition of the Reformation. This would bypass the secularizing dangers of which the intellectual upheavals of Hindu College had merely been the latest example. Raising the specter of the French Revolution, Duff added that *"knowledge without religion"* would only result in the "wildest forms of European infidelity" threatening British rule in India.[49] Through the method he had described, however, the Church of Scotland, "though powerless, as regards carnal designs and worldly policies, has yet the divine power of bringing many sons to glory."[50]

Duff's speech had a profound impact — Principal Patrick Macfarlan and Doctors Duncan Mearns, George Cook, Alexander Black, Robert Burns, and John Brown, all men of influence in the Kirk, declared their fullest support.[51] The assembly appointed Duff to publicize "the great affairs of the Assembly's scheme" throughout Scotland, and the speech itself was published as a separate pamphlet reaching sales of over ten thousand copies.

Alexander Duff had succeeded in presenting the General Assembly's mission in Calcutta as a sophisticated, modernizing institution supremely placed both to create and to take advantage of the civil and intellectual revolution he predicted would occur in India. There would be fundamental criticism of his position from those working with other mission societies in Calcutta, but Duff's speech to the General Assembly of May 1835 and the subsequent publicizing tour of the Scottish presbyteries marked a turning point. By effectively displacing the evangelical, biblicist paradigm of mission method, Duff had changed the way the institution and, indeed, mission itself, was perceived by the Scottish Presbyterian public. Ironically, he had also ensured that, when the evangelical Calvinists broke away in 1843 to form the Free Church of Scotland, their paradigm of mission method would be one originally undergirded by the Enlightenment theology of rational Calvinism.

49. Duff, *The Church of Scotland's India Mission*, pp. 18-19.
50. Duff, *The Church of Scotland's India Mission*, p. 27.
51. For MacFarlan (1781-1849), Mearns (1779-1852), Cook (1772-1845), Burns (1789-1869), and Brown (1784-1849) see N. M. De S. Cameron, ed., *Dictionary of Scottish Church History and Theology* (Edinburgh, 1993). Alexander Black, D.D. (1789-1864) was appointed Lecturer on Practical Religion at Marischal College, Aberdeen, in 1831. He joined the Free Church in 1843 and was Professor of New Testament Exegesis at New College, Edinburgh, from 1844 to 1856 (Scott, *Fasti Ecclesiae Scoticanae*, 7:363).

CHAPTER SEVEN

"Civilizing the African": The Scottish Mission to the Xhosa, 1821-64

NATASHA ERLANK

This chapter analyzes the influences that formed the thinking of early and mid-nineteenth-century Scottish missionaries serving in one particular field — the Cape of Good Hope — and examines the links — representational, discursive, intellectual, and organizational — between Scotland and Xhosaland that connected them through nearly a century of mission work.[1] The theological and philosophical framework of the missionaries was, directly or indirectly, a product of the intellectual creativity of the Scottish Enlightenment. Once at the Cape the missionaries maintained close links with Scotland, particularly through their contributions to the literate culture of the period. Their letters appeared in a succession of journals and papers, which provided the Scottish Christian public with news about their missionary work and the people among whom they worked. The way in which they wrote helped to create ideas about the mission field and the Xhosa that fed into existent discourses on the people of the non-Western world. Although their writing helped to publicize the mission

1. An earlier draft of this chapter was presented at the North Atlantic Missiology Project seminar, at Westminster College, Cambridge, in January 1998. I am very grateful to Brian Stanley, John de Gruchy, and the rest of the seminar participants for their valuable comments. The text is based on a chapter in my Ph.D. thesis, "Gender and Christianity among Africans Attached to Scottish Mission Stations in Xhosaland in the Nineteenth Century," University of Cambridge, 1999. The rest of the thesis focuses on the working of the mission in South Africa, the responses and reactions of the Xhosa to the missionaries and Christianity, and the role of gender in the encounter.

cause, this chapter will argue that they were often unable to evoke much interest in it because of a pronounced Scottish preference for missions in India, whose population were perceived to be more civilized, and where work appeared to provide a more guaranteed return on support. Their writings also helped to inspire a later generation of missionaries to Xhosaland, who often had very different ideas of mission as a result of shifts in domestic theology and the influence of a steadily more racist discourse on the subject of Africans.

The Scottish Enlightenment, the Moderates, and the Evangelicals

The Glasgow Missionary Society was formed in 1796 to "advance and maintain the mission of the Gospel of Jesus Christ, to those quarters of the earth where it is unknown."[2] The GMS was formed when the idea of foreign missions was seizing the imagination of evangelical Christians, and towards the end of the period in which the Moderate party within the Church of Scotland had dominated the intellectual life of the Scottish Enlightenment. The ideas of both the evangelical movement and the Scottish Enlightenment were to have a continuing effect on both mission work and representations of it throughout the century.

Eighteenth-century Scotland was home to a cultural and intellectual florescence, reaching its peak between the 1750s and 1790s, which has come to be known as the Scottish Enlightenment. There is some disagreement as to the temporal, social, and intellectual extent of the Scottish Enlightenment.[3] According to R. B. Sher, it can be recognized as "the culture of the literati of eighteenth-century Scotland," the literati being people who subscribed to a shared body of humane values and principles.[4] The "literati" were, however, no marginal group of intellectuals and included some of the most influential ministers of the Church of Scotland. A growing body of scholarly opinion now insists that the distinctiveness of the Scottish Enlightenment lay pre-

2. M. Berning and S. Fold, "Scottish Missionaries on the Frontier," *Annals of the Grahamstown Historical Society* 17 (1987): 9.

3. For general discussions see A. Chitnis, *The Scottish Enlightenment* (London, 1976); R. B. Sher, *Church and University in the Scottish Enlightenment* (Princeton, 1985); P. Flynn, *Enlightened Scotland* (Edinburgh, 1992). Sher sees the 1750s to the 1790s as the critical years of this "profound cultural transformation" (p. 3). Sher discusses different definitions of this movement at the start of his book (pp. 5-6).

4. Sher, *Church and University*, p. 8.

cisely in the fact that "its ideas were very widely diffused, in all areas and among a very wide span of social groups, in what was for the time a remarkably well-educated and highly literate population, in country as well as in town."[5]

What is beyond dispute is that many of the philosophers of the Scottish Enlightenment — Francis Hutcheson, Thomas Reid, Adam Ferguson, Adam Smith, and David Hume among others — were expressly interested in making observations about humankind based upon inductive and experimental study, according to a methodology derivative from Newtonian and Baconian thinking.[6] In this they were drawing on ideas current in natural philosophy, but since they were (with the exception of Hume) concerned to preserve religious interpretations of human life, their thinking evolved under the rubric of natural theology. According to natural theology, the phenomena of human experience afforded evidence of moral, and hence divine, design of the created order.[7] In this respect their thinking was teleological in that it was possible to see final causes in the designs of nature. This framework influenced thinking on both individual and social morality, on the science of moral philosophy, and on the subject of social change.[8]

Theorizing social change was particularly important in a society itself in the process of transformation as the "civilized" values of Edinburgh and the Scottish Lowlands began to penetrate the Highlands.[9] The Scottish literati were essentially interested in the evolution of society and the bonds that held society together. Many of them theorized about the evolution of society according to a trajectory in which humans progressed through primitive, pastoral, agrarian, and commercial phases.[10] This type of social analysis, called stadialism, was a defining characteristic of the Scottish Enlightenment.[11] The literati drew on Scotland's own experience, as well as history, travel literature, and the Bible, for specific examples to prove their

5. Donald J. Witherington, "What Was Distinctive about the Scottish Enlightenment?" in *Aberdeen and the Enlightenment: Proceedings of a Conference Held at the University of Aberdeen* (Aberdeen, 1987), p. 15. See also David J. Allan, *Virtue, Learning and the Scottish Enlightenment: Ideas of Scholarship in Early Modern History* (Edinburgh, 1993), p. 233.

6. Flynn, *Enlightened Scotland*, pp. xvi-xvii.

7. Flynn, *Enlightened Scotland*, pp. xvii, 118, 120.

8. Flynn, *Enlightened Scotland*, pp. 116, 264.

9. Flynn, *Enlightened Scotland*, p. 264.

10. Flynn, *Enlightened Scotland*, pp. 266-67; Chitnis, *The Scottish Enlightenment*, p. 102.

11. C. Kidd, "Gaelic Antiquity and National Identity in Enlightenment Ireland and Scotland," *English Historical Review* 109.2 (1994): 1198.

general points.[12] They viewed the operation and development of the economy as responsible for a society's progress through these phases. Property was a central economic concept, the possession of which was seen as the distinguishing mark between barbarous, or savage, and civilized societies.[13] This, however, was not a materialist theory of history, as the Scottish philosophers maintained that it was possible to see the evidence of final causes, or the guiding hand of providence, in the progress of humankind through these stages of economic development.

The ideas of the Scottish Enlightenment had their religious base among the Moderate clergy of the established church. The Moderates had emerged as a distinctive party under the leadership of William Robertson (historian, Moderator of the General Assembly, and Principal of Edinburgh University) in the 1750s.[14] As the previous chapter has shown, theirs was a distinctively rational form of Calvinism. Rather than insisting on the primacy of revelation in the attainment of faith, they preferred to see revelation as a support for the moral truths that humans come to through the exercise of rational, moral faculties.[15] They believed that religion was only meaningful if it adapted itself to secular life, and that it was the Church's duty to become interested in the new social philosophies in order to understand the running of society.[16]

By the end of the eighteenth century the Moderates were losing their influence and intellectual vitality. The older Moderates were all moving into retirement and had no successors among the younger clergy, because of the increasing impoverishment of the clergy and the abuse of patronage by magistrates and landowners who were reluctant to appoint ministers of any intellect.[17] The mantle of intellectual innovation in the area of philosophy passed to the legal profession, and the Moderates' interest in social philosophy was taken up by the Popular or evangelical party of Thomas Chalmers.[18] The evangelicals were more socially responsive and blended science and

---

12. Flynn, *Enlightened Scotland*, p. 267.

13. Chitnis, *The Scottish Enlightenment*, p. 100.

14. Sher, *Church and University*, p. 16; on Robertson see S. J. Brown, ed., *William Robertson and the Expansion of Empire* (Cambridge, 1997).

15. Flynn, *Enlightened Scotland*, p. 120.

16. I. D. L. Clark, "From Protest to Reaction: The Moderate Regime in the Church of Scotland, 1752-1805," in *Scotland in the Age of Improvement*, edited by N. T. Phillipson and R. Mitchison (Edinburgh, 1970), pp. 204-5; also Chitnis, *The Scottish Enlightenment*, pp. 58-59.

17. Sher, *Church and University*, p. 319.

18. Sher, *Church and University*, pp. 315, 321.

evangelical Christianity into a theory designed to combat the social evils of the early nineteenth century.[19]

The evangelical upsurge in the Church of Scotland was part of the wider evangelical movement within Protestant churches on both sides of the Atlantic in the eighteenth century. Evangelicalism had at its theological core the doctrines of sin and redemption, but this did not necessarily imply a low evaluation of human reason or a lack of interest in the social dimensions of providence. "The world-view of the Evangelicals was primarily theological and it was distinctive. None the less it had more affinities with the thought of the eighteenth century as a whole than is commonly supposed."[20] The evangelical party in Scotland were very concerned about social dislocation, which they linked to a state of spiritual sinfulness. They believed, nevertheless, that the moral philosophy and scientific knowledge of the Scottish Enlightenment could be harnessed to the gospel and thus contribute towards the solution of these problems. Education, science, and moral philosophy, as well as evangelical Christianity, had a part to play in averting social dislocation.[21] The prime architect of this amalgam of evangelical zeal and Scottish Enlightenment philosophy was, of course, Thomas Chalmers.

By the end of the eighteenth century both evangelicals and some Moderates within the Church of Scotland had become convinced of the need for the propagation of the gospel overseas, but, as the previous chapter has shown, they had quite different approaches to the question of how Christianity and civilization were related. Whereas the Moderates looked to the communication of rationality as a necessary precursor to the acceptance of the gospel, evangelicals believed that missionary preaching held the key to social regeneration. They were confident that religious vitality and revelation would carry the day. As Chalmers asserted, "the man who speaketh from the heart speaketh to it."[22] The distinction between Moderate and evangelical philosophies of mission outlined in the previous chapter was to be fundamental to

19. A. Murdoch and R. B. Sher, "Literary and Learned Culture," in *People and Society in Scotland*, vol. 1: *1760-1830*, edited by T. Devine and R. Mitchison (Edinburgh, 1988), p. 138.

20. R. T. Anstey, *The Atlantic Slave Trade and British Abolition, 1760-1810* (Basingstoke, 1975), p. 158; see also D. W. Bebbington, *Evangelicalism in Modern Britain: A History from the 1730s to the 1980s* (London, 1989), pp. 57-74; Boyd Hilton, *The Age of Atonement: The Influence of Evangelicalism on Social and Economic Thought, 1785-1865* (Oxford, 1988).

21. Murdoch and Sher, "Literary and Learned Culture," p. 138.

22. T. Chalmers, *The Two Great Instruments Appointed for the Propagation of the Gospel* (Edinburgh, 1812), p. 6.

the operation of Scottish missions in South Africa and to the level of domestic support that they received. Here evangelicals worked among those regarded as "savages," whereas the Moderate-instigated mission in India from 1824 was directed at a people whose level of "civilization" was held to signal their readiness to accept the Christian message.

As the leading Scottish advocate of the evangelical school of missions, Thomas Chalmers continually defended and propounded the role of revelation in the attainment of faith. He argued consistently according to Romans 10:17: "So then faith cometh by hearing, and hearing by the word of God," but he also held that "we have no right to sit in indolence, and wait for the immediate agency of Heaven, if God has told us, that it is by the co-operation of human beings that the end is accomplished."[23] For Chalmers this meant that faith could precede civilization, and that therefore any society was in principle open to the work of evangelical missionaries. It did not, however, mean that faith could then dispense with civilization, and this approach was to be followed by the Scottish missionaries to the Xhosa in South Africa and, as chapter eight will show, by the majority of English missions.

The Beginnings of Scottish Foreign Missions

David A. Currie has demonstrated that the primary issue at stake in the celebrated debate in the General Assembly of the Church of Scotland in 1796 was not whether the church should sponsor missionary work on its own account, but whether it should give official approval to the local voluntary missionary societies that groups of evangelicals had initiated earlier that year.[24] The decision of the assembly meant that for the next thirty years Scottish foreign missionary endeavor remained in the hands of a large number of small, independent, mostly interdenominational societies, though only the largest of these — the Edinburgh Missionary Society (later known as the Scottish Missionary Society or SMS) and the GMS — regularly sent out missionaries of their own.[25] The societies were initially rooted in particular localities in Scotland. As Peter Hinchliff has noted, "The distinctive characteristic of the Scottish societies was that they were local. . . . They were local associations of people

23. Chalmers, *The Two Great Instruments*, p. 4.

24. David A. Currie, "The Growth of Evangelicalism in the Church of Scotland, 1793-1843," Ph.D. thesis, University of St. Andrews, 1990, pp. 162-65.

25. According to A. F. Walls, "Missions," in *Dictionary of Scottish Church History and Theology*, edited by N. M. de S. Cameron (Edinburgh, 1993), p. 569, at least sixty-one other local mission societies were founded between 1796 and 1825.

with an interest in and enthusiasm for missions."[26] The majority were more properly auxiliary societies that forwarded funds to missionary causes of their choice, notably the London Missionary Society (LMS).

The SMS and the GMS both began their overseas work in Sierra Leone in 1797, but these early Scottish missionary ventures on African soil proved disastrous and short-lived.[27] The GMS did not resume active involvement in mission work until the early 1820s, when a visit to Glasgow by George Thom, a Dutch Reformed Church minister from the Cape, reawakened the idea of an active foreign mission.

The early missionaries of the GMS shared many of the attitudes of independence of mind that were characteristic of the English Nonconformist societies at this time. Many had been lay preachers before their call and were in training for the church when they felt the call. Scottish Presbyterian missionaries differed from their English Dissenting counterparts in the academic level of their education. They were all university educated and received the same training as those destined for the home ministry.[28] Most of the early missionaries to the Xhosa had obtained their degrees and theological training at Glasgow University, though one, James Laing, had studied moral and natural philosophy at Edinburgh University.[29] Later missionaries were trained at the Free Church's seminary at New College, Edinburgh.

The influence of Thomas Chalmers was apparent among the early Scottish missionaries in the Cape, as it was among their colleagues in India. The Reverend John Ross, the first minister to be set apart by a Church of Scotland presbytery for overseas missionary work, who arrived in the Cape in 1823, was particularly taken with Chalmers's work. Chalmers's ideas on evangelization and poverty are reflected in Ross's own work in South Africa.[30] In addition to Chalmers, the missionaries were clearly influenced by other leading contemporary evangelicals. From Ross's example, and various lists

26. P. Hinchliff, "Whatever Happened to the Glasgow Missionary Society," *Studia Historia Ecclesiastica* 18 (1992): 108-9. It should, however, be pointed out that the Baptist Missionary Society was originally local or regional in character, being supported primarily within the area of the East Midlands covered by the Northamptonshire Baptist Association.

27. Hinchliff, "Whatever Happened?", p. 111; Walls, "Missions," pp. 574-75.

28. See S. Piggin, *Making Evangelical Missionaries, 1789-1858: The Social Background, Motives and Training of British Protestant Missionaries to India* (Abingdon, 1984), p. 219.

29. D. Williams, "The Missionaries on the Eastern Frontier of the Cape Colony, 1799-1853," Ph.D. thesis, University of the Witwatersrand, 1959, p. 32.

30. This is evident as a general influence throughout Ross's writing; see Ms. 2613-3696 in the Cory Library.

kept by the missionaries in South Africa, it is clear that they read works considered standard for evangelicals at the time — works by Jonathan Edwards (particularly his life of Brainerd), Thomas Boston, William Wilberforce, and Hannah More — all of which pointed to the socially regenerative force of evangelical religion. It is also clear that they continued their reading as much as possible when they were in South Africa.

The Xhosa mission, no less than any other foreign mission, depended on a supporting constituency nourished by regular supplies of printed information from the field. There is not much information on the support base of the GMS. Most of the directors appear to have been local clergymen. Support came from local collecting societies, such as the Dunfermline Ladies' Association, as well as individuals from all sectors of society. Special projects (once the missionaries were in South Africa) were often funded by single donations, most of which were anonymous. In all likelihood these emanated from members of Glasgow's rising middle class, which had developed both in numbers and wealth particularly towards the end of the eighteenth century.[31] Merchants of various description formed a large part of this developing class, many of whom had made their wealth through trade with America and through trade in slaves. Though the source of the wealth of the large donors to the GMS is unclear, they were increasingly important to the society from the 1830s onwards, and especially after the adoption of the mission by the Free Church of Scotland. Equally important to the financial maintenance of the mission was the print community that managed and sustained news of it. The example of the Xhosa mission, however, suggests that news from the field was often refracted through the interpretative lens of editorial comment. What the missionaries wrote and what their supporters read were not identical, and the gaps that sometimes appeared between the two reveal the tensions between enlightened theory and evangelical experience.

The GMS in South Africa

When in 1821 the first GMS missionaries — William Ritchie Thomson and John Bennie — arrived in Xhosaland, which was then an independent territory, they joined a station at Tyumie established by John Brownlee, a Scottish missionary of the LMS. In 1824 Bennie and a third missionary, John Ross, es-

---

31. S. Nenadic, "The Rise of the Urban Middle Classes," in *People and Society in Scotland,* vol. 1: *1760-1830,* edited by T. Devine and A. Mitchison (Edinburgh, 1988), pp. 112, 114.

tablished a new station of their own on the Incehra River. This was to become the celebrated Lovedale, named after John Love, Secretary of the LMS and later of the GMS. The station was destroyed in Hintsa's War of 1834, but subsequently rebuilt on a new site four miles distant. These two stations formed the base of GMS work in Xhosaland, which adhered to the missionary model advocated by Thomas Chalmers in its emphasis on preaching and teaching both on the stations and on itinerations. However, in 1841 the missionaries founded a seminary at Lovedale, which they modeled on advice received from Alexander Duff and John Wilson of Bombay. Lovedale was designed as an interracial institution for the higher education of Africans alongside the sons of missionaries and traders.[32]

The affairs of the stations and the mission were decided in a presbytery, formed in January 1824. Until the 1830s the presbytery of Caffraria also ran the financial affairs of the mission. The missionaries were allowed to draw on the GMS for money to run their stations, and to build churches and houses, as well as to run their printing press. Their bills were drawn successively on members of the religious and merchant community in Cape Town. They each earned £100 p.a.[33] Any major outlay had to be approved by the directors of the GMS, who would consult among themselves in Glasgow. It is not too clear how often the directors met, but one or another director was in more or less constant correspondence with the missionaries. Letters began the two- to three-month trip to Scotland as soon as the missionaries were established in Xhosaland. They wrote to their families, friends, as well as to the directors. These letters were distributed widely, and so news of the mission reached an extensive audience. In 1828 friends of Mrs. Weir, stationed at Tyhumie, wrote to her that her letters from the field were being read out loud at her old Bible society in Glasgow, and that one of them had also been printed in an Irish provincial journal.[34] In the early years of the mission all the missionaries wrote home regularly, and remembered their obligations to write in such as way as to provide news of the South African mission. There is little in the correspondence from this period to suggest the lack of attention and funding of which missionaries complained in later years.

32. The foundation of the Lovedale Seminary may in part have been a response to Duff's General Assembly speech of 25 May 1835, but the missionaries had been planning to start a seminary since 1834.

33. Ms. 7714, John Ross to his mother, 17 December 1826; Ms. 3204, John Ross to Alexander Duff, 9 July 1865.

34. Cory Library for Historical Research, Grahamstown, South Africa, Ms. 8379-80, James Greir to Mrs. Weir and then James Weir, 20 Sept. 1828 and 21 March 1831. Hereafter Cory Ms.

In 1822 the GMS printed its first *Annual Report* on the South African mission. This periodical, and the *Quarterly Papers* that were published after 1827, formed the major source of news on the mission for its Scottish public until the 1840s. They consisted of editorial comment and letters from the missionaries (mostly to the directors rather than personal). After the Disruption, publication of these papers ceased, and South African news began to appear in the *Home and Foreign Missionary Record* of the Free Church of Scotland. The content of the first few annual reports and quarterly papers followed a consistent pattern. In the course of their anecdotes and discourses about their work the missionaries tended to describe the Xhosa according to standard stereotypes. Descriptions of Xhosa men as lazy or addicted to cattle thieving, or of Xhosa women as passive and degraded, would be followed by descriptions of the missionaries' efforts to raise them up out this state, to enlighten benighted Africa. A matrix of gradual progress underlay almost every account from the field, coupled with a consistency of metaphoric description in which dyadic tropes involving light and dark, sowing and reaping, depth and height, featured regularly.[35] Progress between the extremes was to be effected by the attainment of the means of grace, administered by the missionaries. John Bennie's comment of 1822, where he referred to "[a] people sunk in ignorance and wickedness, but who are capable of the highest improvement, [through] telling them of the glad tidings of salvation" is typical of this style.[36] This teleology was constantly present in their writing, and it reflects their characteristically evangelical concern with the attainment of faith as a necessary prerequisite for the progress of civilization.

These kinds of descriptions and metaphors formed a mainstay of accounts from the field during most of the nineteenth century. This trend has been discussed by Leon de Kock in his provocative book on missionary discourse at the Cape: "In my reading of missionary documents and books . . . I was struck by the near-stupefying tenacity of Manichean description. Everywhere I looked I came across missionaries . . . reducing heterogeneity and plurality to a binary scheme in which one term predominates and determines the other."[37] De Kock argues that the very existence of such a discourse in a sense prevented the missionaries from writing in a different vein about their work. He refers to this as "entrapment within a particular mode of expression"[38] and locates the mis-

---

35. For a much more detailed discussion of these tropes, see L. de Kock, *Civilising Barbarians: Missionary Narrative and African Textual Response in Nineteenth-Century South Africa* (Johannesburg, 1996), pp. 82-85.

36. *Annual Report of the Glasgow Missionary Society,* 1822, p. 27. My addition.

37. De Kock, *Civilising Barbarians,* p. 17.

38. De Kock, *Civilising Barbarians,* p. 82.

sionaries' writing within a particular ideological framework: "Typical of neo-classical, empirical rendering of knowledge, their mission was never to discover heterogeneity, but always to confirm pre-existent notions of the nature of 'reality' which they regarded as objectively true."[39] De Kock refers only to the general projects of the Enlightenment, but more specifically this rendering of knowledge had its roots in the Scottish Enlightenment philosophies of the development of man and society. Before the missionaries arrived in Xhosaland they already had preconceived ideas of how to write about Africans, through exposure to the literature of the abolition movement as well as previous European writing about Africans, as well as the general "conjectural" histories produced by the Scottish philosophers.[40]

Although the missionaries may have been incapable of portraying Africans any differently, there was another reason for their writing in such a way. As good evangelists they knew the value of publicity. They knew how important it was to write about their work, both in order to publicize their cause and to provide material that served as an example of virtuous Christian living. The traffic in information was crucial because it was on the basis of the news they received that people donated money to the mission. Earlier letters, and especially those from the people at home, explicated the link between knowledge and zeal. "Keep a journal of what you see hear & do and send it home. It will stir up our zeal when we hear particularly the wants of the interior."[41] De Kock attributes such writing to the need to satisfy preconfigured notions of Africans as "'depraved' barbarians," which was necessary to demonstrate differences between Africans and Europeans, and the need to raise the former. Only such reports would awaken Christian sympathy.[42]

The missionaries, however, were not so completely trapped within the boundaries of domestic discourse as de Kock implies. They did not write as often as they were expected to, nor did they always write in the form that people in Scotland would have understood. As they became more isolated from home, and more aware of the fact that standard metaphors did not always describe adequately their experiences, their narratives sometimes failed to conform to domestic expectations. This is clear from repeated admonitions (es-

39. De Kock, *Civilising Barbarians*, pp. 82-83.

40. See Jean and John Comaroff, *Of Revelation and Revolution*, vol. 1: *Christianity, Colonialism, and Consciousness in South Africa* (Chicago and London, 1991), ch. 3, and M. Ferguson, *Subject to Others* (London, 1992), introduction, p. 5, for a discussion of the way in which Africans were written about and the creation of European discourses around Africans.

41. Cory Ms. 3218, Struthers to Thomson, Bennie and John Ross, 6 June 1827.

42. De Kock, *Civilising Barbarians*, p. 83.

pecially in the 1840s) to write more frequently, as well as the growing volume of editorial intervention that occurred in their letters.[43] These were home interventions designed to keep them on the discursive straight and narrow.

Analysis of the editing of missionary narratives reveals a concern to elevate description of social change into a normative statement of the pattern of "civilization." Thus in 1827 William Ritchie Thomson wrote: "Where formerly a wilderness of long grass was, and the soil never turned up since the flood, we have now growing many of the necessaries, and even some of the luxuries of life. A neat village has been formed, inhabited by those who a little while ago roamed the world at large, as wild and savage as their old neighbours, the lions and tigers of the forest."[44] This description appeared, significantly altered, in the editorial comment in the next *Annual Report:* "As might be expected, civilization keeps pace among the Caffers with their advancement in religion. Their bold ferocious character is now considerably tamed and softened down. Instead of roaming the country in search of elephants, lions and tigers, they are gradually acquiring the staid and peaceful and industrious habits of the agriculturist."[45] Although Thomson had employed stereotypical forms of description, he was describing a process of transition to an agrarian economy that had actually occurred. The unnamed editor of the paper, however, used his narrative to essay an opinion of the state of unredeemed Xhosa society, formulated in specifically moral terms, digesting Thomson's information and turning observation into homily for the benefit of the home readership. The teleological assumptions of the Scottish Enlightenment about the development of human society are clearly at work in this description. The experiences of the missionaries in South Africa were being distilled to reinforce existing general principles. Such examples of editorial generalization on the basis of a mixture of empirical and moral observation were fairly common in the journal reports. Editors ensured that the missionaries' reports were presented in a familiar code.

The process of editorial homogenization and generalization that was applied to the news sent home by the missionaries did not always pass without contestation. The missionaries, forgetful of the need to present news from the field in a particular way, were quite alarmed at some of the inaccuracies that appeared. Shortly after the war of 1835, John Ross wrote to the directors complaining about several such in the annual report, and charged them with the injudicious alteration of personal accounts.[46] Editorial interference was not

43. Cory Ms. 3171 and Ms. 3172, Macfarlan to John Ross, 30 April 1845 and 14 September 1845.
44. William Ritchie Thomson, *Annual Report*, 1827, p. 16.
45. *Annual Report*, 1828, p. 19.
46. Cory Ms. 3128, John Ross to directors, no date.

limited to the refashioning of narrative. In 1839 Duncan Macfarlan (an influential member of the GMS Committee) requested John Ross to supply a sketch of Pirrie Station, to be published in the *Spring Quarterly Intelligence* of 1840:

> Allow us to express a wish, that you would at convenience, furnish us with an individual sketch of your own station, such a little picture, as will enable the reader of our Quarterly Intelligence to see before them, your little church with the Caffre Congregation, gathering under the sound of your morning Bell. . . . Something of this kind is necessary, towards securing for each station, a good hold of the mind. And without this, we [illegible] proper access to the heart.[47]

A series of letters followed in which John Ross objected to such pictorial changes, and in which Macfarlan attempted to justify them. In a letter to John Ross in September 1840 he wrote: "We have modified Pirrie by throwing in forest ground in the [foreground] and adding a Belfry on your house [and] a Bell. You will excuse this as well meant. If the sketch is not like Pirrie you might just try to make Pirrie like the sketch?"[48] While Ross was being his usual pedantic, dogmatic self, he did have a point.

Clearly then, missionary accounts from the field were not merely photographic representations of their own work. Home needs — for appropriately uplifting news in correct form — also drove and reshaped missionary writing. These needs, however, had a very real as well as a discursive impact, just as the missionaries' writing itself had real and discursive impact on domestic perceptions. The complex interplay between these different forces is well demonstrated by trends in the organization of the mission after the GMS merged with the Foreign Missions Committee (FMC) of the Free Church of Scotland.

Years of Lean

In 1838 the GMS — both the missionaries and the home congregations — split over the voluntary principle.[49] At the Cape the two mission societies that resulted continued to work together as one presbytery, since they felt that a di-

---

47. Cory Ms. 3159, Macfarlan to John Ross, 19 February 1839.
48. Cory Ms. 3163, John Ross to Macfarlan, 10 March 1840, and Ms. 3165, Macfarlan to John Ross, 10 September 1840.
49. E. G. K. Hewat, *Vision and Achievement, 1795-1956* (London, 1960), p. 180. Hewat is not necessarily the best source for information on the South Africa mission.

vision would only confuse their African members, and moreover it would not have an effect on their work.[50] "[C]onscientious objections . . . have never occasioned its members any practical difficulty, or obstructed its evangelistic labours among the heathen."[51] However, the split divided domestic support for the mission, especially with regard to funding. The directors of the original society who supported the body now known as the GMS of the Church of Scotland (the other half of the society being known as the Glasgow African Missionary Society, and associated with the United Secession and then United Presbyterian Church) decided they had insufficient funds to continue, and after the Disruption of 1843 attempted to hand over their mission to the FMC. From this point on the missionaries began to complain about a lack of attention from Scotland — a lack of communication and a lack of funding. This lack of attention extended to both the FMC and to the evangelical public.

In early May 1844 Duncan Macfarlan of Renfrew, by now the principal spokesperson in Scotland for the GMS Committee, wrote to the FMC seeking a transfer of the GMS to the Free Church of Scotland.[52] His inquiry prompted a favorable reply, and later that month the two societies had a joint meeting in which the Free Church requested the GMS to furnish details of its missions. In September of that year articles of agreement for the transfer of the mission were drawn up and included details of the FMC's expectations of the mission, a memorandum from the Glaswegians as to the personnel, extent, and financial worth of the missions in Caffraria, as well as an "understanding that the following gentlemen [the Glaswegian GMS committee members] shall continue to act as a Sub-Committee in Glasgow for the management of these missions till the next meeting of the Assembly."[53]

Over the next few years the Glasgow subcommittee continued to administer the Xhosa mission, though all important and financial decisions were referred to the FMC. The minutes of the FMC reveal a lack of interest in the Xhosa missions, as well as a tussle for resources and financing that was to continue well into the 1850s.[54] As early as October 1846 Macfarlan and Wil-

---

50. Williams, "Missionaries on the Eastern Frontier," pp. 103-10. Nor did debates at home on the establishment of self-supporting churches have any effect at the Cape, where the missionaries were becoming increasingly convinced of the need for government intervention in order to promote the spread of Christianity.

51. Cory Ms. 9038, Minute, Robert Niven on the reasons for accepting non–Church of Scotland Presbyterian missionaries into the presbytery, 7 July 1841.

52. NLS, Edinburgh, Dep. 298 no. 106.

53. NLS, Dep. 298, no. 106, 20 September 1844.

54. See also Williams, "Missionaries on the Eastern Frontier," pp. 108-10, and S. Brock, "James Stewart and Lovedale: A Reappraisal of Missionary Attitudes and African

liam Govan, principal of Lovedale, who was in Scotland at the time, petitioned the FMC for more adequate instructions for the missionaries in Xhosaland because they felt the status of the Xhosa mission to be very unclear. The FMC would not commit themselves to a definite course of action on the Xhosa missions, and in fact several of its members recommended that the affairs of the Xhosa mission be dealt with solely by a special committee in Glasgow (in effect suggesting that there should be no Glasgow representation on the FMC).[55] This vacillation on the part of the committee where it came to making positive decisions about the Xhosa mission was typical of the first two decades of FMC control.

In 1848, four years after the GMS had become part of the Free Church, financial difficulties caused the FMC to suggest abandoning the Xhosa mission. According to the FMC, their missionary work was running at a deficit of approximately £2,400 p.a. (annual expenditure exceeding annual income of approximately £7,300 by the above amount).[56] The only way in which they could suggest freeing themselves from debt was to get rid of some of their expenditure in the form of established missions: "And in the whole circumstances of the case and after the most serious deliberation the Committee consider themselves bound and warranted to recommend to the Church the discontinuance of the Mission in Africa."[57]

This resolution was passed at a meeting of the committee at which none of the Glasgow members were present. At the next meeting Macfarlan stated his opposition to the resolution and called for a rethinking of the issue. The item was carried over to the next meeting, when it was resolved to postpone a decision until the next meeting of the General Assembly of the Free Church, who promptly threw the decision straight back to the FMC.[58]

Despite these efforts and money raised through extraordinary collections, the abandonment of the Africa mission was mooted again the following year. The *Foreign Missions Report* for 1849 stated that, in order to cut costs, those missions that had been received most recently into the Free Church should be dissolved.[59] This would have been the end of the Xhosa mission had it not

---

Response in Eastern Cape, South Africa, 1870-1905," Ph.D. thesis, University of Edinburgh, 1974, pp. 24-27.

55. NLS, Dep. 298, no. 106, 14 January 1847.

56. *Home and Foreign Missionary Record of the Free Church of Scotland* 3.19 (July 1848): 475.

57. NLS, Dep. 298, no. 106, 19 January 1848.

58. NLS, Dep. 298, no. 106, 29 February and 15 March 1848.

59. These were Nagpur (6 October 1843), Xhosaland (17 May 1844), and the Cape Mission (30 June 1845); *Home and Foreign Missionary Record* 3.6 (July 1849): 160. As far as

been for support received directly from Glasgow. In July 1849 Macfarlan wrote to the committee that friends of the mission in Glasgow proposed to bear the costs of Lovedale Seminary, including Govan's salary, if the FMC would bear other costs, for the next five years.[60] The committee agreed on the understanding that the decision was not binding.[61]

This was the most serious attack that the Xhosa mission experienced in Scotland. However, funding over the next few years was still limited, and more than once the Glasgow brethren had to contribute extra money, such as to provide a salary for John Ross's son, Bryce, who wished to follow his father as a missionary to the Xhosa.

It might be supposed on the basis of the concerns shown by the FMC that the Xhosa mission was a rather large drain on the FMC coffers. In fact the Africa mission cost the FMC only £1,179-5-11 in 1844, £1,469-17-10 in 1845, and £1,161-15-10 in 1847.[62] The salaries for Indian missionaries alone came to £6,501-2-3, £5,342-18-8, and £7,358-15-4 in the same years.[63] The costs of the India missions of the Free Church of Scotland were increasing while the costs of the Africa mission were decreasing. According to Elizabeth Hewat, the FMC suggested abandoning the Africa mission because of their financial difficulties, and because the two Frontier Wars had made that mission a particularly cumbersome charge.[64] This is not totally accurate, however, since the FMC did not bear the costs of the destruction occasioned by the 1835 war, and, when they suggested abandoning the mission in 1848, they had not yet spent any money on rebuilding the Africa mission. In the light of previous costs the FMC had no grounds for supposing that the costs of rebuilding would be excessive in any way; in the end they voted each missionary £25 to cover total personal losses of £525-9-3, and paid only £103-11-8 of the general damages estimated at £1,069-7-8.[65] By the time of their second attempt to close the mission in 1849 the FMC was aware that the British government proposed to grant £190 for repairs at Lovedale, as well as £100 p.a. for the

---

I can gather, the Cape Mission was both partially dissolved and handed over to the Colonial Churches Scheme of the Free Church.

60. NLS, Dep. 298, no. 106, 24 July 1849.

61. NLS, Dep. 298, no. 106, 3 September 1849.

62. *Home and Foreign Missionary Record* 2.6 (June 1845): 135; 2.18 (June 1846): ix; 3.18 (June 1848): vii.

63. *Home and Foreign Missionary Record* 2.6 (June 1845): 135; 2.18 (June 1846): ix; 3.18 (June 1848): vii.

64. Hewat, *Vision and Achievement*, p. 180.

65. *Home and Foreign Missionary Record* 3.20 (August 1848): 499; and 4.6 (June 1849); Ms. 3175, Macfarlan to John Ross, 10 December 1847.

running of the seminary.[66] While there was some reason to discontinue the Africa mission on financial grounds, these grounds were slender. It is clear that there were other reasons for the Free Church's unwillingness to support the mission.

The missionaries were well aware of this neglect and apparent indifference to their mission, as is poignantly apparent from their writing during this period. John Ross's letters to his sons, Bryce and Richard, in Edinburgh at this time, are particularly full of references to the neglect of the Africa mission.

At the same time I received [a letter] of same date from Dr Macfarlan, with the missy Record of Feby. You may have seen [7] letters of his in the Witness: yet it has been contemplated by the Mission Commee. of the Free Ch., or rather the acting Comm. to give up the Missions in Africa, because of financial difficulties. Such a proposal is not so painful as was their unexpressed sympathy with our sufferings. Such a proposal too throws how or why there was a want of sympathy. I can not bring my mind to entertain the thots of such a course. Abandon or suspend a mission in which I have spent all but as much as a levites time of service! A great deal more than twice the best part of my life. Yet what tho' all my life & twice as much as a levites period of service had been spent? Are the members of the church of Christ to be abandoned without a shepherd? Are those who are seeking the Lord to have cause to say, no man cares for my soul! & all among whom we laboured to be left at such a time when, it may be said, Satan seems to be raging more than ever in this land! . . . Have the Foreign M[issionar]y Commee done anything to sustain the Mission & if not how can the members answer to the Great head of the Church?[67]

William Govan, who was in Scotland at the time, wrote confirming John Ross's fear: "Meanwhile the Comm. have declined to come to any definite resolution about the Kafir mission . . . no pledge was made, nay this seems to have been carefully avoided."[68] He added that matters with respect to the mission were gloomy indeed, and that Macfarlan was their only publicist.[69]

Bryce Ross, then a student at New College, wrote to his father in equally depressed vein:

66. *Home and Foreign Missionary Record* 4.7 (July 1849): 158.
67. Ms. 7754, John Ross to Bryce Ross, 21 April 1848.
68. Cory Ms. 3442, Govan to John Ross, 27 April 1847.
69. Cory Ms. 3442, Govan to John Ross, 27 April 1847.

Instead of hailing with joyful lips the rise of the morning star of learning on the shores of Caffreland, and giving it all the countenance and support they could both at home and abroad, and which they ought to have regarded as a high honour and privilege to have been able to do, secret thunderbolt after secret thunderbolt was hurled at it while it stood, and for aught I know these may still be sent against its ruins; it is very likely however, that the contrary may be the case — that more are now awake to their true interests when alas! however, it might be too late. We look with patience to see the result of the dark and gloomy state of Caffraria.[70]

Bryce Ross attributed much of this neglect to the lack of publicity given to the Africa mission: "In reading the Home and Foreign Missionary record of the Free Church one would think that Mr Laing was almost the only missionary of that Church in Caffraria. The name of John Bennie seldom occurs, that of John Ross never. Now this operates very injuriously against the Mission. Old friends lose interest in it, and others take almost none."[71]

It was, however, not lack of publicity alone but lack of the right kind of publicity that acted detrimentally towards the South Africa mission, and to home perceptions of it. By the 1840s the South Africa missionaries were writing about their work in a much less optimistic way than previously. Owing to the succession of wars that had disrupted their work and to local opposition to Christianity, they had few converts. Their reports continued to be full of stories of their life and work, but the stories were not of success in terms of numbers of converts. This lack of achievement on the ground — the absence of stirring news — had a deadening effect on Scottish enthusiasm: "You have no conception what injury those dark and gloomy pictures which have from time to time come from the Free church Mission field in Caffraria have done."[72] These gloomy pictures were framed within the inevitable Enlightenment metaphors of progress, or rather of progress that had ground almost to a halt. The African night was dawning with painful slowness. By 1843 the Xhosa were no longer being described as animals in the field, but as those who had "sunk lower than the beasts."[73] The results were a freezing of interest in the Africa mission, a

70. Cory Ms. 7893, Bryce Ross to John Ross, 2 March 1847.

71. Cory Ms. 7906, Bryce Ross to John Ross, 31 October 1849.

72. Cory Ms. 7910, Bryce Ross to John Ross, 14 March 1851.

73. *Winter Quarterly Intelligence,* Miss Thomson, p. 5. The *Home and Foreign Missionary Record* during the 1840s and 1850s contains many similar examples of highly pejorative metaphoric language.

falling off in support for the mission, and the creation of a discourse on the Xhosa that constantly recirculated the same knowledge. This last point is important because it cut the nerve of the teleology that was intrinsic to evangelical mission thought.

The Scottish dislike of the African mission was, therefore, a result not of that mission's financial status but of its perceived failure to deliver the social and moral transformation that Scottish evangelicals of the Chalmers school expected the gospel to effect in all cultural contexts. That failure appeared to confirm the caution of the Moderates about the capacity of the "uncivilized" to absorb the Christian message, and to reinforce the case that Scottish missionary effort should instead be concentrated on the apparently more promising field of India. The problems of the Xhosa mission were in part the result of a decided Scottish preference for India.

The missionaries in South Africa were well aware of the Indian competition that threatened their continued existence:

> I gather from the report in the [illegible] Guard. [ian] . . . that the Church has had little or no interest in the mission. . . . Yet you may well conceive what a contrast we must sometimes draw on reading in the Miss[ionar]y Record that kind answers of the Convenor of the F. M. Co[e.] have been re[ceive]d to the letters of their Miss[ionarie]s in India.[74]

Ross was not incorrect in his assumption that the India missions of the Free Church were viewed more favorably by the FMC. Macfarlan's reply to this letter contained details of the financial settlement on the amalgamation of the societies:

> At the time the Mission was placed under the Assembly we as a Society were not in circumstances to carry it on. Our Constitution especially in the Free Church were [sic] absorbed and our friends [would] no longer support — I myself proposed in private that if the Assembly would allow us to appropriate to the Kafir Mission our own contributions and such as we could rouse and allow us credit for these in name of the church we would still charge ourselves with the financial responsibility.

74. Cory Ms. 3174, John Ross to Macfarlan, 29 July 1847. It should be added that while the missionaries in South Africa were aware of a preference for India, this did not turn them against the Indian mission, and on other occasions they recognized that the Indian missions too did not have sufficient funding (Cory Ms. 2984, John Ross to Richard Ross, n.d.).

But this proposal was at once rejected on the grounds of its deverting [*sic*] monies from the Indian Mission.[75]

There was truth in this fear about a preference for India.[76] After 1843 the India missions of the Free Church grew continuously. A new mission station (Nagpur) was established in 1843, and the number of buildings and paid native agents on each station was also increasing. India missionaries drew an average salary of £350 p.a., while the South Africa missionaries were paid at £100 p.a.[77] The India missions were the only ones to receive special grants throughout this period. In 1844 Duff at Calcutta was given £600 extra for special payments, while Nisbet and Wilson at Bombay were given £10-0-0 and £83-11-1, respectively. Lovedale received an extra (its only extra) £5-0-6 for books.[78] In the columns of the *Home and Foreign Missionary Record* that listed donations to the FMC, the India mission was singled out more regularly than the Xhosa one to be the recipient of special donations. Quite obviously, because the India mission was run on a larger scale, it needed more money, but the point should be made that it was run on a larger scale because the FMC preferred to allocate funding to it and because people preferred to donate to its cause.

The preference of the FMC for India was also reflected in its publications. The *Home and Foreign Missionary Record* regularly devoted more of its section on foreign missions to the India rather than the South Africa mission. The Xhosa mission was first mentioned in the pages of the journal in March 1845, where it referred to the joining of the two missions in India and Africa and included a brief description of the situation in the eastern Cape. That same year the *Home and Foreign Missionary Record* included extracts from three letters from South Africa. Letters from India, however, appeared in every edition (bar the mid-year financial report), and Alexander Duff alone had extracts from eight letters printed in one edition of the magazine. In 1846 the longest pieces on the Xhosa field were a biography of George Schmidt, one of the founders of the Moravian mission, and a letter from Dr. Macfarlan on the war on the Cape frontier. The year 1847 was singularly lean, with no letters

75. Cory Ms. 3175, Macfarlan to John Ross, 10 December 1847.

76. See Piggin, *Making Evangelical Missionaries*, p. 14; also A. L. Drummond and J. Bulloch, *The Church in Victorian Scotland, 1843-1874* (Edinburgh, 1975), p. 167.

77. NLS Dep. 298, no. 107, 17 October 1854, 22 March 1859. See also Cory Ms. 7895, Bryce Ross to John Ross, 16 June 1847; Cory Ms. 7898, Bryce Ross to John Ross, 17 January 1848.

78. *Home and Foreign Missionary Record* 2.6 (June 1845).

from the Xhosa mission, which received mention only in the General Report of the Foreign Missions Committee.

The results of this preference for India were visible not only in the amount of material published in the *Home and Foreign Missionary Record,* but also in the kind of material published. Whereas the missionaries in the Cape could offer only general narratives of their work, the letters of the Indian missionaries featured stirring tales of conversion, often presented in the converts' own words.[79] Editorial comment in the journal tended to reinforce the point, contrasting the lack of Xhosa converts with reports from India bringing "joyful intelligence of hopeful conversion" and the "energy with which the friends of the truth are proceeding in their efforts."[80]

Several explanations may be offered for the preference for the India mission. The first lies in an east coast–west coast division in Scotland as far as the running and funding of the FMC were concerned. The first mission stations adopted by the Free Church were originally stations of the SMS in western India. The majority of committee members of the FMC during its early years seem to have come from Edinburgh, which may go some way to explaining a bias for the India missions.[81] Glasgow had few representatives on the FMC, and all the missionaries to Xhosaland either came from Glasgow or had studied at the University of Glasgow.

Alexander Duff, who was trained at the University of St. Andrews, had a tremendous influence on the Scottish public's preference for India missions. In his speeches and writing he urged the cause of India continually. "Whatever may be alleged of other heathen lands; if it can be shown of India, in particular, that it is now 'our own,' will it not follow as an inevitable consequence . . . that we are specially bound to provide for its spiritual necessities."[82] The influence of his oratory and writing affected both the FMC and the Scottish evangelical public as a whole. He had more letters printed in the *Home and Foreign Missionary Record* than any other missionary, and his letters were often reprinted in its juvenile counterpart, the *Children's Missionary Record.*

This prominence was the result of Duff's careful endeavors to raise his

79. It is also possible that the editors of the home journals did not want to print material on South Africa, even when it was available.

80. *Home and Foreign Missionary Record* 3.14 (February 1848): 330; and 2.21 (September 1846): 481.

81. NLS Dep. 298, nos. 106 and 107, Lists of Committee Members. Edinburgh is listed as the address for the majority of committee members.

82. A. Duff, "A Vindication of the Church of Scotland's India Missions," in *Missionary Addresses, Delivered before the General Assembly of the Church of Scotland in the Years 1835, 1837, 1839* (Edinburgh, 1850), p. 124.

own profile and the profile of the India mission in the Scottish public, with a view to raising greater funds for this mission. He was well aware of the importance of publicity: "And are [the people of Scotland] not apt to measure the relative importance of subjects by the relative prominence given to them in [journals and periodicals]?"[83] Duff's three-hour address to the 1835 General Assembly on the subject of the India mission and subsequent fund-raising tour of northern Scotland were extraordinarily effective in attracting evangelical support for a mission founded on Moderate principles.[84] The support he raised was sustained by his regular writings on India so that by the 1840s his work and the work of the India mission had gained widespread publicity. Duff was a favorite of the Scottish evangelical public, who donated readily to his particular causes. India seemed an intellectually more exciting field of work than Africa. Whereas Africa was regarded as a curiosity, India was a treasure house of sophisticated if idolatrous religion and philosophy that called for the deployment of the most powerful intellectual weapons in the missionary armory.[85] According to Duff's blend of evangelical zeal and Enlightenment philosophy, India offered both challenge and opportunity, while the Xhosa field in the 1830s and 1840s seemed stony ground.

By the late 1850s, however, the Xhosa mission was starting to gain new recognition. More regular reports from the Xhosa missionaries were appearing in the *Home and Foreign Missionary Record,* and the FMC was beginning to take greater interest in the mission. There were several reasons for this, all connected. By this time more members both of the Free Church public and of the FMC would have acquired personal knowledge of some of the Xhosa missionaries and thus forged a more personal connection with the Xhosa mission. Laing and Govan had both been back to Scotland during the 1840s, and Richard Ross (the younger son of John Ross) had spent several months arranging special collections for the Free Church in various parishes around Scotland prior to his departure for the Cape. This work was quite influential in publicizing the mission. The letters appearing after this point in the *Home and Foreign Missionary Record* are almost invariably written by Govan, Laing, and Richard Ross. The visits of these missionaries and the work of Richard Ross gained the Xhosa mission more support on the FMC. This was transferred into greater coverage in the *Record,* to which the Xhosa missionaries

83. A. Duff, "Farewell Address on the Subject of the Church of Scotland's India Mission," in *Missionary Addresses,* p. 134.

84. I. Maxwell, "Enlightenment and Mission: Alexander Duff and the Early Years of the General Assembly's Institution in Calcutta," North Atlantic Missiology Project Position Paper No. 2 (Cambridge, 1996), p. 1.

85. Piggin, *Making Evangelical Missionaries,* p. 14.

contributed more regularly, aware as they were of the need to maintain interest in their mission. The presence of Tiyo Soga in Scotland, preaching at the John Street Presbyterian Church in Glasgow for just over a year from late 1856, also roused the interest of the United Presbyterians in their South African mission.[86]

More important than all of these was the fact that a publicist of Africa who rivaled Duff in charisma had finally emerged. The publication of David Livingstone's *Missionary Travels and Researches in South Africa* in 1857 brought Africa, the "savage continent," into European vogue.[87] He popularized and reinvigorated interest in Africa and Africa missions on a scale unknown before. "Had foreign missions been mentioned midway through the century outside the ranks of the most devoted, it would have been India that came first to the minds of most ordinary church members." This changed with the publication of Livingstone's work.[88] "It would seem as if God were about to remember in mercy Poor Africa. The explorations of Livingstone, and other missionaries, have all at once awakened an uncommon degree of interest."[89] At the conjunction of these different forces the FMC began to devote more time, interest, and money to the Xhosa missions.

Years of Plenty

The renewal of the FMC's interest in its African missions in the 1860s had a number of repercussions. In 1863 and 1864 two events occurred that were to change the course of the mission in South Africa irrevocably. In July 1863 James Stewart visited the Scottish mission stations on his way home to Scotland from his travels on the Zambezi. In March 1864 Alexander Duff, on his way home to take up a post as convenor of the FMC (having been forced to retire from the field due to ill health) also called on the various mission stations in Xhosaland. These two visits were of crucial importance for the future of Scottish policy on the mission. Duff used his new position within the FMC both to promote the interests of Xhosaland in Scotland and to implement changes in the mission that reflected his own and Stewart's ideas.

It is not clear what happened in Scotland once they had both returned,

86. D. Williams, ed., *The Journals and Selected Writings of the Reverend Tiyo Soga* (Cape Town, 1983), p. 2.
87. See Leon de Kock, *Civilising Barbarians,* pp. 162-70, for Livingstone's discursive impact.
88. Drummond and Bulloch, *The Church in Victorian Scotland,* p. 167.
89. *Home and Foreign Missionary Record* 3.3 (October 1858): 58.

but both of them (especially Duff) felt that "the mission required radical changes in organisation and educational policy."[90] According to Duff, mission initiative in Xhosaland was making no progress, partly because of infighting within the presbytery, and the constant recourse to the FMC that was necessary in consequence. This was to be remedied by an alteration in organization of the mission at the Cape, perhaps the most radical move being the separation of the Lovedale Institution from the control of the presbytery.[91] While the changes to the Xhosa mission have been viewed as a response to the dire straits the mission was in (financially and organizationally), less attention has been paid to the desire of outside parties to mold the Xhosa mission in light of their views on education, theology, and mission.

As convenor of the FMC, Duff was now in a powerful position to implement his mission theory in other fields than India. In South Africa he saw a field that had had limited success but was now in a position — as a result of the imposition of British rule and some degree of development — to yield greater benefits. His belief in the necessity of national conversion through elites, and his preference for advanced Christian education rather than proselytization, lay behind the move to separate the Lovedale Institution from the rest of the mission still being run on evangelical principles. The nonproductive side of the mission could thus be marginalized in favor of the concentration of resources at Lovedale under Stewart. Stewart supported this view of the importance of the seminary and education, as is clear from the amount of attention he devoted to it in a series of pieces on the Xhosa missions that he wrote in the *Monthly Record* in 1864. After visiting the African congregation at Lovedale, Stewart wrote:

> The preaching of the everlasting word, which exercises such potent and marvellous influences on human hearts whenever the Spirit's blessing goes along with it, is the means by which these results [referring to work previously done] are effected. But in every mission field, whether amid the stationary barbarism of Africa or the stationary civilization of India, a very little experience soon shows how important a part education plays in paving a way for the gospel *to pass through the intellect* to the heart.[92]

90. Brock, "James Stewart and Lovedale," p. 31.

91. Brock, "James Stewart and Lovedale," pp. 31-35. Brock's thesis discusses the nature of the changes at greater length.

92. *Monthly Record of the Free Church of Scotland* 21 (April 1864): 482-83. My emphasis. From 1862 the *Monthly Record* replaced the *Home and Foreign Missionary Record* as the missionary paper of the FCS.

This comment suggests that Stewart's mission theory differed significantly from Duff's original position. In Stewart's view Christian education was necessary for conversion, irrespective of the level of civilization attained by a society. In his description of the congregation at Burnshill, where he found "purely evangelistic services," Stewart dwelt on the length of time it took the missionary to convey "the elements of that knowledge which, when received into the heart and devotedly believed in, makes the possessor wiser than the wisest of the world's sages." But the next generation of worshippers would have "fewer grey-headed candidates for baptism acquiring in this laborious fashion the knowledge of divine truth," because education would by then have given people the power to read for themselves.[93] The theme of faith through education, as opposed to faith through hearing of the word, dominates his writing on the African mission and heralds his intentions towards it.

Stewart's version of Duff's missionary vision thus emphasized method rather than Scottish Enlightenment assumptions about the need for civilization as a prerequisite to evangelization through education. In fact, by the 1860s the earlier marked differences in mission theology between Moderates and evangelicals had settled into differences in method between those who shared a broadly evangelical theological consensus. The rational Calvinist view of mission, while still current (especially for Duff), was now more of a philosophy of mission practice, with a particular emphasis on education. Stewart combined an evangelical theological framework with a pragmatic conviction that far more needed to be done than had been done in the Xhosa mission towards the promotion of education. His ideas differed from Duff's earlier theory in some important respects. It is not at all clear that Stewart thought that he was dealing with a civilized elite at the Cape, nor is it clear that he envisaged the education of such an elite. He does not appear to have held out such great hopes of the African intellect as Duff did of the Indian. Commenting on Lovedale Institution, shortly to be under his charge, Stewart compared the mental faculties of Xhosa and Fingo boys, and European boys, favorably. Later in life, however, the mental accomplishments of the Africans were not so much in evidence:

> It may be that a different class of faculties from those receptive ones that chiefly act in earlier years, must be called into play in maturer life, involving more the exercise of the reasoning and moral powers, and from this cause certain differences arise; or it may be in greater probability due to the very unfavourable circumstances in which the natives find

93. *Monthly Record* n.s. 22 (May 1864): 507-8.

themself [*sic*] when commencing the struggle of life in competition with the white race.[94]

Although he did not think it likely that differences between white men and black men could be explained by lesser reasoning powers, Stewart thought it was possible. His belief that racial differences explained mental differences was to become more apparent over the period of his principalship at Lovedale (1870-1905).[95] He directed Lovedale away from an emphasis on academic training to the same level for Europeans and Africans, to one in which African education would be designed to produce only a small elite, with the majority of men being trained in practical skills.[96]

Stewart was not the only missionary for whom racial differences were becoming more important. In 1863 the *Monthly Record* contained a description of a visit to one of the out-stations: "[Y]ou see groups of fierce-looking fellows chatting together, with no clothing upon them whatever, while others are lying beside their huts basking in the sun, enjoying the savage luxury of utter laziness."[97] No improving metaphor followed. While no author is mentioned, the content of the piece suggests that it was written by Simon Colquhoun, a teacher at Lovedale since 1860. This sort of description, the presumption and contempt in the gaze, was something not present in the letters of the older missionaries in the field. It contrasts, for example, with an assertion made in the *Home and Foreign Missionary Record* in 1840: "[T]he knowledge which has been acquired by the negro during his residence among white men . . . has completely proved that he needs only to be educated and treated as a man, in order to be capable of doing all that other men can do. . . . [L]et it not be said that the negro is essentially an inferior being."[98]

Stewart was the epitome of the late nineteenth-century missionary, more highly educated and more inclined to view missionary work as a profession, and thus quite suited for the new mission project that Duff envisaged for South Africa. He had grown up in a different intellectual and discursive context than his predecessors. By the end of the nineteenth century Scottish missionaries were no longer reading the moral philosophers of the eighteenth

94. *Monthly Record* n.s. 26 (September 1864): 602.
95. De Kock, *Civilising Barbarians*, p. 71. De Kock both examines Stewart's language for this and also cites other support for this view.
96. De Kock, *Civilising Barbarians*, pp. 72-73. For Stewart's view see his speech in *The Educated Kafir, An Apology and Industrial Education: A Sequel* (Lovedale, 1880), pp. 6-7.
97. *Monthly Record* n.s. 6 (January 1863): 123.
98. *Home and Foreign Missionary Record* 1.9 (March 1840): 141.

century and had moved away from the expressly teleological visions of human potential held by the earlier missionaries. Stewart and his generation had been fed on a steady diet of news about the savages in Africa and went to the field with the African template contained in this literature fixed in their heads. They were caught up in the upsurge of interest in Africa that succeeded Livingstone and had a half century's worth of additional literature on Africa to read. They were influenced by the evolutionary theories of the second half of the nineteenth century, and they knew from the example of the Indian Mutiny what happened when British control was allowed to slip. Their minds were formed by the discourse of the preceding half century, as articulated in the Scottish missionary magazines, which itself had roots in peoples' ideas about the goals of missions and the status of savages.[99]

Conclusion

This chapter has outlined the intellectual and theological context of Scottish missions in the early nineteenth century and shown how this context, itself shifting during the century, continually affected mission projects and views of mission work. The first Scottish missionaries to the Cape were intellectually influenced (if not convinced) by much of the philosophy of the Scottish Enlightenment, as well as by the evangelical revival of the same period. The ideas of the former, especially emphases on the teleological development of human societies, acted as a blueprint for what the missionaries hoped to achieve among the Xhosa, yet ironically at the same time increasingly limited the expectations that the Scottish religious public entertained of the mission. The early missionaries among the Xhosa were driven by a belief, founded on Thomas Chalmers's version of the "evangelical Enlightenment," that the gospel was capable of propelling even African "savages" along the staged pathway of social development. With time, however, as the predicted social transformation failed to materialize, such evangelical optimism became increasingly tempered by the Moderate emphasis on the necessary priority of civilizing educational effort.

Enlightenment assumptions could thus exert a direct influence on the operation and funding of different missions. Until the 1860s the Xhosa mission did not receive much support from Scotland, both because of a preference for India reinforced by the personal advocacy of Duff and, crucially, because of

---

99. Again see the Comaroffs, *Of Revolution and Revelation*, ch. 3, for a discussion of this.

the perceived lack of progress of the Africa mission. Such disappointment appeared to confirm Duff's view that the attainment of a certain level of civilization was necessary before people would be receptive to Christianity. Part of the FMC's (and to some degree the evangelical public's) relative neglect of the South African mission was as a result of this thinking.

The message of lack of missionary progress in southern Africa was imparted to the Scottish public through the medium of print, both through the very paucity of the information that was conveyed and through the rhetoric employed to describe the African mission. Through a diet of information that ceased to emphasize the possibility of equality and progress, the Scottish supporters of the Africa mission came to believe neither was possible. As the missionaries and the editors of the *Home and Foreign Missionary Record* resorted to more benighted metaphors to drive home the needs of their mission, they neglected to emphasize what progress was occurring and thus created the erroneous impression in the Scottish mind that progress was not possible. Lack of belief in the mission led to lack of funding in the 1850s; this resulted in a dispirited, disheartened missionary community, who knew perfectly well that the Xhosa mission was being short-changed. Matters began to change in the 1860s, partially through an invigorated interest in Africa, and partially through the personal intervention of Alexander Duff. Duff tackled the lack of progress in South Africa through a set of drastic interventions, designed to separate the evangelical and educational areas of work in the Cape. Duff's response resulted in the appointment of Stewart as Principal of Lovedale, and from that point Stewart's estimate of African potential dictated the course of events at Lovedale as well as the tone of reports back home. Stewart's views on Africa had been shaped in a different context than that of the earlier missionaries. This tone was picked up by new missionaries to the field, who arrived on the field less sanguine and more racially dogmatic than their older colleagues. Expectations of Christian achievement at the Cape now revived, but confidence was now placed in the capacity of a particular missionary method — education — to compensate for the supposed innate backwardness of the African mind. No longer did the union of evangelicalism and the Scottish Enlightenment engender a profoundly egalitarian dynamic.

CHAPTER EIGHT

Christianity and Civilization in English Evangelical Mission Thought, 1792-1857

BRIAN STANLEY

I

The missionary enterprise of the last two centuries appears to most contemporary Western minds as an audacious attempt at religious conversion on a global scale. At first glance it appears to have been about the elimination of religious and cultural difference and the imposition of ideological conformity, whether of a Catholic or a Protestant hue. Yet, as Anthony Pagden and Nicholas Thomas have recently emphasized, the enterprise could not predicate the *absolute* difference of the "heathen" without collapsing into futility.[1] Missionary support in the nineteenth century thrived on lurid tales of "heathen" blindness and the savage cruelties of idolatry, but these tales would have been pointless if the blindness and savagery were innate. "If savages are quintessentially and irreducibly savage," Thomas points out, "the project of converting them to Christianity and introducing civilization is both hopeless and worthless."[2] Those rare missionaries who have absolutized the difference of the "heathen" by placing them under the curse of Ham have usually done so out of evangelistic frustration. Thus the Huguenot Jean de Léry, chronicler of the abortive Calvinist mission to Brazil from 1556 to 1558, was so de-

---

1. Anthony Pagden, *European Encounters with the New World: From Renaissance to Romanticism* (New Haven and London, 1993), p. 43; Nicholas Thomas, *Colonialism's Culture: Anthropology, Travel and Government* (Cambridge, 1994), pp. 126-28.

2. Thomas, *Colonialism's Culture*, p. 128.

pressed by the obdurate resistance of the Tupinamba to conversion that he abandoned all hope of their election, concluded that they were under the curse of Ham, and from that perspective of ineradicable difference was able to give a remarkably objective ethnographic description of their "otherness."[3]

In contrast, evangelical missionary advocates in the eighteenth and nineteenth centuries, while notoriously prone to gross and offensive caricatures of the "heathen" whom most of them had never seen, did so precisely in order that they might magnify the capacity of the gospel to emancipate the "heathen" from their barbarism. The barrier separating "civilized" from "savage," though formidable at first sight, was in principle and practice surmountable.[4] For example, Alexander Waugh, minister of the Scots Secession Church in London, preaching at the third general meeting of the LMS in May 1797, though prepared to identify Africa with the "land of Ham" in which the scorching sun fanned the "unsubdued tempers of the depraved mind," urged his hearers to share their overflowing cup of spiritual privilege with "our thirsty African brother" so that even in Africa the promised blessed age of gospel regeneration might come.[5] The Congregationalist, Isaac Nicholson, president of Cheshunt College, in a sermon preached the following day, gave voice to even more extreme statements about "filthy Hottentots" and "ferocious Jaggas," but utilized these to prove his point about the ability of the gospel to save to the uttermost even the most degraded of the human species.[6]

The numerous historians who understandably brand such statements as racist obscure the paradoxical union of extreme statements of cultural difference with assertions of humanitarian identity that was integral to the missionary enterprise. They also thereby minimize the contrast between missionary views of the relative and erasable singularity of non-Christian peoples and those increasingly influential later nineteenth-century perspectives that posited an absolute and essential difference between "civilized" and "uncivilized" peoples. These essentialist perspectives paradoxically supplied the intellectual apparatus both for hierarchical forms of colonialism and for the distinctively

---

3. Pagden, *European Encounters with the New World*, p. 43; Jean de Léry, *Histoire d'un voyage fait en la terre du Brésil*, facsimile ed., edited by J.-C. Morisot (Geneva, 1975), pp. 259-61.

4. Doug Stuart, "'Of Savages and Heroes': Discourses of Race, Nation and Gender in the Evangelical Missions to Southern Africa in the Early Nineteenth Century," Ph.D. thesis, London, 1994, p. 209.

5. *Four Sermons, Preached in London at the Third General Meeting of the Missionary Society, May 10, 11, 12, 1797* . . . (London, 1797), pp. 70-72.

6. *Four Sermons*, p. 90. I owe thanks to Mrs. Nancy Stevenson for this and the previous reference.

modern understanding of the plurality of cultures as discrete and autonomous systems of custom and value. From this standpoint, it is clear that nineteenth-century missions sit more comfortably within a framework that was common to both Renaissance and Enlightenment eras than to the alternative framework introduced by the subsequent reaction against Enlightenment assumptions. Bernard McGrane and Nicholas Thomas have argued cogently that, in the "Renaissance world of resemblance and the sovereignty of the like," non-Western peoples were defined primarily in terms of what they lacked (but could be supplied) — supremely clothes and Christianity — rather than in terms of absolute ethnic difference. However, more questionable is their corresponding claim that, by contrast, Enlightenment thought, being predicated on analysis and differentiation, divided humanity into distinct unitary types, distinguished by both physical and psychological characteristics and hence analogous to species differences, and then increasingly ranked these types on a time-scale of historical evolution.[7] In fact, there was great diversity among Enlightenment thinkers on the question of race. At one extreme stood David Hume, who held an Aristotelian position that racial differences were innate, constant, and independent of climate. At the other extreme were those, such as his fellow Scot and philosophical opponent, James Beattie (1735-1803), who explained difference of cultural and technological achievement in terms of the historical process of "civilization."[8] An intermediate position was held by the French natural historian, Buffon, who attributed difference not to human initiative but to the effect of climate and living conditions on human nature; according to Buffon, the resulting differences became genetic but were in principle capable of elimination if the determining circumstances were to change, at least over a long period.[9] The answer to the question of which of these three positions (and of other positions advanced by Enlightenment thinkers) may be termed most typical of "the Enlightenment" will depend on one's definition of the Enlightenment, but, in the English-speaking evangelical world, at least, it was the Scottish repudiation of Hume's skepticism, as represented by Beattie's Christian philosophy and more broadly by the mainstream of the Scottish Enlightenment, that exercised the most extensive influence. The majority of Enlightenment thinkers in England and America, as well as Scotland, subscribed to an ideal of progress towards civilization that, no less than the mis-

7. Bernard McGrane, *Beyond Anthropology: Society and the Other* (New York, 1989), pp. 87-103; Thomas, *Colonialism's Culture*, pp. 72-76, 80-96.

8. On Beattie see *Dictionary of National Biography* (London, 1885-1900), vol. IV, pp. 22-25, and E. H. King, *James Beattie* (Boston, 1977).

9. The preceding summary draws on Emmanuel C. Eze, *Race and the Enlightenment: A Reader* (Oxford, 1996).

sionary hope of global conversion, depended on a presumption of ultimate human commonalty. That presumption was increasingly eroded as the nineteenth century proceeded. Late nineteenth-century anthropology, by ascribing to each ethnic group its essential cultural characteristics, belongs to the post-Enlightenment Romantic reaction that followed Herder in insisting on the absolute incommensurability of all cultures.[10]

To be sustainable, the missionary project could not escape a commitment to assimilationism and the fundamental unity of humanity.[11] The antislavery slogan "Am I not a man and a brother?" which was probably coined by the decidedly rationalist Cambridge churchman, Peter Peckard, in 1788, gained common currency in missionary circles primarily because it enabled evangelicals to articulate their sense of essential identity with, and urgent moral responsibility towards, the African people who were the victims of the slave trade.[12] Evangelicals employed the language of the brotherhood of man with reference to those whose seemingly incontrovertible "barbarism," in the minds of many in polite society, appeared to place their moral entitlement to the full privileges of humanity in question. It is noteworthy that they seldom did so with reference to Indians or Chinese, perhaps because the entitlement of Eastern peoples to the full privileges of humanity was not felt to be in such jeopardy. As Jane Samson emphasized in chapter five, the unity of humanity was a foundational principle that early nineteenth-century Christians found in their Bibles but that in practice they found necessary to qualify under the influence of theories of ethnic differentiation and the apparent evidence of major variations in degrees of "civilization."[13] Where the gulf in "civilization" between "heathen" and "Christian" peoples was large enough to be used to justify practices such as slavery, which infringed the unity of humanity, many evangelicals were prepared to resort to the politically sensitive ideology of human rights and brotherhood to reinforce their claims of missionary and humanitarian obligation.

The unity of humanity in evangelical thought was thus not undifferentiated. It was customary, for example, for missionaries to compare the industri-

10. Pagden, *European Encounters with the New World*, pp. 172-81.

11. Thomas, *Colonialism's Culture*, p. 134.

12. Peckard, who was Master of Magdalene College from 1781 to 1797, is generally accepted as the author of the anonymous tract, *Am I not a Man? and a Brother? With all Humility Addressed to the British Legislature* (Cambridge, 1788). See John Walsh and Ronald Hyam, *Peter Peckard: Liberal Churchman and Anti-Slave Trade Campaigner*, Magdalene College Occasional Papers No. 16 (Cambridge, 1998), p. 17. A. T. Yarwood, *Samuel Marsden, The Great Survivor* (Carlton, Victoria, 1977), pp. 8, 12, 16, is incorrect to describe Peckard as an evangelical.

13. See above, pp. 103-22.

ous and intelligent savagery of the Maoris with the extreme degradation of the aborigines of New South Wales, but at least some of the blame for the latter was placed at the door of the convicts and European settlers who had literally demoralized the aborigines.[14] The position that a particular people occupied on the scale between savagery and civilization was not fixed. The scale could function as either snake or ladder, and its natural propensity was towards the former role. At least in the early nineteenth century, the evangelical emphasis, as Samson's analysis of mission ethnography in the Pacific illustrates, was not on the inevitability of human progress towards the ideal of civilization, but rather on the capacity of universal human depravity to drag even the most ostensibly enlightened societies down the scale of degeneracy towards moral barbarism.[15] It is this central feature of evangelical anthropology that prevented missionaries from giving a blank check to the forces of civilization and places in question recent interpretations of the missionary impact, for example by Leon de Kock, which claim that if one takes "the long view," distinctions between evangelical philanthropy and secular colonialism pale into ultimate insignificance in the light of a common pursuit of European hegemony.[16] Evangelical theology prescribed the medicine of the gospel as the only remedy capable of moving a society back up the scale towards the goal of a just, humane, and godly community. Where evangelicalism betrayed its Enlightenment parentage, however, was in its predisposition to believe that, in the relative or even total absence of true spiritual regeneration, a rational education infused by Christian principles nevertheless possessed the power not simply to check the slide towards barbarism but even to lay the foundations for subsequent spiritual recovery.[17] In certain mission contexts, supremely in India, this conviction could foster a mission policy that in practice virtually inverted theoretical evangelical orthodoxy about the relationship of Christianity and civilization.

The missionary movement developed within an intellectual context whose methodological emphasis on rational inquiry and empirical observa-

---

14. See the evidence of the CMS missionary, William Yate, to the Aborigines Committee in 1836, in *Parliamentary Papers* (hereafter P.P.) 1836, VII (538), qq. 1601, 1786-92, 1854-55.

15. See above, pp. 112-13; for the frequent appearance of theories of religious degeneration in the southern African context, and see Stuart, "Of Savages and Heroes," pp. 38-39, 206-9; and David Chidester, *Savage Systems: Colonialism and Comparative Religion in Southern Africa* (Charlottesville, Va., and London, 1996), pp. 90-94.

16. Leon de Kock, *Civilising Barbarians: Missionary Narrative and African Textual Response in Nineteenth-Century South Africa* (Johannesburg, 1996), pp. 42-43.

17. See D. W. Bebbington, *Evangelicalism in Modern Britain: A History from the 1730s to the 1980s* (London, 1989), pp. 123-25.

tion was liable to nurture among missionaries and serious students of missions increasing dissatisfaction with the simple antitheses of Christian and pagan inherited from pre-Enlightenment tradition. The evangelical commitment to empirical analysis contained the seeds of forms of differentiation between peoples that later generations would develop in directions that earlier evangelicals might not have approved. William Carey's survey of world religions in his famous pamphlet of 1792, *An Enquiry into the Obligations of Christians to Use Means for the Conversion of the Heathens,* followed conventional Renaissance discourse in its classification of adherents of non-Christian religions simply as Pagans, Mahometans, or Jews, but here and there Carey's categorization became more precise. Persian Mahometans were described as being "of the sect of Ali," and the inhabitants of some of the Caribbean islands were labeled "Native Caribbs" rather than simply pagans.[18] The comprehensiveness of Carey's geographical and demographic data (generally fuller than that provided in the first two editions of the *Encyclopaedia Britannica*) demonstrated a characteristically eighteenth-century concern for encyclopedic analysis that many of his successors on the mission field were to follow.[19] Christopher Herbert goes so far as to argue that early evangelical missionaries in Polynesia, impelled by the need to supply clinching empirical evidence of the depravity of raw humanity, developed techniques of ethnographic research, that, for all their tendentiousness, anticipated modern anthropology's methodology of the participatory observer.[20] Rod Edmond has similarly described the "oscillation between science and sermon" that forms the rhythm of the text of missionary ethnographic works such as William Ellis's *Polynesian Researches.*[21] In a similar way in India the enthusiasm

---

18. William Carey, *An Enquiry into the Obligations of Christians to Use Means for the Conversion of the Heathens* (1792), facsimile ed., edited by Ernest A. Payne (London, 1961), pp. 46, 60-61; see David A. Pailin, *Attitudes to Other Religions: Comparative Religion in Seventeenth- and Eighteenth-Century Britain* (Manchester, 1984), pp. 45-46.

19. The article on "Geography" in the first edition (1771) of the *Encyclopaedia Britannica,* 2:682-84, contained a table of countries, less detailed than Carey's, and without figures for population or religion. The article in the second edition (1778-83), 5:3251-368, contained no table or systematic population estimates but included articles on individual countries whose geographical data may have been one of Carey's sources.

20. Christopher Herbert, *Culture and Anomie: Ethnographic Imagination in the Nineteenth Century* (Chicago and London, 1991), ch. 3.

21. Rod Edmond, *Representing the South Pacific: Colonial Discourse from Cook to Gauguin* (Cambridge, 1997), pp. 105-8; see also his "Translating Missionary Cultures: William Ellis and Missionary Writing," in *Science and Exploration in the Pacific: European Voyages to the Southern Oceans in the Eighteenth Century,* edited by Margarette Lincoln (Woodbridge, Suffolk, 1998).

of evangelicals such as Charles Grant, Claudius Buchanan, and William Ward to observe, classify, and label the religious phenomena of the Indian subcontinent contributed to the broader intellectual process whereby the supposedly coherent entity of "Hinduism" was constructed and systematized in the Western mind.[22] Even if such interpretations as those of Herbert and Edmond are thought to underplay the distorting effect of evangelical polemic against idolatry or superstition, the conclusion is hard to escape that it was missionary observation that laid the foundations of the modern scientific and taxonomic study of religions. While the very scientism of missionary ethnography entailed a stylized construction of other religions and cultures in terms that served to bolster European self-identity, the commitment of missionaries to empirical observation of other religions laid the foundation for the subsequent emergence of stances that stressed "justice, courtesy and love" rather than confrontation. In this respect, Enlightenment methodology deserves a more measured evaluation than it has received in Kenneth Cracknell's recent book.[23]

Evangelical missionary apologists frequently transposed gospel values into an Enlightenment key. Carey's close associate, John Sutcliff, preaching to the Northamptonshire Baptist ministers in 1791, urged that the duty of Christian benevolence to one's neighbor must extend even to the "ignorant Negro" of unexplored Africa, or the "untutored Savage, wandering in the inhospitable forests of America," since he was a fellow creature, neighbor, and brother and possessed of an immortal soul.[24] In deducing consequences for Christian action from the unity of all those who bore the imprint of the *imago dei,* Sutcliff was, however, drawing on an older pre-Enlightenment Christian tradition, which included de las Casas in the sixteenth century. Christian theology stressed the unity of humanity even more strongly than did the Greeks, whose adherence to the essential unity of the human genus was qualified by their awareness of the gradations that separated the barbar-

---

22. Geoffrey A. Oddie, "The Protestant Missionary Movement as a Factor in the Hindu Construction and Refashioning of 'Hinduism,'" in *Missionary Challenges in India since 1700,* edited by R. E. Frykenberg (Curzon Press, forthcoming). See also Frykenberg, "Constructions of Hinduism at the Nexus of History and Religion," *Journal of Interdisciplinary History* 23.3 (1993): 523-50.

23. Kenneth Cracknell, *Justice, Courtesy and Love: Theologians and Missionaries Encountering World Religions* (London, 1995), pp. 14-20.

24. *Jealousy for the Lord of Hosts: and, the Pernicious Influence of Delay in Religious Concerns: Two Discourses delivered at a Meeting of Ministers at Clipstone . . . The Former by John Sutcliff of Olney . . .* (London, 1791), p. 7; cited in Brian Stanley, *The History of the Baptist Missionary Society, 1792-1992* (Edinburgh, 1992), p. 10.

ian from the civilized man of virtue. Although the medieval Church took over the Greek concept of the *oikumene,* the civilized community from which barbarians were excluded, and gave it Christian dress as the *congregatio fidelium,* the brotherhood of all those incorporated by baptism into Christ, the Christian *oikumene* was an open community. Through baptism, barbarians could become Christians and in so doing be incorporated within the civilized community.[25] Catholic sacramentalism rendered the process of incorporation relatively straightforward by focusing attention on the sacramental act and actor rather than the spiritual and moral condition of the one to be baptized. Protestantism made the feasibility of incorporation more of an open question by the emphasis that it placed, particularly in its evangelical forms, on individual understanding of and voluntary response to the Christian message. Protestants thus faced a choice. A few, such as de Léry in 1578 or Dissenters of hyper-Calvinist leanings in eighteenth-century England, were inclined to deny the "heathen" the possibility of saving grace on the grounds of their inadequate capacity (either rational or spiritual) for conversion, given the absence of miraculous apostolic means of effecting this object.[26] More common in the eighteenth century was the Scottish rational Calvinist qualification of this position, as outlined in chapter six, which asserted that conversion was possible only as a sequel to a preliminary process of rationalization — civilization must come first. A third option was for Christians to insist that the resources for the reception of the gospel even by the barbarous were to be found within Christianity itself. It was precisely here that Enlightenment empiricism and "common-sense" philosophical method supplied evangelicalism with the ammunition it needed to counter both hyper-Calvinist and rationalist forms of skepticism about the potential of the "heathen" for salvation. Yet that same confidence in experience and common sense, as we shall see, left evangelical mission theory open to a great variety of modifications.

II

The substantial majority of mission thought in the English evangelical tradition from the late eighteenth to the mid-twentieth centuries was fully commit-

25. Anthony Pagden, *The Fall of Natural Man: The American Indian and the Origins of Comparative Ethnology* (Cambridge, 1982), pp. 17-20.

26. It is clear from Carey, *An Enquiry,* pp. 8-11, that hyper-Calvinist Dissenters believed that the heathen could not be converted without a renewed display of the apostolic supernatural gifts.

ted to the priority of Christianity over civilization. The gospel itself was believed to be the great engine of social change, the horse that pulled the cart of moral and cultural transformation. For most evangelical Christians, to attempt to civilize the "heathen" without reliance on the transforming power of the cross was to put the cart before the horse.[27] This emphasis marked a clear reversal of the orthodoxy prevailing in New England Protestant missions until the 1760s, which insisted on the priority of reducing Native American savages to a state of civility.[28] John Eliot believed that, just as the law paved the way for the gospel, so civilization must precede Christianity.[29] The transition from the presumption that gathering Native Americans into ordered civil communities must take precedence over the formation of Native American churches to the claim of David Brainerd and Jonathan Edwards that Native Americans could and should be converted on the frontier, well away from the baneful influence of civilization, has been identified by R. H. Pearce as a crucial marker signaling the mutation of Puritanism into evangelicalism.[30] Bosch by implication agrees, contrasting Eliot's theocratic approach with the relegation of religion to the private sphere characteristic of the Enlightenment.[31] Although the shift of emphasis from Eliot to Brainerd may have been prompted by disillusionment with the moral influence exerted by English traders, it cohered with the quintessential evangelical belief in not simply the universal necessity but also the unlimited potential of conversion. Carey's *Enquiry* in 1792 was in part a polemic against the view that it was a waste of time preaching the gospel to barbarous people. Most of the barbarous acts inflicted by savages on their Western visitors Carey believed to be prompted by self-defense, rather than evidence of innate ferocity.[32] Here also, when all due qualifications are made, re-

27. The best exposition of this theme remains Niel Gunson, *Messengers of Grace: Evangelical Missionaries in the South Seas, 1797-1860* (Oxford and Melbourne, 1978), pp. 267-79.

28. See James Axtell, *The Invasion Within: The Contest of Cultures in Colonial North America* (New York, 1985), ch. 7.

29. Andrew Willey, "Transforming Heroes: Seventeenth-century Puritan Missions to Native Americans," M.Phil. thesis, University of Birmingham, 1998, pp. 64-65.

30. R. H. Pearce, *Savagism and Civilization: A Study of the Indian and the American Mind* (Baltimore, 1965), pp. 29-34; see also W. R. Hutchison, *Errand to the World: American Protestant Thought and Foreign Missions* (Chicago and London, 1987), pp. 27-29. The contrast may, however, be overdrawn, for Eliot did not deny that preaching the word of God was itself a civilizing force; see Sidney H. Rooy, *The Theology of Missions in the Puritan Tradition* (Grand Rapids, 1965), pp. 236-38.

31. David J. Bosch, *Transforming Mission: Paradigm Shifts in Theology of Mission* (Maryknoll, N.Y., 1991), p. 259.

32. Carey, *An Enquiry*, pp. 68-71.

mains the nub of the difference separating the Moderates from the Popular or evangelical party in the celebrated and much misrepresented debate in the General Assembly of the Church of Scotland in 1796. The Moderates, though far from blind to the vices that Western civilization might bring in its train, argued for the priority within missionary endeavor of the inculcation of natural religion and learning. The evangelicals, while still highly respectful of civilization, insisted from New Testament evidence that the gospel must be proclaimed to the barbarian no less than to the Greek.[33]

Protestant convictions regarding the appropriate means to bring the "heathen" to conversion matured from the 1740s onwards in response to reports of Moravian work in Greenland and Jonathan Edwards's edition of the journal of David Brainerd, published in 1749. Brainerd struggled with the difficulty of how to bring the Native American Delaware tribe, who conceived of sin purely as a contravention of social norms, "to a rational conviction that they are sinners by nature." The second appendix to his journal recounts the various homiletical strategies that he employed in order to surmount the difficulty, but also concludes that, in the final analysis, it was God himself who had taken the work into his own hand by "making them *feel at heart,* that they were both sinful and miserable."[34] A palpable and sudden demonstration of God's power, rather than any slow process of cultural amelioration, offered the only hope of conversion.[35] Brainerd thus tended to evaluate the success of his evangelistic preaching by the degree of "melting" or weeping that it induced among his hearers.[36] Although the emphasis was on the divine work of convicting the senses, there was an implicit recognition that even Native American hearts possessed the capacity to be moved in this fashion. Edwards's crucial distinction, in his tract on the *Freedom of the Will,* between natural and moral inability to respond to the gospel supplied later Calvinistic

33. Gavin White, "'Highly Preposterous': Origins of Scottish Missions," *Records of the Scottish Church History Society* 19.2 (1976): 111-24; see also Friedhelm Voges, "Moderate and Evangelical Thinking in the Later Eighteenth Century: Differences and Shared Attitudes," *Records of the Scottish Church History Society* 22.2 (1985): 142-43. These accounts now need to be supplemented by David A. Currie, "The Growth of Evangelicalism in the Church of Scotland, 1793-1843," Ph.D. thesis, St. Andrews, 1990, pp. 162-71.

34. Jonathan Edwards, *The Life and Diary of the Rev David Brainerd: With Notes and Reflections,* in *The Works of President Edwards,* edited by E. Williams and E. Parsons (London, 1817-), 3:455-56. This second appendix is omitted from the 1985 Yale University Press edition of the journal.

35. Pearce, *Savagism and Civilization,* p. 34.

36. David Murray, "David Brainerd and the Gift of Christianity," *European Review of Native American Studies* 10.2 (1996): 26; see, for example, Brainerd's journal for 6-8 August 1745, in Edwards, *The Life and Diary of the Rev David Brainerd,* 3:329-32.

missionary advocates with further resources for affirming the universality and feasibility of the evangelistic commission.[37] In his *The Gospel Worthy of All Acceptation* (1785) the Baptist theologian Andrew Fuller used Edwards's distinction to rebut hyper-Calvinist objections to the free offer of the gospel to all. Since the inability of sinners to perform any spiritual good was not natural but rather the result of a culpable rebellion of the human will, it was neither absurd nor cruel to urge them to repent and believe.[38] Fuller had Fenland villagers rather than the "heathen" overseas in the forefront of his mind when he first wrote his tract in 1781, but his advocacy of the duty of Christians to offer the gospel to all laid the foundations not simply for Carey's *Enquiry* but more broadly for the theological motivation of the Baptist Missionary Society.[39] By the early nineteenth century, the accent in evangelicalism on both sides of the Atlantic was shifting decisively from the tradition-oriented confessional orthodoxies of the Reformation towards theologies that stressed the autonomy and capacity of the individual human will.[40] Increasingly, evangelicals began to assert that the preaching of the cross could in and of itself be expected to exert an effective impression on the "heathen" mind.[41] This view depended on an anthropology that attributed at least an embryonic form of rationality to the uncivilized. Evangelicals both north and south of the border discovered a credible basis for such an anthropology in Thomas Chalmers's fusion of Reformed theology and common-sense philosophy.

It seems to have been his reading of published accounts of Moravian missionary work in Greenland and Labrador that impressed upon Chalmers's inductive philosophy the lesson that no preparatory process of civilization was necessary before "savages" could respond to the gospel.[42] Chalmers regarded it as a "wonderful fact, that a savage, when spoken to on the subject of his soul, of sin, and of the Saviour, has his attention more easily compelled, and

37. Jonathan Edwards, *A Careful and Strict Enquiry into the Modern Prevailing Notions of that Freedom of the Will, Supposed to be Essential to Moral Agency . . .* , edited by Paul Ramsey (New Haven, 1957).

38. Andrew Fuller, *The Gospel Worthy of all Acceptation: or, the Duty of Sinners to Believe in Jesus Christ,* in *The Works of the Rev. Andrew Fuller* (London, 1824), 1:171.

39. See Stanley, *History of the Baptist Missionary Society,* pp. 5-6.

40. Mark A. Noll, "The Americanization of Christian Theology in the Evangelical Surge, 1790-1840," unpublished paper read at the Anglo-American Conference of Historians, 1996.

41. See Gunson, *Messengers of Grace,* pp. 267-68.

42. See [T. Chalmers,] "Journal of a Voyage from Okkak," *Eclectic Review* n.s. 3 (1815): 1-13, 156-73; cited in John Roxborogh, "Thomas Chalmers and the Mission of the Church with Special Reference to the Rise of the Missionary Movement in Scotland," Ph.D. thesis, Aberdeen, 1978, p. 304.

his resistance more effectually subdued, than when he is addressed upon any other subject whether of moral or economical instruction."[43] As a disciple of Calvin, Chalmers believed that all those who bore the *imago dei* possessed a "natural virtue" that was the raw material on which the Holy Spirit could work through the proclamation of the cross. Natural virtue implied neither moral rectitude nor acceptance before God, but it did mean that, given a proper conjunction between prayer and diligent human agency,[44] the gospel message could be expected to arouse a sense of sin in even the most savage mind. This innate moral sense or conscience, which Chalmers later habitually referred to as the "portable evidence of Christianity," was, more than any external evidences, the basis for the universality of the missionary enterprise and the foundation of Chalmers's contention that gospel preaching need not wait for the soil to be prepared by civilization. The universality of conscience guaranteed that all, whether Greek or barbarian, possessed the capacity to respond to that conjunction of word and Spirit that was the divinely appointed means for the spread of Christianity.[45]

It was precisely this confidence in empirical method, however, that ensured that important variations developed among the formulae that different sections of the evangelical community employed to encapsulate the relationship of Christianity to civilization. Scottish evangelicals, Chalmers included, were deeply influenced by the experience afforded by the Society in Scotland for Propagating Christian Knowledge (SSPCK) of a program of Christian civilization in the Scottish Highlands. The SSPCK recipe that successfully blended itinerant preaching, a network of local schools, and Bible distribution convinced evangelicals as well as Moderates that education had a crucial role to play in Christianization.[46] Chalmers spoke for many of his new evangelical friends in 1812 when he assured the Fife and Kinross Bible Society that if "schools and bibles have been found . . . to be the engines of civilization to the people of Britain, it is altogether a fair and direct exercise of induction when these schools and bibles are counted upon . . . as equally powerful engines of

43. [T. Chalmers,] "Journal of a Voyage from Okkak," p. 4.

44. Thomas Chalmers, "The Necessity of the Spirit to Give Effect to the Preaching of the Gospel," in *Sermons, Preached in the Tron Church, Glasgow* (Glasgow, 1819), pp. 50-52.

45. Thomas Chalmers, "The Manifestation of the Truth to the Conscience," in *Select Sermons* (Glasgow and London, 1859), pp. 193-221. This account is indebted to Roxborogh, "Thomas Chalmers and the Mission of the Church," pp. 305-7, 377-79; see also Bebbington, *Evangelicalism in Modern Britain*, p. 59.

46. See A. F. Walls, "Missions: Origins," in *Dictionary of Scottish Church History and Theology*, edited by N. M. de S. Cameron (Edinburgh, 1993), pp. 567-68.

civilization to the people of other countries."[47] Yet he also regarded the experience of the SSPCK as a decisive refutation of the Moderate view that proclamation must be delayed until the foundations of civilization had been laid. He reminded an Edinburgh congregation in 1814 that the Society's agents

> have been found among the haunts of savages. They have dealt with men in the very infancy of social improvement, and their zeal for proselytism has far outstript that sober preparatory management, which is so much contended for. Why, they have carried the gospel message into climes on which Europe had never impressed a single trace of her boasted civilization. They have tried the species in the first stages of its rudeness and ferocity, nor did they keep back the offer of the saviour from their souls, till art and industry had performed a sufficient part. . . . This process which has been so much insisted upon, they did not wait for.[48]

Chalmers's most celebrated pupil, Alexander Duff, was similarly skeptical about any attempt to regenerate Hinduism purely by the inculcation of the precepts of political economy or useful knowledge. All endeavors to propagate reason *without* true Bible religion would, as in eighteenth-century France, result in terror and anarchy.[49] Duff's missionary theory adhered to the SSPCK recipe inasmuch as he enjoined the closest possible relationship between the three evangelistic media of preaching to adults, instructing the young, and translating and circulating the Scriptures. Yet Duff sought to convince his evangelical supporters that higher education should occupy pride of place by pointing out that all three media would be effective only if trained Indian agents were available to implement them.[50] At a deeper level, as Ian Maxwell has shown in chapter six, Duff was very much influenced by the "rational Calvinism" of George Hill, with its insistence, as against Chalmers's theory of the "portable evidences," that the reception of the gospel was empirically dependent on the prior acceptance of common standards of rationality. On arrival in Bengal, Duff was confirmed in his divergence from Chalmers's principles by his observation that the economics of the employ-

---

47. *Edinburgh Christian Instructor* 6 (1813): 66; cited in Roxborogh, "Thomas Chalmers and the Mission of the Church," p. 298.

48. Thomas Chalmers, *The Utility of Missions Ascertained by Experience: A Sermon Preached before the Society in Scotland . . . for Propagating Christian Knowledge . . .* (Edinburgh, 1815), pp. 11-13.

49. Alexander Duff, *India, and Indian Missions* (Edinburgh, 1839), pp. 261-69.

50. Duff, *India, and Indian Missions*, pp. 284-89.

ment market in Bengal gave any mission that majored on advanced English education a passport to success. He was subsequently able to use the commercial models of Scottish political economy to convince objectors to his "Anglicist" policy that his approach would soon overstock the limited market for native servants who needed a bare modicum of English, and as a result drive those anxious for preferment to secure an ever higher level of English-medium education.[51] The commercial logic of the market combined with the evidential logic of Hill's rational Calvinism to overbalance Duff's theoretical triple alliance on preaching, education, and Bible translation in favor of a predominant emphasis on educating the Bengali élite. The success of Duff's methods ensured that it was his highly literary variant of the classic SSPCK missionary recipe, rather than Chalmers's more populist conjunction of preaching with elementary Christian education, that increasingly set the pattern for English as well as Scottish missions in India, and, as chapter seven has shown, for Scottish missionary activity elsewhere.

Most English evangelicals, not having had the Scottish experience of a major civilizing mission on their own doorstep, saw education as a less immediate priority. More consistently than Duff, they tended to derive its importance from the need to raise up an indigenous ministry rather than seeing education as an evangelistic medium in its own right. English evangelicals, drawn as many of them were from the ranks of the artisan classes, tended to define the civilizing function of mission less as the inculcation of a polite education than as the practical instruction in the "useful arts." There were, of course, important exceptions, not least because many English Nonconformists owed their theological education either to Scottish universities or to Dissenting academies profoundly influenced by Scottish models. The traces of Scottish theory are most noticeable in the early years of the LMS, whose first secretary (until 1800), James Love, was a Presbyterian from Paisley formerly identified with the Moderate party. Love sought to model the LMS Tahiti mission on the Moderate principle of inculcating natural religion first.[52] Although Love himself met with scant success, experience in Tahiti was soon to provide the first major test of evangelical confidence in the regenerative power of the preaching of the cross. For the modern historian, the Tahiti case supplies a telling example of the degree to

---

51. Duff, *India, and Indian Missions,* p. 521; see M. A. Laird, *Missionaries and Education in Bengal, 1793-1837* (Oxford, 1972), p. 208.

52. John Morison, *The Fathers and Founders of the London Missionary Society: A Jubilee Memorial,* new ed. (London, n.d. [1845?]), pp. 261-62. Love became Secretary of the Glasgow Missionary Society and as such gave his name to the society's station at Lovedale (see ch. 7 above).

which evangelical mission theory was pliable in response to the apparent "facts" thrown up by field experience.

III

The Tahiti mission owed its origins to Thomas Haweis, and hence ultimately to Captain James Cook's narratives of his South Sea voyages, the reading of which had such a pronounced impact on Haweis, as on Carey.[53] Haweis repeatedly assured the founding supporters of "The Missionary Society" (later the London Missionary Society) in 1795 that the South Sea islands offered the best prospects of missionary success, precisely because their inhabitants were "uncivilized." Although Haweis, as a good evangelical, believed that nothing could "ultimately stand before the standard of the cross," he saw civilization more as an obstacle than as a friend to the gospel: "where civilization hath long obtained, — where false religions are deeply rooted — formed into casts — and plead immemorial antiquity — these present a wall of brass around the people."[54] The inhabitants of Tahiti, however, being in an "uncivilized" state, would, in Haweis' judgment, be struck by European superiority in knowledge, and, even more, the mechanic arts.[55] Hence his recommendation that the first missionary party should comprise those who could teach "the common arts of labour." What was required was not learned missionaries who would seek through education to eliminate the differential in civilization between Tahiti and Europe, but rather "plain" men, "full of faith and of the Holy Ghost," who could employ their mechanical skills to turn that differential to gospel advantage: "I am persuaded all the learning of the schools would not be of half the efficacy of a good artisan, with a heart touched with real grace, and well informed of divine truths, disposed to communicate them with zeal and patient perseverance."[56] Success beckoned in the Pacific, for there people beyond the reach of civilized learning would be attracted to Christ by the simple words and deeds of "godly mechanics."[57]

These expectations were cruelly disappointed. The first LMS party to Tahiti met with a reaction that varied from violence to indifference. Since

53. A. S. Wood, *Thomas Haweis, 1734-1820* (London, 1957), pp. 170, 195.
54. *Sermons Preached in London, at the formation of the Missionary Society, September 22, 23, 24, 1795* (London, 1795), p. 165.
55. *Sermons Preached in London*, p. 170.
56. *Sermons Preached in London*, p. 15; T[homas] H[aweis], "The Very Probable Success of a Proper Mission to the South Sea Islands," *Evangelical Magazine* 3 (1795): 266-67.
57. Gunson, *Messengers of Grace*, pp. 34-37.

Cook's last visit to the island in 1777, about twenty European vessels had called at Tahiti and introduced a flourishing traffic in European musketry that had wrought havoc with the existing balance of power and (one might have thought) destroyed any claim of Tahiti to be a virginal (if postlapsarian) Eden unsullied by "civilization."[58] In March 1798 eleven out of the eighteen missionaries who had sailed on the *Duff* for Tahiti abandoned the island for the safe haven of Port Jackson in New South Wales. The unenviable task of retrieving this missionary flotsam and jetsam washed up in New South Wales and of advising the LMS on how to salvage some achievement from the disaster fell to Samuel Marsden of Parramatta, who had arrived four years earlier as the assistant chaplain to the colony.[59] It was this challenge that transformed Marsden, an Anglican of impeccable evangelical pedigree, into the most celebrated missionary advocate of what at first sight appears to be the Scottish Moderate view that missionary activity was doomed to failure unless civilization had first paved the way for the gospel.[60]

On 30 January 1801 Marsden addressed a lengthy memorandum to the LMS directors that, in the light of the manifest moral failure of some of the *Duff* party, urged the importance of sending to the South Seas men who were properly qualified, properly subordinate to appointed leaders, and properly married.[61] It also argued at length that, since the Tahitians were "in the strictest sense in a state of Nature," it was the duty of missionaries "to use every means for their Civilization and not to imagine they are already prepared to receive the Blessings of Divine Revelation." Models drawn from New Testament evangelism could not be woodenly applied to the Pacific, for Paul had preached the gospel to the sophisticated societies of the Greco-Roman world, whose people had been prepared for the reception of the gospel by "the highest degree of Civilization." Future recruits for the mission must be "guarded against all erroneous notions" and not taken in by the "flowery language" of navigators. This could be read as an implied rebuke for Haweis's romanticism,

58. C. W. Newbury, ed., *The History of the Tahitian Mission, 1799-1830: Written by John Davies Missionary to the South Sea Islands* (Cambridge, 1961), p. xli. Even in 1795, however, Haweis had acknowledged that the "untutored offspring of fallen nature" found in the Pacific had been "contaminated by our vices" (*Sermons Preached in London,* pp. 12-13).

59. J. R. Elder, ed., *The Letters and Journals of Samuel Marsden, 1765-1838* (Dunedin, 1932), pp. 40-41.

60. The best biography of Marsden is A. T. Yarwood, *Samuel Marsden: The Great Survivor* (Carlton, Victoria, 1977).

61. London, School of Oriental and African Studies, Council for World Mission archives, LMS Australia Incoming Letters, Box 1, S. Marsden to LMS Directors, 30 January 1801.

and, at first glance, Marsden appears to have inverted Haweis's belief in the priority of evangelization over civilization. Indeed, Marsden's nineteenth-century biographer made much of the contrast between Haweis's expectations of immediate conversion and Marsden's insistence on the precedence of civilizing effort.[62] There is, however, ample evidence to refute the supposition that Marsden and Haweis were fundamentally at odds over mission policy. Marsden retained Haweis's confidence throughout, and very probably drew from Haweis the idea of a missionary ship, which would not only supply the islands with necessities but also transport Polynesians to the New South Wales colony for intensive training in the useful arts.[63] The vessel was to be the crucial means of linking Tahitians "with the more enlightened Parts of Society," and hence of opening and enlarging their minds for the entrance of the gospel.[64] When in 1818 Marsden gained his ship, it was named *The Haweis*.

Marsden's emphasis that civilization must pave the way for the gospel implied neither that missions should leave the initial task of civilizing to secular agencies, nor even that missionaries should initially refrain from preaching and devote themselves wholly to manual work. This he made very clear in 1808 in his advice to the CMS committee on the mission that he projected to New Zealand:

> Though the Missionaries might employ a certain portion of their time, according to local circumstances, in manual labour, this neither would nor ought to prevent them from constantly endeavouring to instruct the natives in the great doctrines of the Gospel, and fully discharging the duties of Catechists. The arts and religion should go together. . . . I do not mean that a native should learn to build a hut or make an axe before he should be told any thing of Man's Fall and Redemption; but that these grand subjects should be introduced at every favourable opportunity, while the natives are learning any of the simple arts. To preach the Gospel without the aid of the Arts will never succeed amongst the heathen for any time.[65]

---

62. J. B. Marsden, ed., *Memoirs of the Life and Labours of the Rev. Samuel Marsden, of Paramatta . . .* (London, n.d. [1858]), pp. 36-44, 56, 82-83. J. B. Marsden was no relation of Samuel.

63. Wood, *Thomas Haweis*, pp. 234-35, 245, 247, 255, 259.

64. London, School of Oriental and African Studies, Council for World Mission archives, LMS Australia Incoming Letters, Box 1, S. Marsden to J. Hardcastle, 20 July 1805; cited in Yarwood, *Samuel Marsden*, p. 106.

65. S. Marsden to J. Pratt in *Proceedings of the Church Missionary Society* 2 (1806-9): 362.

The principal thrust of Marsden's remarks on civilization in the 1801 memorandum was, similarly, to attack "the absurdity of the idea of the Missionaries employing their time *only* [my italics] in conversing and instructing the Natives in the principles of Religion. It is not to be expected that the Natives will be so anxious for instruction as willingly to support the Missionaries in idleness." Repeatedly Marsden urged the necessity of missionaries being active and industrious: "An idle Lounging Missionary will be a dangerous character. A missionary should on no account be suffered to spend an idle Vagrant Life."[66] For Marsden, as befits one whose time was principally divided between reforming convicts and rearing sheep, the process of "civilization" began, not with mind or manners, but with instilling the discipline of manual labor and developing means of subsistence capable of sustaining an ordered "civil" life. The "heathen," even the Maoris, whom Marsden admired for their natural intelligence, suffered from "wandering minds." The CMS annual report in 1808 commented, in language drawn directly from Marsden, that missionaries would be unable to "fix" any idea of religion in the "vagrant minds" of the New Zealanders without the visual aid of a regular settlement in which European superiority in industrious habits could be exemplified.[67] Marsden's institutions at Parramata were intended to provide such a visual aid to Australian aboriginals, visiting Polynesians, and Maoris. Various levels of explanation are possible for such statements, and a full understanding of Marsden's concept of civilization requires a subtle integration of these different levels of analysis. Clearly Marsden regarded idleness as partly to blame for the liaisons that two of the Tahiti missionaries had formed with native women.[68] Also apparent is the horror of one who had risen from relatively humble social origins (as a youth he had worked in his uncle's smithy)[69] at the prospect of those who ought to be always diligent in the work of the Lord descending into the ranks of the undeserving poor. Missionaries who had no fixed abode would be prey to moral temptation as well as physical danger. A permanent settlement where crops could be grown and useful arts practiced was essential. Civilizing activity was as much for the material and moral benefit of the missionary as for the good of the "heathen." Nevertheless, the "heathen" would profit from observing such activity: their curiosity would be ex-

66. London, School of Oriental and African Studies, Council for World Mission archives, LMS Australia Incoming Letters, Box 1, S. Marsden to LMS Directors, 30 January 1801.

67. *Proceedings of the Church Missionary Society* 2 (1806-9): 337, cited in J. R. Elder, ed., *Marsden's Lieutenants* (Dunedin, 1934), p. 19.

68. Newbury, *The History of the Tahitian Mission*, pp. xl-xli.

69. Yarwood, *Samuel Marsden*, p. 4.

cited and their confidence gained, and they would be thus more inclined to listen to the missionary's teaching.

At a deeper level, Marsden's emphasis could be interpreted as broadly consistent with the sequential understanding of social progress developed by the Scottish Enlightenment. The Scottish political economists' formulation of history implied that the preconditions for the emergence of the commercial economy on which civilized society was believed to depend were the substitution of settled communities for a nomadic existence, and an agrarian economy for more primitive modes of subsistence.[70] However, Marsden expected the combination of Christianity and the useful arts to effect their transformation far more rapidly than conventional Scottish theory about the stages of civilization postulated. What drove Marsden to despair and racial cynicism was that, in the case of the aboriginals, the visual aid of a civilized settlement failed to achieve the desired effect: they "had no wants, they lived free and independent," and it proved impossible "to attach them, either to places or to individuals in the Colony who wished to benefit them."[71] Experience in Australia was impelling this evangelical towards the distinctly unevangelical conclusion that those who obdurately preferred vagrancy to civilization must be reckoned as beyond the reach of the power of the cross.[72] Marsden's antipathy to vagrancy conforms to a European pattern of hostility to nomadism as the very antithesis of "civil" life that long predates the Enlightenment. In the language of Christian theology, nomadism was identified as one of the distinguishing marks of the degeneration of humankind from the settled and cultivating mode of existence that characterized the Garden of Eden.[73] In classical terminology, "pagans" were originally and literally those who dwelt in the "country districts": only through the settled community of the city could barbarism be kept at bay.[74] Missionaries can thus be interpreted as heirs to a centuries-old Western tradition, stretching back through Columbus ultimately to Homer, of the intrepid voyager into the unknown. Pagden has shown how, precisely because of their own rootlessness, such travelers have needed to develop mechanisms of "attachment" to give sense and stability to their unfamiliar new world.[75] The immobility of the "mission station," against which the Anglican mission theorist

---

70. See Philip Flynn, *Enlightened Scotland* (Edinburgh, 1992), p. 267.

71. Cited in Yarwood, *Samuel Marsden*, p. 160.

72. Yarwood, *Samuel Marsden*, pp. 102, 216, 277; contrast the view of Daniel Tyerman and George Bennet, cited in Yarwood, *Samuel Marsden*, pp. 237-38.

73. Stuart, "Of Savages and Heroes," p. 215.

74. Pagden, *European Encounters with the New World*, pp. 2, 157.

75. Pagden, *European Encounters with the New World*, pp. 2-3, 17-49.

Roland Allen was later to direct his withering critique, was just such a means of attachment.[76]

Both Marsden and Haweis looked to the industry of godly artisans as an indispensable ally of the preaching of the gospel to uncivilized people. Haweis seems to have understood "civilization" as the inculcation of "polite" rational learning through education; he believed that to attempt such a strategy without first seeking spiritual and moral regeneration was folly. In the light of what had befallen the Tahiti mission, Marsden was more inclined to stress the importance of a missionary being a person of some education rather than "a gloomy ignorant clown,"[77] but he was no nearer than Haweis to advocating a policy of civilization in isolation from proclamation. Marsden, therefore, should be interpreted not so much as an adherent of the eighteenth-century Moderate tradition of "education first" as a slightly eccentric representative of that widespread spirit of evangelical industriousness and economic improvement that Jean and John Comaroff have rather too closely identified with the nonconformist strand of the missionary movement. The sources of Marsden's prescription for mission policy lie not so much in Scottish Enlightenment theory as in the tendency of evangelical Christianity, whether Anglican or Nonconformist, to define vital religion in terms of productive "usefulness," as interpreted by the work ethic of the artisan and yeoman classes from which Marsden and most evangelical missionaries came.[78]

The policy that Marsden enjoined with considerable success on both the LMS and the CMS enjoined the closest possible linkage, rather than any absolute temporal divorce, between civilization and evangelization. However, the men on the spot remained skeptical about the value of the plow or the adze as a converting ordinance. From 1801 onwards, Marsden's informal influence within the LMS grew in step with the succession of further bad news from Tahiti and culminated in his appointment as a foreign director in 1812. In April of that year the directors sent a letter to Tahiti chiding the missionaries for the "small degree of Improvement made amongst the natives in respect of Industry and Civilization." John Davies's history of the mission reveals something of the resentment this criticism aroused, and comments that the missionaries were

---

76. Roland Allen, *The Spontaneous Expansion of the Church and the Causes which Hinder It* (London, 1927), pp. 142-45.

77. Marsden to LMS Directors, 30 January 1801, cited in Gunson, *Messengers of Grace*, p. 65.

78. Jean and John Comaroff, *Of Revelation and Revolution,* vol. 1: *Christianity, Colonialism, and Consciousness in South Africa* (Chicago and London, 1991), 1:59; Jean and John Comaroff, *Ethnography and the Historical Imagination* (Boulder and Oxford, 1992), pp. 238-40, 246-50.

"not at all disappointed as to their small degree of improvement in those things for they could not see how it could take place without the overthrow of their religious system."[79] After 1812, however, Tahitian resistance to Christianity did in fact crumble, not because of any drawing power exercised by the display of mechanical and agricultural skills, but rather in response to the lure of literacy. Tahitians had perceived that the key that unlocked the power of the encroaching new world was the written word, and their enthusiasm to become people of the book now gave the missionaries the entrance they had been seeking.[80] The LMS directors were naturally jubilant but continued to repeat Marsden's favorite mottoes about the importance of introducing "a knowledge of the more useful arts," "a system of productive labour," and "regular industry." No longer, however, were these activities seen as a *praeparatio evangelica*. Rather, they were "absolutely indispensable to the preservation" of the religious and moral habits of the infant Christian community, a bulwark against regression to idleness and idolatry.[81] On Marsden's advice, the society sent out in 1817 an agriculturist from the West Indian slave plantations, John Gyles, to teach the islanders how to cultivate sugar cane, coffee, and cotton. Two others, Elkanah Armitage and Thomas Blossom, followed in 1821, charged with instruction in cotton spinning and weaving.[82] These endeavors met with mixed success and indifferent enthusiasm from the older LMS missionaries, who regarded the directors' new expectation that civilization would follow speedily in the wake of conversion as scarcely more realistic than their previous conviction that the mechanical arts would pave the way for conversion. John Davies anticipated that, "notwithstanding the mighty assistance derived from the Laws and institutions of Christianity," it would take as many centuries for the islanders to reach the present standard of European civilization as it had taken Europeans to climb out of barbarism.[83] W. P. Crook agreed, commenting that "Capt Cook could never have read Robertsons Histy of America or he would have seen that savage life is not quickly to be changed into civilized life."[84] Field experience was thus forcing

79. Newbury, *The History of the Tahitian Mission*, pp. 150-51.

80. G. S. Parsonson, "The Literate Revolution in Polynesia," *Journal of Pacific History* 2 (1967): 39-57.

81. London Missionary Society, *Report of the Directors to the Twenty-Fifth General Meeting of the Missionary Society, Usually Called the London Missionary Society, on Thursday, May 13, 1819* (London, 1819), pp. 11-12.

82. Gunson, *Messengers of Grace*, pp. 40, 203, 271.

83. Newbury, *History of the Tahitian Mission*, pp. 329-31; see Edmond, *Representing the South Pacific*, p. 121.

84. Newbury, *History of the Tahitian Mission*, p. 346. See William Robertson, *The History of America*, 2 vols. (London, 1777); and S. J. Brown, ed., *William Robertson and the Expansion of Empire* (Cambridge, 1997).

some evangelical missionaries to endorse the view of the greatest of the Scottish Moderate historians about the inevitably long-term character of the civilizing process, a view that stood in sharp contrast both with Marsden's confidence in the converting efficacy of agricultural improvement and with domestic evangelical orthodoxy on the transforming power of gospel preaching. Evangelical theory had telescoped into a few short years of miraculous transformation a process of natural (but not irreversible) social development that the Scottish "conjectural history" of writers such as Robertson traced over centuries.[85] Now that this optimistic time-scale had been placed in question, the dominant intellectual framework for conceptualizing the typical evolution of barbarism into civilization began to look more persuasive to some missionaries than domestic evangelical enthusiasm had initially suggested.

IV

As criticism of Marsden's theories strengthened, the CMS and the LMS became more sensitive to charges that their Pacific missions were conducted on the principle of the priority of civilization over evangelization. Such a view of the New Zealand mission, affirmed the CMS committee in 1815 with considerable justification, was "wholly a mistake."[86] First-hand exposure in New Zealand to civilized vices reinforced Marsden himself in his typically evangelical conviction that the gospel was "the only remedy for the evils that sin hath introduced amongst men into the world."[87] The Australian aboriginal experience appeared to many to indicate the failure of Marsden's theories. The civilizing achievement in Tahiti, however, could plausibly be explained in terms of the capacity of the gospel finally to cast down the strongholds of idolatry and bring what Thomas Chalmers termed "a wondrous transformation" in its wake, for a conversion movement driven by the hunger for literacy was bound to be a powerful engine of cultural change.[88] More broadly, missionary experience in the Cape Colony and the West Indies seemed to reinforce the message coming from the Pacific that "civilization first" was a foolish policy.[89]

85. See H. M. Höpfl, "From Savage to Scotsman: Conjectural History in the Scottish Enlightenment," *Journal of British Studies* 17 (1978): 19-40.

86. J. B. Marsden, *Memoirs . . . of Samuel Marsden,* p. 57.

87. Elder, *The Letters and Journals of Samuel Marsden,* p. 324.

88. Thomas Chalmers, "The Manifestation of the Truth to the Conscience," in *Select Sermons,* pp. 218-21.

89. Andrew Porter, "'Commerce and Christianity': The Rise and Fall of a Missionary Slogan," *Historical Journal* 28 (1985): 609-10.

The Scottish mission theorist, Ralph Wardlaw, assured a London congregation in 1823 that "experience has refuted the opinion, that civilization is necessary, as a preparatory step, to the introduction and success of the gospel."[90] As the power of settlers and traders grew, it tended to be forgotten that the advocates of a civilizing missionary policy had always insisted that it must be the godly who were doing the civilizing. "Civilization first" was now regarded as a secular and antimissionary slogan, to be dismissed as having been decisively refuted by the inductive power of field experience. John Morison's *The Fathers and Founders of the London Missionary Society*, first published in 1839, when discussing John Love's Moderate theory that natural religion must precede the proclamation of the gospel, commented that "the very reverse of this notion has been inculcated by the stern lessons of experience."[91] Even two decades later, in 1858, Samuel Marsden's biographer, J. B. Marsden, displayed considerable embarrassment when discussing this aspect of his thought.[92]

When the secretaries of the London, Church, and Wesleyan Methodist Missionary Societies were called to testify before T. F. Buxton's Parliamentary Select Committee on Aborigines in 1836-37, they were unanimous in rejecting the view that civilization should precede the preaching of the gospel. All the missionary witnesses to the committee agreed that Christianity must come first, and that civilization would follow.[93] John Philip went so far as to claim that the facts of the Frontier Wars in the Cape Colony indicated that the "Caffres" possessed a higher level of moral virtue than was evident in the "barbarous and unjust policy" of the supposedly civilized whites.[94] Philip, though indebted, as Andrew Ross has emphasized, to Adam Smith for his confidence in the civilizing function of commerce, here departed radically from the insistence of the Scottish Enlightenment on the indissoluble connection between sound learning and virtue.[95] While Philip's contention, like Carey's before him in 1792, that any aggressive behavior by non-Western peoples was provoked rather than innate contains echoes of the noble savage, to

---

90. Ralph Wardlaw, *The Early Success of the Gospel and Evidence of its Truth, and an Encouragement to Zeal for its Universal Diffusion* . . . (London, 1823), p. 38.

91. Morison, *The Fathers and Founders of the London Missionary Society*, p. 262.

92. J. B. Marsden, *Memoirs* . . . *of Samuel Marsden*, pp. 41-43, 56-59, 82-83.

93. See D. Coates, J. Beecham, and W. Ellis, *Christianity the Means of Civilisation: Shown in the Evidence Given before a Committee of the House of Commons, on Aborigines* (London, 1837). For the full minutes and report of the committee see P. P. 1836, VII (538) and P. P. 1837, VII (425).

94. P. P. 1836, VII (538), q. 4473, pp. 556-57.

95. Andrew Ross, *John Philip (1775-1851): Missions, Race and Politics in South Africa* (Aberdeen, 1986), pp. 66-67, 96; David Allan, *Virtue, Learning and the Scottish Enlightenment: Ideas of Scholarship in Early Modern History* (Edinburgh, 1993), pp. 205, 232.

attach the label "barbarous" to the ostensibly civilized was a bold inversion of centuries of Western thought. Yet, when pressed by committee members, the missionary witnesses tended to agree that the wisest mission policy was in fact to conjoin the preaching of the gospel with civilization. John Williams, for example, having affirmed without hesitation that "you cannot get a barbarous people to attend to anything of a civilizing process, or to aspire to any European habit, till you give them Christian principle," was then asked by Edward Baines whether the most effectual process was not in fact for Christianity and the useful arts of civilization to assist each other. "Undoubtedly," replied Williams, "that is what I would advise. The idea I would convey is this: I would not advise an attempt to civilize a people leaving Christianity out of the question. I think the attempt would fail; but I would advise that Christianity should be accompanied with a civilizing process. It is what we have united in all our attempts."[96] Similarly, William Yate of the CMS New Zealand mission, while insisting that civilization should never precede Christianity, described the process of civilization in New Zealand as proceeding "hand in hand with Christianity" from the "very moment" when the gospel had first gained a foothold.[97]

Thus by the mid-1830s English mission theorists, while doctrinally committed almost without exception to the rhetorical priority of Christianity over civilization, were prepared to admit that experience suggested the wisdom of a practical partnership between the two that was much closer to Marsden's ideas than their apparent inversion of his formula suggests. John and Jean Comaroff come close to an accurate perception of this paradox in their argument that nineteenth-century missions among the Tswana turned to the everyday practicalities of the civilizing quest in response to the frustration of their hopes of an immediate conversionist breakthrough.[98] This reorientation, however, was not just a pragmatic step, but one example of the ways in which nineteenth-century evangelicals committed to inductive principles of truth sought to harmonize the divergent indications of conversionist enthusiasm, Scottish historical theory, and the indifferent pattern of mission success.

It is against this background that the famous conjunction of civilization, commerce, and Christianity articulated by T. F. Buxton and subsequently by David Livingstone should be interpreted. As early as April 1834, Buxton was

---

96. Coates, Beecham, and Ellis, *Christianity the Means of Civilisation,* pp. 294-96.
97. P. P. 1836, VII (538), q. 1783, p. 200.
98. John L. and Jean Comaroff, *Of Revelation and Revolution,* vol 2: *The Dialectics of Modernity on a South African Frontier* (Chicago and London, 1997), pp. 8, 67-68, 118.

persuaded that the only force capable of civilizing the West Indian slave population, soon to be emancipated, and imparting industry and commerce would be "a flood" of Christian instruction.[99] John Philip's visits to the Buxton family home at Northrepps Hall from December 1826 had impressed on Buxton gratifying "facts" about the fruits of missionary labor on the Kat River. By 1834 his missionary addresses were using examples from South and West Africa and New Zealand to prove that industry, commerce, honesty, peace, education, sobriety, and freedom, as well as Christian conversion itself, were the products of missionary endeavor.[100] In harmony with the evangelical consensus formed in the 1820s in the wake of the Tahiti experience, Buxton argued that the first step towards the conversion of any people must be the translation of the Bible into their own language.[101] Yet Buxton was able also to draw from Philip an emphasis on the development of free commercial exchange between European and non-European peoples as the most effective counter to slavery and other forms of exploitation. Christianity was the ultimate source of civilized and industrious values, yet the successful planting of a church in a context where indigenous labor resources were subject to monopolistic control required a partnership between preaching the gospel and the encouragement of indigenous agricultural production for the market. Buxton's Niger Expedition of 1841-42 applied these ideas to West Africa.[102] By 1851 Livingstone was looking to the same medicine to remedy the ills of southern Central Africa. Like Buxton and his predecessors, Livingstone believed that "if the love of Christ enters the heart, civilization follows in due course." It was "Christianity alone" that reached "the very centre of the wants of Africa and of the world." Commerce without Christianity would not produce civilization worth the name, as was testified by Arab slave traders, or (as Livingstone told his Senate House audience in Cambridge in the Mutiny year of 1857) the British record in India.[103] Yet Livingstone, like Buxton, urged that Christian missionary work must proceed in association with legitimate commerce if God's purposes for Africa's liberation were to be achieved. Just as Marsden's apparent advocacy of "civilization first" reduces on closer inspection to a prescription for a partnership

---

99. Oxford, Rhodes House, T. F. Buxton Papers, vol. 10, pp. 51-52.

100. Oxford, Rhodes House, T. F. Buxton Papers, vol. 10, pp. 64-66, 84-86; cf. Ross, *John Philip,* p. 105.

101. Oxford, Rhodes House, T. F. Buxton Papers, vol. 10, p. 69.

102. Porter, "Commerce and Christianity," pp. 610-14.

103. I. Schapera, ed., *Livingstone's Missionary Correspondence, 1841-1856* (London, 1961), pp. 187, 301-2; W. Monk, ed., *Dr Livingstone's Cambridge Lectures,* 2nd ed. (Cambridge, 1860), p. 165.

between preaching and the industrious arts, so the reiteration by Buxton and Livingstone of the older motto of "Christianity first" did not in fact imply any chronological separation between evangelization and the introduction of commerce.

V

How, in conclusion, does this complex story relate to our overall theme of Christian missions and the Enlightenment? On one level, the Enlightenment character of the utterances of Buxton or Livingstone on the benefits of Christianity and commerce is so obvious as scarcely to warrant comment. Buxton, in his notes for a speech in April 1834 celebrating the achievement of emancipation, observed that, however praiseworthy the contribution made by Lord Stanley and other politicians, "It is a higher power who smiles on intention & sends his blessing on the endeavour to diffuse liberty & with liberty happiness civilization & Christianity."[104] Clendennen has aptly remarked that "One can easily detect the 'hidden hand' of Adam Smith and the Scottish Enlightenment in Buxton's, and hence Livingstone's, economic philosophy."[105] Furthermore, Livingstone's acknowledged debt to Thomas Dick's Enlightenment philosophy of inductive science is well known. Behind Livingstone's celebrated dictum in his *Missionary Travels and Researches in South Africa* that "I view the end of the geographical feat as the beginning of the missionary enterprise" lay Dick's touching belief that a minute and comprehensive knowledge of the facts of geographical science would preserve directors of missionary societies from groping in the dark and spending their money in vain.[106] Nevertheless, simply to invoke the Enlightenment as a device to explain the philosophy of missions typical of the era of Buxton or Livingstone is to wield an instrument too blunt for the task. Mid-nineteenth-century evangelical mission *theory* stressed the intrinsic capacity of Christianity to effect the transformation of barbarism even without (and indeed, *preferably* without) any preparatory civilizing work of disseminating rational knowledge. To that extent it contradicted the central tenet of the Scottish Enlightenment that vir-

---

104. Oxford, Rhodes House, T. F. Buxton Papers, vol. 10, p. 57.

105. G. W. Clendennen, ed., *David Livingstone's Shire Journal, 1861-1864* (Aberdeen, 1992), p. xix.

106. David Livingstone, *Missionary Travels and Researches in South Africa* (London, 1857), p. 673; Thomas Dick, *The Christian Philosopher; or, the Connection of Science and Philosophy with Religion,* 3rd ed. (Glasgow, 1825), pp. 238-39. On Livingstone's scientism see de Kock, *Civilising Barbarians,* pp. 166-69.

tue came though learning, rather than vice versa. The juxtaposition between heathen idolatry as the source of barbarism and Christianity as the source of civilization is emphatically a premodern theme. Yet evangelicals argued for this position on the basis of a typically modern inductive appeal to the "facts" of missionary experience. Moreover, this principled insistence on the priority of evangelization, repeated in countless missionary meetings throughout the nineteenth century, was for missionaries themselves and serious thinkers such as Buxton qualified by a pragmatic recognition that Christianity could not be left to effect economic or social regeneration in its own time — a managed partnership between spiritual, economic, and social change offered the only hope of lasting transformation. Again, this qualification, though consonant with emphases characteristic of the Scottish Enlightenment, arguably owed more to reports of mission experience than to philosophical reflection. In India the lessons of experience, as urged by Alexander Duff in particular, seemed for a time to point less ambiguously towards a mission policy whose degree of emphasis on the dissemination of useful knowledge was in conformity with Enlightenment presuppositions; for here bazaar preaching seemed singularly sterile whereas education on Scottish principles had by the 1830s become a prized commodity.[107] However, even in India, the accumulated weight of disappointed missionary hopes of a high-caste breakthrough began to bear down on the fragile structure of a mission policy constructed on Scottish Moderate foundations. By the final quarter of the nineteenth century, even Scottish missions in India had followed the path blazed by English evangelicals in the South Seas earlier in the century. "Civilization first" had patently not worked, and the partnership between Christianity and commerce was looking increasingly suspect also. The dawning signs of an evangelistic harvest among the rural poor of south India renewed hopes that the simple evangelical recipe might after all be substantially correct: preach the gospel, build the indigenous church, and generate a hunger for literacy and economic improvement from the bottom up rather than by downwards diffusion from an educational or commercial élite.[108]

Possibly the most common thread running through the diverse expressions of English evangelical mission thought in the late eighteenth and nineteenth centuries was thus a commitment to abide by the supposedly objective facts established by field experience. Yet this commitment was less straight-

107. See chapter six above, pp. 135, 137-39.
108. See Andrew Porter, "Scottish Missions and Education in Nineteenth-century India: The Changing Face of 'Trusteeship,'" *Journal of Imperial and Commonwealth History* 16 (1988): 35-57.

forward than it professed to be. Domestic writing on missions claimed by the 1830s that field experience was unanimous in its rejection of the motto of "civilization first." In fact, this was not yet the case in India, and even in southern Africa or the Pacific the repudiation of this creed did not necessarily imply acceptance of the converse theory that the road from conversion to civilization was a short and straight one. This chapter has suggested that further investigation of the impact of the Enlightenment on mission thought and policy will yield relatively little illumination if it simply engages in a pursuit of the ostensibly Enlightenment origins of the dominating ideas of the missionary movement. Scholarly inquiry ought instead to focus on the diverse and complex ways in which the epistemological method characteristic of the Scottish Enlightenment intersected both with long-established Christian traditions of thinking about barbarism and civilization and with the "facts" thrown up by the new experience of evangelization along and across the extending imperial frontier of the nineteenth century.

The pragmatism that was nurtured by evangelical empiricism might be thought to signify a commendable readiness to modify "dogma" in the light of practical realities. It has been argued that such modification did eventually take place on a very significant scale, especially in relation to Christian attitudes to other religions. To this extent, it is appropriate to warn against too absolute an interpretative divorce between "ideas" and "method." Commitment to inductive method could and did encourage a pluralism of approach, even ultimately of theology. However, as is well known, common-sense empiricism too often masked the inability of Enlightenment Europeans to grasp the relativity of their own perceptions of other cultures and religions. On this count, Bosch is surely correct when he identifies a false separation between facts and values as one of the distinguishing features of mission thought in the Enlightenment era.[109] This consistent yet visually impaired inductivism explains not simply why it is of limited value to attempt to delineate any recognizable body of "Enlightenment ideas" within the missionary movement but also, as Andrew Walls has reminded us, why Western missions have found it so difficult to come to terms with non-Western assumptions about the open and permeable nature of the frontier between the world of material phenomena and the unseen world of the transcendent.[110] Missionaries found it fatally difficult to see dimensions of non-Western consciousness that could

109. Bosch, *Transforming Mission*, pp. 266, 272.
110. Andrew F. Walls, "Introduction: African Christianity in the History of Religions," in *Christianity in Africa in the 1990s*, edited by C. Fyfe and A. F. Walls (Edinburgh, 1996), pp. 8, 12.

not be reduced to the hard tactile level of facticity. Even when Protestant missionaries began to see such dimensions, they could interpret them only through religious lenses colored not simply by the Enlightenment but also by the Reformation, with its tendency to categorize the mysterious as superstition and miracle as magic. Further back still, they continued to be affected by the legacy of the medieval tradition of rationality, with its conception of the world as a single land mass, with Jerusalem at its center, and the threatening oceans marking the perimeter of human vision.[111] Although the discovery of the New World had shattered this unicentric geographical vision, almost all European Christians continued to think in essentially Eurocentric categories until very recent times; it may be suggested, indeed, that the majority do so even today. In so far as one aspect of the Enlightenment was the pushing back of the intellectual horizons of European Christendom to accommodate new fields of knowledge, awareness, and moral sensitivity, one of the broader conclusions of this volume may ironically be that part of the malaise of Western Christianity is that this dimension of the process of Enlightenment has not gone far enough.

111. McGrane, *Beyond Anthropology,* pp. 32-34.

CHAPTER NINE

Upholding Orthodoxy in Missionary Encounters: A Theological Perspective

DANIEL W. HARDY

Introduction

Missions are not undertaken without good reason and clear, strong motivation, and they do not continue without assurance of their value. Although all sorts of other factors may be present, the ultimate basis of this motivation and assurance is "theological." It does not lie in *any* conception of "theology" but in what is taken to be *normatively* theological — in what is called "orthodoxy." Operating from "orthodoxy" is central to the nature and practice of mission.

That simple consideration can easily be overlooked in the study of missions, which, as this volume itself witnesses, usually concentrates on "history," on the sequence of events, the institutions and movements, and the interactions between persons, involved. However valuable in its own terms, this kind of history will prove somewhat limited unless it adverts to the motivations that generate missions, to the fundamental orientations that guide them, and to the basic criteria operative in assessing their success. A corrective move would be to extend "historical" study to include the study of the normative theological notions underlying the motivations and assurances of missions,

---

An earlier version of this chapter was delivered at the North Atlantic Missiology Project Symposium on "Christian Missions and the 'Enlightenment' of the West" at Boston University, 21-24 June 1998.

so that the pertinent "events, movements, institutions, and people" are traced to the "orthodoxies" they represent. In that case, the result would be a "history of missionary orthodoxies," which would be a form of the *history of theology*.

Even then, the study of missions would not be located where — from an authentically theological viewpoint — it must be, that is, in *historical theology* or *theology of history*. What distinguishes this from the history of theology is the attempt to uncover the purposes and work of God in the history of mission, including the orthodoxies that underlie it. Historical theology is notable for its rarity in our time, and in all recent theology. It is very important nonetheless, and it is what will concern us here: establishing ways by which to trace the purposes of God in mission, and in the orthodoxies involved. For reasons of practicality, it will be necessary to limit ourselves to discovering the issues involved. There will be little opportunity to locate these by reference to the history of missionary activity.

To attempt such a thing presents forbidding difficulties. Most acutely, in a situation shaped by modern movements opposed to such questions (largely originating in the European Enlightenment), it raises the question of *how* the purposes of God are found in missions and their history. This question is usually answered by adopting a particular vantage point that establishes how the purposes of God are known.

Such a vantage point is supplied, for example, by the tradition of Western Reformed theology often employed in Christian approaches to the history of missions. In that case, the purposes of God are traced to God's self-revelation proclaimed and received in faith — to a deep conviction of the *gracious act* by which God makes himself known to faithful human beings. However, the adoption of this view brings two problems. First, the main concern is with *God's purposes and actions,* and although missions themselves will be taken very seriously as the occasions for the proclamation and reception of the work of God, the *history of missions* will be seen as only very uncertainly related to God's purposes.[1] Second, this view implicitly limits the recognition or use of alternative positions about how God's purposes are found: in created existence, in the transformation of human lives, in the church, or in particular historical movements — all of them powerful theological alternatives. Of course, if any of these alternatives were to be adopted instead, it might prove equally limiting.

What is the alternative to adopting one such framework or another for

---

1. This may, indeed, be the cause of the inattention to strictly theological questions that is usual in mission studies.

knowledge of God's purposes in the history of missions? It is at least possible to trace the dynamics through which *God's* purposes appear in the interconnection of events, movements, and people in the history of missions, and in the "orthodoxies" that figure in them, to locate their basic characteristics, and to ask what mission *truly is* and *should be* with respect to hope in the true God and the hope of true humanity — which are arguably central to biblical Christianity. Beginning the pursuit of that kind of "theological history" is the concern of this essay.

Orthodoxy and the Question of Theological Criteria

It may be best to begin by looking more carefully at the notion of orthodoxy. It has to do with the focusing of a way of being — usually one already intrinsic to the existence, understanding, and life of people — by which they orient themselves and guide their interaction with others, especially in adverse circumstances. In that sense, it is what might be called a "method of reason."

In the usual sense of the term, to specify orthodoxy is to establish "sufficient conditions" (criteria) for the presence of a property or the truth of a proposition. In the case of Christianity, we may take it that the property whose presence is sought is "conformity to God's work in Jesus Christ by the Holy Spirit." If this is expressed in the form of propositions, such as confessional statements, orthodoxy will be the specification of sufficient conditions for approximation to these propositions. In this case, "the word expresses the idea that certain statements accurately embody the revealed truth content of Christianity and are therefore normative for the universal church."[2]

To determine "orthodoxy" is to establish sufficient conditions for such conformity throughout the range of Christian activity, in knowledge and the means of justifying it, in expression and meaning, in intention or action, or even in morality and moral identity. Hence, if mission is to "uphold orthodoxy," its basis, conduct, and assurance must meet the conditions thus established.

This is not an abstract "philosophical" exercise. The *Christian identity* of life, knowledge, communication, and action — always a matter of theological orthodoxy — is at stake at every point in the history of mission before, during, and since the Enlightenment of the West. Theological orthodoxy is operative in

---

2. J. I. Packer, "Orthodoxy," in *Evangelical Dictionary of Theology,* edited by W. A. Elwell (Basingstoke, 1984), p. 808.

- generating determinate missionary activity from the movement of God toward humanity as that *orders* and *intensifies* human energies for people to be "sent" to others,
- providing a rationale for this activity,
- determining the conduct of mission, and its practical rules,
- selecting the possible partners in mission,
- deciding the value to be assigned to those to whom people are sent, and how others' self-established difference is engaged with, including:
  - their standing in the sight of God,
  - the "religious" convictions that order and govern their understanding and the conduct of their lives,
  - their cosmological understanding and their conception of their relation to their environment,
  - the dynamics of their social and political life, and
  - their convictions about the possibilities of human life,
- how this engagement is undertaken, whether
  - governed by "Christian principles" alone, or
  - allowing that which is not excluded by "Christian principles," or
  - through dialogical engagement, with the principles established through mutual interaction.
- what is the goal of mission, whether
  - preservation and transference of "orthodox" belief and practice, or
  - making "space" for the fulfillment of the other in the renewal of Christian faith,
- how theological orthodoxy is ascertained, whether
  - unilaterally, or
  - bilaterally, through mutual discovery.

In other words, that, how, and why mission is undertaken are not simply casual matters, but implicitly issues of theological orthodoxy: Do mission, its practice, and its goal satisfy the conditions for "Christianity"?

It is especially important to notice that "orthodoxy" does not operate simply as a set of inert principles by which activity is measured. It is the dynamic internal to theology by which missionary activity is *moved, shaped,* and *directed.*

Studying Theological Orthodoxy

Since theological orthodoxy has been under discussion throughout Christian history, it is not surprising that no common standard of orthodoxy is entirely shared among those responsible for missions. It is possible, therefore, that missions are always pluriform in purpose and different in operation, and must vary "all the way down," even in their most fundamental orientation. If so, the question of the *truth* of the theological bases and criteria of particular missionary ventures cannot be answered except within one or another of these orientations. Given the centrality of the theological impulse and rationale for such missions, that is a major problem; they are driven by passionate convictions that are ultimately *theological* in kind.

Even if there are no *common* standards of orthodoxy employed in different missionary ventures, *theological* orthodoxy is utilized in each that is distinctive to the sponsoring organization or group. Missing this is likely to locate the significance of missions wrongly. The most common alternative today is to judge it in pragmatic terms, measuring it by some standard of practical success: for example, its production of Bible translations, or how many "Christians" resulted from the mission, and so forth. Considering it by reference to a standard of orthodoxy, however, measures the achievements of missionary activity by the deep dynamic that motivates it. Exploring the theological standards of orthodoxy therefore raises the study of mission to another level, where it is understood and its "success" is tested by reference to its highest aims. In practice, how well did it succeed in following this dynamic?

This dynamic does not emerge only where there is confrontation with other religions and worldviews — where Christian missions engage, for example, with Muslims or Hindus. It is there beforehand: it concentrates what is distinctive and fruitful about Christian faith and makes it possible to *distinguish* it from alternatives. This is the basis for developing the *differences* between them, which may become *contrasts* as each is developed in contradistinction to the other. Hence, this dynamic constitutes a different level of explanation than accounting for them as contrasting "cultures" or "worldviews." It concentrates the main and deep features of the one and elicits a comparable concentration of the other, showing their manifest theological difference. Since it goes beyond surface differences, it may well open possibilities for deeper engagement between them. These features are typically those in terms of which "reality" is ordered and energized by religious factors — in the end profound issues of the God who so orders and energizes them. They are not superficial items of one intellectual and practical landscape as distinct from another, but the rocklike foundation and structure of the "city" inhabited.

Viewing them in these terms places them at a more fundamental level of explanation than designating them as "cultural." The word "culture" in its modern usage designates *human* construction, holding, or operation. Using it of orthodoxy prejudges the nature of orthodoxy, indicating that it is a humanly constructed "standard of rightness," thus relocating the *theological* criteria being employed from the dynamic of *God's* revelation or grace as actively received by human beings to *human* holding and use. That is, using such a word as "culture" for them begs the most important question of all, the basis of "meaning" and "rightness" in God's action in and among human beings — as distinct from human activity alone. That was not the case with the usage of "orthodoxy" in earlier centuries to designate what is necessary for the preservation of Christianity in conditions of disagreement.

The importance of the dynamic of theological orthodoxy can also be seen in the historical study of theological orthodoxy. Suppose we set about providing a history of theological criteria of orthodoxy, exploring how they — in their variety — are used by Christian faith in missionary encounter, and proceed to compare their use in the measurement of understanding and practices. In doing so we may be taken as presenting a comparative history or phenomenology of humanly developed standards. Although this might possibly be quite illuminating in its own terms, it would necessarily eschew the question of the basis of these theological criteria in the dynamic of God's self-gift to human understanding and life. It would detach the theological criteria and their use from the action of God in which they are founded.

It is not that there are not eminent precedents for this relocation of theological criteria. Indeed, the thrust of all thought since Immanuel Kant is to do just that, to place categories within the sphere of human operations, whether cognitive or moral, suspending the question of their derivation from God's self-giving. Yet even if such a thing is considered legitimate — and there are now serious questions as to whether it is — it is not permissible where the theological basis of missions is concerned, for it and they are rooted in a *first-order* relation, immediate or mediated, between the self-giving God and those who think and live from the gifts of this God. That is, they begin and continue in trusting the God who is self-giving in such a way as to elicit their faith.

These considerations suggest that theological orthodoxy must be explored in a manner appropriate to its level. That is, we must attempt to grasp the *dynamics* of the history of theological orthodoxy by reference to the nature and activity of God who is grasped therein. Studying theological orthodoxy by reference to God will enable us to assess *theologically* what is actually occurring historically in conceptions of orthodoxy as they develop in the Enlightenment and in missionary encounters. This is somewhat like focusing on the *idea* of measurement in and through the *process* of measurement, as it operates through particular kinds of measurement such as imperial or metric.

We will need to trace the dynamics of theological orthodoxy as this oper-ated in the history of the encounter of Christians with the patterns of thought and life known as "the European Enlightenment" and of their encounter with others in missionary practice. We will see how — in these encounters — the dynamics of theological orthodoxy and its maintenance became congealed or fixed, and what the effects were.

Later we will to try to attend especially to the testing of these dynamics not only by conventional Western views of orthodoxy but by the "nature" of God's dynamic relationship with "reality" as this unfolds in missionary en-gagement — an extraordinarily deep and difficult matter.

Studying History Theologically

The normative theological notions — the theological orthodoxies — under-lying the motivations, orientations, conceptions, and practice of mission have their own history, a history of theology submerged in the outworking of all the issues just mentioned. This history neither is simple in itself, nor does it follow a simple line. It engages with what is thought to be "original" and normative for Christian faith and does so within the pressures and in-fluences of different times. The preceding chapters have suggested that there was, for example, a complex symbiosis between theological orthodoxy, mis-sionary practice, and the European Enlightenment. Because of such "exter-nal" factors, the history of theological orthodoxy cannot be told only by ref-erence to Christian faith and practice as perceived from within; it must refer also to other conceptions and practices that impinge on the character or na-ture of orthodoxy.

Even this complex history amounts only to a species of "history of theol-ogy," however. The more difficult question is that of "historical theology." This is the question how theological orthodoxy — as it appears (for example) in its relation to the Enlightenment — is tested by reference to God and God's manifold work in the world, as that occurs through the dynamic involvement of the Trinitarian God in creation, providence, reconciliation, redemption, and the establishment of the kingdom of God. To put the question another way: How do conceptions of theological orthodoxy, past and present, and the history of missions in which they are embedded figure in the dynamic of God's life and work? If the final goal of theological orthodoxy is to enable the intensity of God's life and purposes to arise fully in *others* for their *salvation*, how is theological orthodoxy to be tested and developed until that purpose is attained?

These, then, are the three areas that we need now to address if the fullness of the concept of orthodoxy in missionary encounters is to be recovered: the way theological orthodoxy operates in the history of missions; its history during this Enlightenment period; and how it figures in God's work.

Enlightenment Orthodoxy

The question of how theological orthodoxy operates in a particular period immediately raises the issue of whether there is not some fixed way in which it always operates. Although there may be different points of reference — whether biblical, doctrinal, confessional, ecclesiastical, traditional, or some combination of them — were they not all used in roughly the same way? Furthermore, weren't they always used that way in the history of Christian faith? These are commonplace assumptions.

Although there was always the concern to be true to normative Christian faith, the ways in which this was done were far more subtle than providing a fixed way of doing so. The *complex form* of Scripture as witness to the Word of God in Jesus Christ, the "grammar" of this Scripture-borne witness as declared in the ancient Creeds, and the life of the Church as the continuation of the gospel were most widely normative. In reaction to the proliferation of "Christian" views and the reduction of Christian expectations in the late Middle Ages, and to the complex world that was emerging with the Renaissance, there were attempts to restate the fundamental points of reference. This was more like "reconcentrating" attention — on the justifying Word of God (the Reformers) or on the sifting of correct Church doctrine (Thomas Aquinas) — than developing fixed norms for Christian faith in doctrinal and confessional terms, although this did happen after the initial "reconcentrations."

How were these "orthodoxies" affected by the new circumstances of the Enlightenment? Something quite distinctive occurred in them as a result. Summary of the Enlightenment as such is notoriously difficult and potentially misleading because of the differing origins, concerns, and pace of the movement in England, France, and Germany. In the broadest terms, it was a highly complex movement beginning in the seventeenth century in which the ideals of human life changed, new attention was given to the constructive and regulative powers of human thought, and new possibilities for human flourishing were seen, which in turn required a release from age-old constraints. Gradually, the goals and means of "progress" were consolidated in various ways — scientific, philosophical, social, political, economic, technological, and artistic — to such a degree that they developed a momentum that was difficult to arrest or divert.

The issues at stake were inherently religious. They had to do with the nature of God and God's work, what is proper to the world and human life, and what were the needs and possibilities of life in the world (material, social, economic, political, cultural, and religious) — developed versions of all the areas that had figured in Christian concerns. Against what were seen as the "darkness" and "superstition" of previous ages (especially the Middle Ages) was set the courageous and independent attempt to develop what was inherently rational in thought and practice. All beliefs needed to be tested and accepted by reason, not because of "authorities," whether texts, traditions, or "divinely appointed" priests or leaders. This would fulfill, even perfect, the natural rationality and goodness of humanity. This in turn constituted a universal standard: through reason, all might be free and equal in society. This universal ideal was to supersede local prejudices and practices.

The orthodoxy of the Enlightenment was distinctive in that it appealed to the powers present but dormant or uncoordinated in human beings themselves. It was directed to enlightenment, without clear predefined criteria or a preestablished set of implications considered decisive. It has been described thus:

> The search for a new stability begins — a stability founded on rational arrangements in social and political life that would embrace both individual morality and the relations between entire states. The measures that were recommended, planned or implemented to this end, however, were not always explicitly envisaged as elements in a programme of Enlightenment; they were undertaken more in an attempt at better understanding or as a form of criticism of existing traditions. It was in fact the multiplicity and diversity of such measures and the tension between them and their divergent motives that formed the driving force of the process we know as Enlightenment.[3]

The orthodoxy that *differentiated* the Enlightenment was therefore more pluriform and dynamic than that provided by the theological orthodoxies that preceded it and reacted to it. To be sure, it *found differences* between its own "attempt at better understanding" and "existing traditions," but these were not predefined.

3. Ulrich Im Hof, *The Enlightenment,* translated by William E. Yuill (Oxford, 1994), p. 9.

Correspondingly, its *response* was to carry "enlightenment" forward by whatever means seemed suitable to the task. Its "mission" was as broad as the manifold spheres in which it operated — all the conditions for what was thought to be the flourishing of human life — and it "met" people by giving them hope for better conditions. Its roots in these concerns were what gave it its power, at least in Europe.

It is easy to develop a catalog of the baleful results of the Enlightenment, and thus to regard it only as highly damaging — which has recently become a popular pastime.[4] Its conclusions could be highly problematic for traditionalist Christian faith: a deistic notion of God remote from the operation of the world, a self-structured/self-maintaining natural world, the best possibilities of human life as within human capability, rationalism as the criterion for legitimacy, life seen as an arena for individual striving, social life seen in human-contractual terms, and so forth. It was understandable that some should find it necessary to reclaim the "high ground" by developing a pure, detached position by which to resist: there was plenty in the "worldly" practices of society and church to justify that response. It was equally understandable that others should attempt to redevelop theological orthodoxy in coordination with Enlightenment ways, for they had brought new vitality to human life. Each could see no better way of maintaining the truth of Christian faith.

The Responses of Theological Orthodoxy

Enlightenment conceptions had a dramatic effect on the way in which theological orthodoxy was construed. It could hardly have been otherwise, for, as late as the eighteenth century, "it was largely the clergy who sustained intellectual life,"[5] and it was they (perhaps more than any other group) among whom Enlightenment conceptions were fostered. There was division among them, however, about the implications of these new currents of thought, and conceptions of theological orthodoxy changed accordingly.

Yet new Enlightenment ideals were also, in important respects, similar to Christian concerns. There had been repeated attempts to reconcentrate faith in an intensive, purified form, both to rescue it from misguided and superstitious practices — those of the Middle Ages for example — and to create a new commonality among Christians — a "faithful tolerance" one might call it. There had been acute concern for the intrinsic truth of Christian faith, as

---

4. This has been especially true of those who espouse "postmodernism."
5. Im Hof, *The Enlightenment,* p. 168.

distinct from reliance on earthly authorities. Furthermore, God-given rationality was seen as the means by which this purification was to occur. Such were the "universal standards" of Christianity, by comparison with which human differences were insignificant. All these suggest a greater affinity between the Enlightenment and Christian faith than is usually supposed, especially by those who see only the damage it has done.

It would be surprising if Christians rejected the Enlightenment; and — on the whole — they did not. Instead, they adapted themselves to it, employing it in different ways. Correspondingly, several notions of the proper relation between theological orthodoxy and the Enlightenment appeared. In order to show these with maximum clarity, we will state them in notional terms as "Enlightenment-reconstituting" (E^R), "Enlightenment-instrumentalizing" (E^I), "Enlightenment-correlating" (E^C), and "Enlightenment-surpassing" (E^S).

E^R: Among some, there was a concerted attempt to employ new ways — although not necessarily recognized as such — as a means of redefining the intrinsic truth and rationality of Christian faith as the basis of Enlightenment.[6] The content of faith could thus be treated as the source and norms for the very rationality, morality, and civilization for which the Enlightenment sought. This can be seen as an "Enlightenment-reconstituting" view, hence the designation "E^R."

E^I: There was a more pragmatic variant of the view just indicated. By supposing, without examining, the credibility of Christian faith, it was possible to enlist the dynamic spread of civilization that arose from Enlightenment conceptions and practices in the service of the proclamation of Christian faith. In this case, the Enlightenment was used as instrumental to the spread of Christian faith, hence the designation "E^I."

E^C: It was also possible to take a still more positive view of Enlightenment ideas, anticipating their value for Christian faith. Hence it was supposed that the truth of Christian faith was intimately associated with — even mediated through — secular forms of human understanding and practice, as well as social institutions. With the onset of the Enlightenment, and despite its radical implications, some sought to perpetuate in new ways the possibility of the mediation of faith in common human practices. We signify this by E^C, to designate the attempt to develop the correlation of faith to the new "critical" reason characteristic of the Enlightenment.

These options were not necessarily compatible. E^C drew on the ancient practice of expressing Christian faith in the visible institutions and practices

---

6. The theology of F. D. E. Schleiermacher was a powerful example of such a strategy.

of society at large, whereas E^R (at least of the Reformed kind) had a "higher" intent, to show the basis of true reason and practice in the self-conferral of God. To the latter (E^R), however, the former (E^C), and even E^I, with its more selective appropriation of Enlightenment ideas, could seem to be less true to Christian faith, or even a *capitulation* to what was alien to faith.[7]

Stated in notional terms, these were the conceptions of the relation of theological orthodoxy to the Enlightenment that might be expected during the period, and since. When we take a broader theological-historical view and ask what view should be the basis for missionary work, it may be necessary for us to consider another position. When major questions are raised both about the value of the European Enlightenment as such, and also about the viability of E^R, E^I, and E^C as responses to it, another strategy appears, a view (E^S) that attempts to *surpass* both Enlightenment conceptions and the usual religious responses. We need first to give careful attention to the others, however, not least because they are so often seen as "the way things have always been done," and consequently as normative for Christian faith and mission.

Reconcentrating Faith in the Face of the Enlightenment

Up to this point, we have stated these alternatives in notional terms. The positions were normally seen, however, in the treatment both of substantial issues of theology and also of other kinds of understanding and practice.

For example, the strategy designated as E^R is exemplified in two changes in the norms of Christian faith. In the first place, there was a change in the use of Scripture and creeds, and, in the second place, they were supplemented by the construction of a systematized doctrinal worldview. The changes were highly significant.

On the one hand, the long-standing — and very subtle and complex — use of Scripture as "realistic narratives" of God's work of creation, redemption, and perfection, and of the creeds as a "grammatical" accompaniment to guide interpretation of Scripture, changed to a simpler kind of use that made it possible to say: "Scripture says . . ." and "Christian faith requires . . ." On the other hand, as Christian faith was being detached from the emerging explanations and the commonplace awareness of the world, a coherent "doctrinal

---

7. For those that wished to avoid the kinds of confessional disputes that had plagued Europe (in the Thirty Years War in Germany, the English Civil War, or the expulsion of the Huguenots from France), E^C or E^I might have seemed a more sensible way.

universe" was substituted, one visibly derivative from Christian faith in ways the emerging world-awareness was not.

These are difficult matters to fathom, and here we can only outline what happened, lest — as one historical scholar admitted of himself — we "disappear into history and never come out."[8] Sketching it should serve to show that the kind of theological orthodoxy often assumed always to have been normative for Christian faith actually employed Enlightenment rational methods to purify what was seen as the intrinsic truth of faith as the basis of the Enlightenment itself.[9] In other words, the effect of Enlightenment "modernity" upon the form of theological orthodoxy was to *change* it: perceptions of Scripture as normative for Christian faith were "purified" or "concentrated" by means comparable to those of the Enlightenment, and the implications of faith for the world were "doctrinalized" by similar means. This was intended to make the criteria and content of theological orthodoxy, and their implications for the world, both more self-consistent and also normative for the Enlightenment. Yet it had the effect of establishing an *alternative* to views then emerging. This effect has shaped Christian faith ever since.

This process deserves a closer look. Central to theological orthodoxy was Scripture. Through most of Christian history, however, Scripture was regarded as "realistic narratives" and read literally as the history of the real world that "embrace[d] the experience of any age and reader." Reading and interpreting the Bible was like a "craft" that followed informal rules guiding the Christian community in doing so. This *sensus literalis* was a very supple way of using Scripture, not bound to particular theories of reading and interpretation, which were always matters for argument.[10] Over a period of years, and culminating in the nineteenth century, the "biblical world" was more and more separated from the "real historical world," which brought questions about the source and authority of Scripture.[11]

These questions were answered by "the concept of revelation, which came to assume the position of the central technical concept in theology, a position

8. A remark made in private conversation by the eminent Calvin scholar, Edward Dowey.

9. See, for example, D. W. Bebbington, *Evangelicalism in Modern Britain: A History from the 1730s to the 1980s* (London, 1989), p. 74 and *passim.*

10. Hans W. Frei, "The 'Literal Reading' of Biblical Narrative," in Hans Frei, *Theology and Narrative: Selected Essays,* edited by G. Hunsinger and W. Placher (New York, 1993), p. 118-19.

11. The attempts of evangelicals, such as the missionaries in the South Pacific described in chapter five, to reconstruct ethnographic history on the basis of early biblical history were regarded with diminishing seriousness as the nineteenth century proceeded.

of eminence to which it has clung through various changes in its own content, brought about by such shifts as that from rationalist to romantic sensibility."[12] In other words, with the separation of the "biblical world" from the "real historical world," Scriptural authority was established by reference to the self-communication of God, and its connection to "historical reality" was sustained by theoretical means — in this case a theory establishing the direct relation of the two, a theory of correspondence.

Such concepts and theories were not accepted as self-evident, however. Indeed, they were the subjects of much disagreement in the seventeenth century, as can readily be seen in the writings of John Locke. Furthermore, the meaning of the texts and their use as a cumulative history (to show that the whole Bible reflects a single, gradually developing and cumulative *history*), as well as their reliability, were open to ongoing controversy.

All this had strange consequences for the reading of the Bible. Thereafter attention was given not so much to literal reading of the Bible as realistic history as to a reading that would uncover "the single meaning of a grammatically and logically sound propositional statement."[13] It then became possible to say: "the Bible says . . ." as if it could be summarized in concentrated ideas. This actually indicates a "hardening" of the way in which the Bible functioned in theological orthodoxy.

In the second place, it came to be accepted that these concentrated ideas should be unfolded in their own right, as if to follow the dictum (gaining ground in those days) "positive theology is a theology, not a history."[14] With this, it became commonplace to suppose that Christian faith was expressible in a series of doctrinal statements and should be explored in discrete thematic fields or *loci* — the basis of modern doctrine.

The preoccupation with the authority of the Bible and its connection to worldly existence, the hardening of the meaning of the Bible, and the "doctrinal thematizing" of belief about the world can all be seen as the Christian reconstitution of the Enlightenment's attempt to trace the basis and rules of reason. The effect was to form a self-consistent and exclusive view of theological orthodoxy, as if to say: "this self-revelation of God, a coherent statement accompanied by doctrinal exposition, is authoritative for all worldly existence." This standard was both simpler and more dogmatic than what had preceded it, in effect claiming to define both the exclusive source of truth and its outworking in norms for the world. Some proponents of this standard saw

---

12. Hans W. Frei, *The Eclipse of Biblical Narrative* (New Haven, 1974), p. 52.
13. Frei, *The Eclipse of Biblical Narrative*, p. 9.
14. Yves M.-J. Congar, *A History of Theology* (New York, 1968), p. 233.

it in quasi-deductive terms (the self-revelation of God leading to coherent propositional forms, leading in turn to normative statements about the world). The position itself relied on concepts and arguments, and these were not allowed to stand unchallenged by the very Enlightenment figures whose techniques and concerns they had co-opted.

It is not to be supposed that these were the only terms in which a Christian position reconstituting the Enlightenment (E^R) could be specified. Construing the Church as itself the continuance of the gospel, whose embodiment of truth was authoritative for the world, provided another self-consistent and authoritative view of theological orthodoxy. Although we will not attempt to analyze it further, this view was another important example of a Christian reconstitution of the Enlightenment.

Such "reconcentrations" were important responses to the Enlightenment. They enlisted Enlightenment methods in the service of Christian faith in order to reaffirm it as the basis of true enlightenment, even if not to the satisfaction of many proponents of the new methods. They operated on "high ground," by reinterpreting the basis of Enlightenment notions. Their "missionary" concern was with the Enlightenment as such, and the European conceptions and institutions involved in it. In and of themselves, they were not likely to generate concern for "foreign" missions.

Yet concern for the intrinsic universality of the truth of the gospel could take a more practical or "extensive" form, where the implications for the well-being of all human beings were primary. The impulse to missions elsewhere arose among those who combined intensive awareness of the universal truth of the Christian message with a sense of the urgency of bringing this truth — the truth of salvation — to those outside the usual spheres of Christianity. Among them, we can discern two kinds of engagement with Enlightenment concepts and practices. One was found in those — designated above as E^I — less concerned about the implications of the Enlightenment as such, who nonetheless used it (or the extension of Enlightenment "civilization") as the "occasion" or "launching pad" for the proclamation of the universal truth of Christianity. As they "instrumentalized" Enlightenment views or practices, or their use among other peoples to influence their social structure, patterns of existence, or culture, they typically reshaped them in a fashion appropriate to this religious proclamation. The resultant interaction between religious views and Enlightenment positions and practices could be diverse and very complex.

Another kind of engagement — designated as E^C before — is seen in those who acknowledged the inherent value of the Enlightenment and sought to preserve it by continuing to engage with it at various levels. For them, the universality of the truth embodied in Christian faith was to be found also *within* Enlightenment convictions and practices, or within their extension throughout the world, and served to enlarge Christian faith. For them, theological orthodoxy furnished the reason and motivation for engaging with these others, and enlarging themselves — to greater or lesser extent — through their concepts and practices. It also furnished the criteria for the dialogical enlargement by these concepts and practices. In this fashion, these "new worlds" should and could be utilized for their own value in a growing Christian faith. To understand how this could be, however, we need to understand more about the Enlightenment and the opportunities and difficulties it offered.

Engagement with Enlightenment

There was a transition in the Enlightenment itself as regards orthodoxy. Only variably and gradually did it develop agreed criteria for understanding and practice. At first, and only in a fragmentary fashion, it practiced a "negative orthodoxy," by which it declared its *difference* from the "dark" and "closed" alternatives that surrounded it, with the intention of reopening all of them to the illumination that would come with clear thought. This "orthodoxy" required "modernity" both to differentiate itself from all hindrances to human progress and to respond to them by surpassing them. This may well have been the secret of its amazing dynamism, as well as the benefits it brought. Later, however, it developed a more consolidated orthodoxy, centered on a closed view of what was deemed to be "rational," and this was much more problematic.

Insistence on the absoluteness of revelation by a personal God proved a natural target for those influenced by the Enlightenment, especially the increasing number of those who could acknowledge an impersonal "transcendent." Such questioning sometimes led to disengagement by civil authorities from church missions, even where there had been alliances of state and church "back home,"[15] for by nature the Enlightenment was a *critical* movement, one that focused on all assumed authorities, traditions, institutions, concepts, and arguments, subjecting them to testing and either refinement or disposal.

Unsurprisingly, a series of intellectual controversies followed about the philosophical and factual credibility of truth validated by special divine self-communication through historical occurrences. The emergence of biblical

---

15. See Brett Christophers, *Positioning the Missionary: John Booth Good and the Confluence of Cultures in Nineteenth-Century British Columbia* (Vancouver, 1998), p. 11.

criticism directed attention to the complexity of the biblical witness and implicitly challenged simple views of revealed truth. The doctrinal universe that had been derived from such views was continuously tested against "reality" as newly understood. The very topics that had been reconstituted through the E^R views — the nature of God, the nature of the world, the basis and character of rationality, the nature of human beings and their responsibilities, and the possibilities for human development of the conditions of life (whether material, economic, socio-political, cultural, or even religious) — were subjected to continuous testing and revision. This meant that they were frequently made into a program of rational explorations — separate pursuits that should be pursued in their own terms, free of the formulations in which "theology" and Christian institutions had confined them.[16]

Some saw these "explorations" as promising to Christian faith, but they were not necessarily committed to the standards of those who attempted to reconstitute the Enlightenment by establishing its basis in Christian faith (E^R), and they could easily be caricatured by those who did. In fact, they saw the priorities being developed in the Enlightenment — natural instincts (including the natural need for religion), the quest for freedom, the need for sound judgment, rational education and scholarship, the reservation to "God" of ultimate questions of morality and truth, egalitarianism, active tolerance of differences — as potentially, if not actually, compatible with Christian faith (E^C). Furthermore, less confined by adherence to concentrated formulations of the meaning of Scripture and to "thematized" doctrinal beliefs, they were committed to forms of Christian faith worked out in the ordinary practices of human life in the world.

As we have now seen, there was a considerable variety in the conceptions of theological orthodoxy formulated in response to the Enlightenment. The difference between them can be summarized: they range from "purist" reconstitutions (E^R) to "purist" instrumentalizations (E^I) to "conciliatory" views (E^C). They did not, of course, exist in watertight compartments. Generally speaking, they coexisted and interacted, often within the same churches or mission organizations, stimulated as much by each other as by anything outside. It was this that made their variety a seedbed for missions, a rich and paradoxical mixture of revival and reason.

16. This was the birth of the discipline that came to be known as "philosophy of religion."

Implications for Mission

In a fundamental sense, missions are "intervals"[17] — the "space" made between one's own situation and that of others — with different ways of construing and using the space. These ways are formed, controlled, and checked by various orthodoxies.

In modern times, the "space" made in missions is always, at least in some respects, generated or affected by Enlightenment orthodoxy. As a direct byproduct of the "universalizing" of the European project for true human progress, the world itself became a field for exploration, rationalization, and utilization. The "space" between Europe and others was construed accordingly. "They" — the others — were to be identified, understood, civilized, and utilized according to the criteria of Enlightenment orthodoxy, with at least some benefit for Europe. Accordingly, the "space" between those who went and those to whom they went was construed as *difference* and the *asymmetrical* provision by one party of the "benefits." This construction of "space" was unavoidably the context for the missionary activity of Christians, and the nature of their activities coalesced with Enlightenment interests in these respects.

To begin at the most concrete level, it is worth noting that Christian missions were made both necessary and possible by Enlightenment advances. They were made necessary by the program of Europeans for advancement and by news of "heathen" peoples brought by prior explorations. They were made possible by the development of means of travel and communication, and, more fundamentally, by the enhanced sense of the unity and potential of humanity that Enlightenment thought and practice embodied.

These "modern" tendencies were exemplified in education. Previous chapters have shown how the commitment to education as a major objective of missionary activity, although long thought to be an essential adjunct of faith, took on a heightened urgency under the influence of the Enlightenment. In missions shaped by the Scottish Moderate tradition, the inculcation of rationality through English-medium education could acquire quasi-redemptive significance. Even where evangelical orthodoxies limited such tendencies, Enlightenment empiricism pushed missions towards investing greater confidence in education as a means of reducing "difference" than was warranted on strictly theological grounds. Although the need of "uneducated" people abroad for literacy and "civilization" was consistent with the Western Christian tradition, the value now given to education was a reflection of Enlightenment assumptions.

17. See Daniel W. Hardy, *God's Ways with the World* (Edinburgh, 1996), ch. 18.

Within the common Enlightenment-generated conceptions of "space," "difference" and "asymmetrical provision" evident in these ways, special emphases were provided by different theological orthodoxies. The significant *differences* between those who went and those to whom they went, and their *relative responsibilities* — those that structured their relationships — varied according to the orthodoxy held. Probably because they were preoccupied with the attempt to reconstitute the presuppositions of the Enlightenment in its European form, and with the wide-ranging controversies to which this gave rise, most adherents of the E^R model simply did not venture into the threatening space created by the expansion of European horizons. The few sectors of Protestantism that reacted entirely negatively to the Enlightenment by attempting to fence themselves in within reinforced confessional orthodoxies were precisely the ones that held back from the missionary movement, with its "dangerous" possibilities of evangelical ecumenism, dilution of doctrinal distinctiveness, dallying with human rights ideologies, and willingness to agitate politically for native interests. The most obvious examples are the Dutch Reformed Church in the Cape colony and Boer republics, and hyper-Calvinist Dissenters, such as Strict Baptists, in England.

Most nineteenth-century missionaries adhered to an E^R or E^I position. Their view of *superordinate* revelation and doctrine as the basis of ordinary understanding strongly differentiated those who preached the gospel from those to whom it was preached. They were the bringers of knowledge of God that would otherwise have remained inaccessible. Such a position supposed a radical deficiency in those who were to hear it, and their need for the profound individual transformation of conversion. Nevertheless, their indebtedness to reason as a handmaid to faith could lead them to value features of the lives of those to whom the gospel was preached as "opportunities" for Christian transformation. Adherents of an E^C position, with its view of a Christian life that might be coordinated with ordinary life, were more fundamentally inclined to find correlatives to the gospel in local cultures.

Identifying differences and needs would also shape the *dynamics* of missionary activity. Those with an orthodoxy of the universal truth of the gospel, as they found themselves more and more at odds with the thrust of life and understanding among those to whom they went, would be more likely to respond (reactively) by concentrating more exclusively on Christian faith and doctrine as derived from revelation and by rejecting "lesser" alternatives. Those more disposed to finding the compatibility of faith with other life and understanding would be more likely to redouble the search for possible "mediations" for Christian faith in existing notions and practices. This makes an important point: theological orthodoxy not only is formative for the

216

"space" between missionary and those to whom he or she is sent, and therefore for differences and tasks, but itself stimulates an ongoing dynamic.

Hence we can conclude that diverse orthodoxies, derived from Enlightenment and theological sources in different mixtures, contain by implication varying views of difference and responsibility — what differentiates the incoming European from those to whom he or she goes, and what their respective responsibilities (usually asymmetrical) are. Such notions of difference and responsibility provide particular *imperatives* and *content* for mission: "they are different, and we need to deal with them in this way." It is significant not only that such orthodoxies are about what is said or done; but also that they establish the conceptions and dynamics of *difference* and *responsibility*.

Sponsoring institutions and procedures embodied the diverse kinds of orthodoxy. It is noticeable, for example, that whereas the missionary organizations shaped by the Scottish, English, and American Enlightenments were predicated on either the E^R or the E^I model, some of their individual missionaries in the field embraced views that correspond more to an E^C model. However, the Protestant missions that were most prepared to regard national cultural forms as expressions of the variegated grace of God were those that reacted most strongly against the French and Scottish versions of the Enlightenment, namely, German missions influenced by Herder's repudiation of unitary models of "civilization." Some Anglo-American missions, such as the (Anglo-Catholic) Universities' Mission to Central Africa or the China Inland Mission, displayed other aspects of the Romantic reaction against the Enlightenment. There is room for much more thorough analysis of different kinds of missionary activity in terms of the "orthodoxies" they represent, but we can pursue the matter no further now.

History of Orthodoxy: Predicting Possibilities and Problems

We have now traced something of the dynamics of orthodoxy, theological and other kinds, and seen something of the history of the interplay between them, the ways in which they collided and colluded.

The orthodoxy of the Enlightenment brought two responses. One was the attempt to reconstitute the basis of Enlightenment views by referring them to a Christian faith redeveloped by Enlightenment methods (E^R). Since this was usually resisted, the result was the firm establishment of the differences between Christian belief and the Enlightenment, and with it a sense of responsibility — on both "sides" — to maintain and express the difference. Taken to the extreme, such a position could lead to separatism or sectarianism, but in its more moderate form it led to an interest in worldly affairs and philosophies only insofar as they served the proclamation of the Christian message (E^I).

The other response was the continuing endeavor to coordinate Christian faith, belief, and institutions with those emerging through the Enlightenment (E^C). This implicated Christianity in the pluriform and dynamic quest of the Enlightenment, in effect making a permeable boundary between Christian faith and Enlightenment aims and practices.

In turn, the Enlightenment's reopening of many of the questions "closed" by traditional answers constituted a different kind of strategy, authorizing independence from the coercive affects of reactive Christianity and giving rise to a drive to enlightenment.

These strategies led to the opening of different "spaces" or "intervals" between European missionaries and the "strangers" to which they went. With these went varying conceptions of difference and responsibility, which were nonetheless alike in the supposition of an asymmetry between missionaries and those to whom they went, missionaries as "bringers" and the others as "receivers." Whether this could ever allow serious consideration of the *inherent* value of the others as the field of God's prevenient activity is a matter of question. The two orthodoxies, theological and Enlightenment, although very different, drew, as chapter eight suggests, on a common Western heritage of difference from a "heathen" world, in which both Enlightenment imperialism and the Christian missionary enterprise were implicated.

If these were the fundamental priorities and practices of mission, it should be possible to trace the *practical implications* of the kinds of theological orthodoxy. Doing so, even in crude summary form, should serve to clarify the ways in which — insofar as they were consistently applied — these orthodoxies operated in practice. As we have seen, one form of orthodoxy, which attempted to redevelop itself as the basis for the Enlightenment, employed a revelation-centered (and sometimes a "logical") version of Scripture accompanied by a doctrinal prescription of the implications of the gospel for the nature of the world and the life of its peoples (E^R). Although it was actually an attempt to reconvert Enlightenment thinkers with their own "tools," resistance to it distanced it from alternatives. For some, this brought a retreat into confessional isolation; for others it brought the attempt to use Enlightenment practices and achievements to proclaim Christian views (E^I). Another form (E^C) was characteristic of those who sought to coordinate faith with, or find its possibilities mediated in, the new forms of thought and life found in the Enlightenment and other cultural situations. It tended to be more open and explorative across the range of the implications of Christianity for the world and its peoples, sometimes to the intense dissatisfaction of sponsoring institutions of a different cast of mind. It involved a less pronounced difference from alternative positions, and a willingness to engage with those who took them.

Theological History of Theological Orthodoxy

Outlining these views in notional or ideal (and admittedly abstractive) distillation allows for a simple comparison of their implications. Yet some of the most interesting views are those in which different orthodoxies were held and pursued simultaneously, as indeed they often were.

It is possible, for example, to combine strong assertions about the universality of Christ with a dialogical engagement with other forms of life and thought, where a strong standard and content for theological orthodoxy is held together with open searching for the implications for, and in, history. In such a case, the one is not merely the background to the other but functions as the *reason for searching for the meaning* in the other. Or the conviction *that* God deals with human beings in history serves as the framework for searching *with* others to find *where* and *how* God does so. One could argue that the primary theological motivation for engagement with the spheres of free inquiry opened by the Enlightenment, or for engaging in mission throughout the world, derived from holding two strategies together. This is illustrated by a quotation from Max Warren that suggests another strategy in theology of mission:

> The question of God's operations in history constantly worries an enormous number of people today, convinced Christians amongst them. Directly one draws an analogy between Isaiah and the Assyrians with Mao-tse-Tung etc., there is a scream of anguish. Yet Isaiah, particularly Isaiah Jr. (!), and Habakkuk arrived at a view of history which enabled them to make sense of their world. And the pertinacious insistence in survival by the Jews derives fundamentally from their faith that God operates in history. And it has not been an easy faith to sustain! It seems to me that here we are at the heart of one of the strongest contributions of the Monotheistic religions.[18]

18. Max Warren, Letter 597 to Roger Hooker, cited in Graham Kings, "A Corresponding Theology of Mission: Letters between Max Warren and Roger Hooker, 1965-1977," NAMP Position Paper No. 89, Cambridge, May 1998.

As this quotation shows, it is possible to appeal to a strong view of faith as the basis for finding how God is operative in the contingencies of history. Warren's view shows a close affinity with pre-Enlightenment Christian conceptions of the undivided unity of biblical history and "real" history but broke new ground precisely in its assertion that the location of ultimate meaning in the secularity of "real," contingent, "Enlightenment" history was paradoxically at the heart of the biblical tradition.

Here we are on the edge of theological history, the attempt to find how history, including the use of conceptions of theological orthodoxy in history, manifests the operation of God in history. There is little doubt that this attempt originates in Jewish tradition, which finds in the Bible the history of true humanity in faithfulness to the God who promises, "I shall be with you." Whether pure monotheism is adequate for the purpose is another matter.

The Theology of Theological Orthodoxy: Intensity and Extensity in Mission

We should recall that to specify orthodoxy theologically in Christian terms is to establish "sufficient conditions" (criteria) for the presence of "conformity to God's work in Jesus Christ by the Holy Spirit." We have now seen three different types of theological orthodoxy, which in response to Enlightenment modernity establish sufficient conditions for that conformity. Are they of equal value? To declare that they are is to avoid a more fundamental level of questioning about theological orthodoxy — the "Enlightenment-surpassing" view (E^S) mentioned earlier.

It is possible that the forms of theological orthodoxy that we have been considering, and their implications for the "why" and "how" of mission, are *approximations* to a level of orthodoxy that has not yet been reached in theology or mission, except perhaps occasionally and informally. It is also possible that difficulties in missionary engagement have been not so much the result of the conceptions of difference ("hardness of heart" or "inadequacy") and mission ("transference" or "education") as the consequence of deficient criteria of theological orthodoxy. Perhaps the difficulties of sustaining Christian faith during the Enlightenment and through missionary engagement have brought a fixation on the criteria and content of orthodoxy that were generated in a *particular historical period*, which prove in the end to be *surface* or *secondary*. How can they be called "surface" or "secondary"? This is because they stop at forms of orthodoxy that express the nature of God and God's work without placing them *within the dynamic of life with God* as such, and without placing them *within engagement with the self-established orthodoxies* of the non-Western world. If so, greater *theological* and *missiological* attention will have to be given to the establishment of criteria of orthodoxy. We must now briefly consider how that is possible.

The most fundamental issue is to shift the criteria for theological orthodoxy to direct relationship with the Trinitarian God as that occurs within the dynamic of this God with human life in the world. This would be to relocate theological orthodoxy within participation in God's life with the world, as formed in the intensity of God's enactment of blessing through discerning love for the whole world. The implications for human life that follow from this "Godly" theological orthodoxy are that it should be lived in the intensity and extensity that marks God's own relation to the world.

In suggesting that, what we have done is to relocate the conceptions of difference and response that we saw in Enlightenment-influenced forms of theological orthodoxy. Difference is not then founded on concentrations of the authority and meaning of the universal truth of the Gospel as found in Scripture and its doctrinal implications for the world (E^R), or indeed on collaborations or compromises with modernity (E^I and E^C), but on participation in the intensity of God's blessing as that is "mapped" onto the extensity of the whole world. This implies certain ways in which Scripture and doctrine should be used, that they are to be "mapped" onto the world to assist it to find and live within the primary intensity of the blessing of the Trinitarian God.

This relocation has definite implications for the issues of mission that we have been tracing:

- Why should there be mission?
  - to raise the standards of orthodoxy
- How there should be mission?
  - for mutual engagement and assistance in the intensity of God's life in the world, through:
    - developing/redeeming the fundamental criteria for participation in the intensity of God's life
    - developing/redeeming the conditions of life in the world for the well-being of humans (e.g., worldly, social, cultural)
- What is the other's difference?
  - a like "space" in the Trinitarian life of God with the world
- How are we to engage with this difference?
  - by following the pattern of God's Trinitarian life, allowing the other to be, and assisting in the raising of God's life in him or her
- How is theological orthodoxy to be ascertained?

- *a posteriori,* by a dynamic multilateral process through which the universality of the Trinitarian work of salvation for all humanity is discerned.

Such a relocation of the criteria for theological orthodoxy rests on intense participation in the dynamic of the life of the Trinitarian God with the world and its implicit "extensity" — the incorporation of all the world's life in this dynamic as the source of its own well-being. It does not impose an alien and triumphal notion drawn from Western theology but proposes a sphere for intensive common life whose basic criterion (the life of the Trinitarian God) is found implicit in the act of achieving the fullest quality of commonality. This commonality is based on forgiveness, making space for others in ourselves, and inviting them in to share. In that we know the intensity of the "embrace" of the Trinitarian God.

> Having been embraced by God, we must make space for others and invite them in — even our enemies. This is what we enact as we celebrate the Eucharist. In receiving Christ's broken body and spilled blood, we, in a sense, receive all those whom Christ received by suffering.[19]

---

19. Miroslav Volf, *Exclusion and Embrace: A Theological Exploration of Identity, Otherness, and Reconciliation* (Nashville, 1996), p. 129.

Bibliography of Printed Sources

A. Printed Primary Sources
(excluding periodical literature, for which see footnotes)

An Abstract of the Annual Reports and Correspondence of the SPCK from the Commencement of Its Connexion with the East India Missions, AD *1709 to the Present Day.* London, 1814.

Alexander, W. L. *Memoirs of the Life and Writings of Ralph Wardlaw, D.D.* Edinburgh, 1856.

Allen, Roland. *The Spontaneous Expansion of the Church and the Causes which Hinder It.* London, 1927.

[Anon.] "A Clergyman." *The Spirit of Christian Missions.* London, 1815.

Brown, George. *George Brown, D.D. Pioneer-Missionary and Explorer: An Autobiography.* London, 1908.

Brown, William. *The History of the Propagation of Christianity among the Heathen, since the Reformation.* 3 vols. Edinburgh, 1854.

Buzacott, Aaron. *Mission Life in the Islands of the Pacific.* London, 1866.

Campbell, George. *Dissertation on Miracles.* Edinburgh, 1762.

————. *The Success of the First Publishers of the Gospel a Proof of its Truth: A Sermon Preached before the Society in Scotland for Propagating Christian Knowledge . . .* Edinburgh, 1777.

Carey, William. *An Enquiry into the Obligations of Christians to Use Means for the Conversion of the Heathens, in which the Religious State of the Different Nations of the World, and the Success of Former Undertakings, and the Practicality of Further Undertakings Are Considered.* Leicester, 1792. New facsimile ed., edited by Ernest A. Payne. London, 1961.

Chalmers, Thomas. *The Two Great Instruments Appointed for the Propagation of the Gospel: A Sermon . . .* Edinburgh, 1812.

————. *The Utility of Missions Ascertained by Experience: A Sermon Preached before the Society in Scotland . . . for Propagating Christian Knowledge . . .* Edinburgh, 1815.

————. "The Necessity of the Spirit to Give Effect to the Preaching of the Gospel." In *Sermons, Preached in the Tron Church, Glasgow,* 17-54. Glasgow, 1819.

————. "The Manifestation of the Truth to the Conscience." In *Select Sermons, 193-221.* Glasgow and London, 1859.

————. *Prelections on Butler's Analogy, Paley's Evidences of Christianity and Hill's Lectures on Divinity.* Edinburgh, 1859.

Church Missionary Society. *Register of Missionaries (Clerical, Lay and Female), and Native Clergy from 1804 to 1904.* Printed for private circulation in 1896 with a supplement ca. 1905.

Clarke, R. *Sketches of the Colony of Sierra Leone and its Inhabitants.* London, 1863.

Clendennen, G. W., ed. *David Livingstone's Shire Journal, 1861-1864.* Aberdeen, 1992.

[Anon.] "A Clergyman." *The Spirit of Christian Missions.* London, 1815.

Coates, D., Beecham, J., and Ellis, W. *Christianity the Means of Civilisation: Shown in the Evidence Given before a Committee of the House of Commons, on Aborigines.* London, 1837.

Codrington, R. H. *The Melanesians.* Oxford, 1891.

Crocombe, Ron, and Marjorie Crocombe, eds. *The Works of Ta'unga.* Canberra, 1968.

Curnock, Nehemiah, ed. *Journal of the Rev. John Wesley.* 8 vols. London, 1909-16.

De Léry, Jean. *Histoire d'un voyage fait en la terre du Brésil.* Facsimile ed., edited by J.-C. Morisot. Geneva, 1975.

Dick, Thomas. *The Christian Philosopher; or, the Connection of Science and Philosophy with Religion.* 3rd ed. Glasgow, 1825.

Dobinson, Henry Hughes. *Letters of Henry Hugh Dobinson.* London, 1899.

Duff, Alexander. *The Church of Scotland's India Mission etc.* Edinburgh, 1835.

————. "Farewell Address on the Subject of the Church of Scotland's India Mission." In *Missionary Addresses, Delivered before the General Assembly of the Church of Scotland in the Years 1835, 1837, 1839,* 131-214. Edinburgh, 1850.

————. *India, and Indian Missions.* Edinburgh, 1839.

Edwards, Jonathan. *The Life and Diary of the Rev David Brainerd: With Notes and Reflections.* In *The Works of President Edwards,* edited by E. Williams and E. Parsons, vol. 3, 73-311. London, 1817.

————. *The Life of David Brainerd,* vol. 7: *The Works of Jonathan Edwards,* edited by Norman Pettit. New Haven, 1985.

————. *Life of the Revd. David Brainerd revised and abridged with an Introductory Essay by James Montgomery.* Glasgow, 1829.

————. *A Careful and Strict Enquiry into the Modern Prevailing Notions of that*

Freedom of the Will, Supposed to be Essential to Moral Agency . . . , edited by Paul Ramsey. New Haven, 1957.

―――. *Religious Affections*, vol. 2: *The Works of Jonathan Edwards*, edited by John E. Smith. 1st ed., 1746; new ed., New Haven, 1959.

Elder, J. R., ed. *The Letters and Journals of Samuel Marsden, 1765-1838*. Dunedin, 1932.

Ellis, William. "Geography." In *Encyclopaedia Britannica*, 1st ed., vol. 2, 682-84. Edinburgh, 1771.

―――. "Geography." In *Encyclopaedia Britannica*, 2nd ed., vol. 5, 3251-368. Edinburgh, 1778-83.

―――. *Narrative of a Tour Through Hawaii*. London, 1826.

―――. *Polynesian Researches*. 2 vols. London, 1829.

Erskine, J. E. *Journal of a Cruise Among the Islands of the Western Pacific*. London, 1853.

Four Sermons, Preached in London at the Third General Meeting of the Missionary Society, May 10, 11, 12, 1797 . . . London, 1797.

Frater, Maurice. *Midst Volcanic Fires: An Account of Missionary Tours Among the Volcano Islands of the New Hebrides*. London, n.d.

Fuller, Andrew. *The Gospel Worthy of all Acceptation: or, the Duty of Sinners to Believe in Jesus Christ*. In *The Works of the Rev. Andrew Fuller*, vol. 1, 1-256. London, 1824.

Gill, William W. *Selections from the Autobiography of the Rev. William Gill*. London, 1880.

Gliddon, George R. "The Monogenists and the Polygenists." In *Indigenous Races of the Earth, or, New Chapters of Ethnological Enquiry*, edited by Alfred Maury et al. Philadelphia, 1857.

Goen, C. C., ed. *The Great Awakening*, vol. 4: *The Works of Jonathan Edwards*. New Haven, 1972.

[Haweis, Thomas]. "The Apostolic Commission." In *Sermons Preached in London*. London, 1795.

Henderson, Thulia Susannah. *Memoir of the Rev. Ebenezer Henderson, Including his Labours in Denmark, Iceland, Russia, etc. etc*. London, 1859.

Hill, G. *Sermons*. London, 1796.

―――. *Lectures in Divinity*. 6th ed. Edinburgh, 1854.

Hodgkin, Thomas. *On the Importance of Studying and Preserving the Languages Spoken by Uncivilized Nations*. London, 1835.

Hough, James. *The History of Christianity in India from the Commencement of the Christian Era*. 5 vols. London, 1839-60.

Inglis, John. *An Examination of Mr. Dugald Stewart's Pamphlet etc*. Edinburgh, 1806.

―――. *The Grounds of Christian Hope etc*. Edinburgh, 1818.

Ivens, Walter G. *Jealousy for the Lord of Hosts: and, the Pernicious Influence of De-*

lay in Religious Concerns: Two Discourses delivered at a Meeting of Ministers at Clipstone . . . The Former by John Sutcliff of Olney . . . London, 1791.

———. *Hints to Missionaries to Melanesia.* London, 1907.

Kaye, J. W. *Christianity in India: An Historical Narrative.* London, 1859.

Keith, A. Berriedale, ed. *Speeches and Documents on Indian Policy, 1750-1921.* 2 vols. Oxford, 1922.

Kennedy, John. *The Natural History of Man, or, Popular Chapters on Ethnography.* 2 vols. in 1. London, 1851.

Kitto, John. *Daily Bible Illustrations . . . Evening Series,* vol. 2: *Isaiah and the Prophets.* Edinburgh, 1852.

Koelle, S. W. *Polyglotta Africana; or a Comparative Vocabulary of Three Hundred Words and Phrases in More Than One Hundred Distinct African Languages.* London, 1854.

Livingstone, David. *Missionary Travels and Researches in South Africa.* London, 1857.

[London Missionary Society]. *Report of the Directors to the Twenty-Fifth General Meeting of the Missionary Society, Usually Called the London Missionary Society, on Thursday, May 13, 1819.* London, 1819.

Lundie, R. *Account of Proceedings and Debate in the General Assembly of the Church of Scotland 27th. May 1796 etc.* Edinburgh, 1796.

Lushington, Charles. *The History, Design, and Present State of the Religious, Benevolent and Charitable Institutions . . . in Calcutta and Its Vicinity.* Calcutta, 1824.

Marsden, J. B., ed. *Memoirs of the Life and Labours of the Rev. Samuel Marsden, of Paramatta . . .* London, n.d. [1858].

Marshman, J. C. *The Life and Times of Carey, Marshman, and Ward.* 2 vols. London, 1859.

Matheson, J. J. *A Memoir of Greville Ewing.* London, 1843.

[Melanesian Mission]. *Isles of the Pacific: Account of the Melanesian Mission.* Melbourne, 1861.

Millar, Robert. *The History of the Propagation of Christianity and the Overthrow of Paganism Wherein the Christian Religion Is Confirmed. The Rise and Progress of Heathenish Idolatry Is Considered. The Overthrow of Paganism, and the Spreading of Christianity in the Several Ages of the Church Is Explained. The Present State of Heathens Is Inquired into; and Methods for their Conversion Proposed.* 2 vols. Edinburgh, 1723.

Monk, W., ed. *Dr Livingstone's Cambridge Lectures.* 2nd ed. Cambridge, 1860.

Morison, John. *The Fathers and Founders of the London Missionary Society: A Jubilee Memorial.* New ed. London, n.d. [1845?].

Moyle, Richard M., ed. *The Samoan Journals of John Williams.* Canberra, 1984.

Mullens, Joseph. "Modern Missions and Their Results." In *Ecclesia: Church Prob-*

lems Considered in a Series of Essays, edited by Henry Robert Reynolds. London, 1870.

Murray, A. W. *Missions in Western Polynesia.* London, 1863.

———. *Forty Years' Mission Work in Polynesia and New Guinea.* London, 1876.

Newbury, C. W., ed. *The History of the Tahitian Mission, 1799-1830: Written by John Davies Missionary to the South Sea Islands.* Cambridge, 1961.

Owen, J. *The History of the Origin and First Ten Years of the British and Foreign Bible Society.* 3 vols. London, 1816-20.

Patterson, George. *Missionary Life among the Cannibals.* Toronto, 1882.

Pearson, Hugh. *A Dissertation on the Propagation of Christianity in Asia. In Two Parts. To Which Is Prefixed, A Brief Historic View of the Progress of the Gospel in Different Nations since Its First Promulgation; Illustrated by a Chronological Chart.* Oxford, 1808.

[Peckard, Peter]. *Am I not a Man? and a Brother? With all Humility Addressed to the British Legislature.* Cambridge, 1788.

Piggott, S., ed. *An Authentic Narrative of Four Years' Residence at Tongataboo.* London, 1810.

[Anon.]. *Polynesia, or, Christianity in the Islands of the South Sea.* Dublin, 1828.

Prichard, James Cowles. *Researches into the Physical History of Man,* edited by George W. Stocking. Chicago and London, 1973.

Rhenius, C. J. *Memoir of the Rev. C. T. E. Rhenius.* London, 1841.

Robertson, William. *The History of America.* 2 vols. London, 1777.

Russell, M. *Polynesia: or, an Historical Account of the Principal Islands in the South Sea, Including New Zealand.* 3rd ed. Edinburgh, 1845.

Schapera, I., ed. *Livingstone's Missionary Correspondence, 1841-1856.* London, 1961.

Scott, Hew. *Fasti Ecclesiae Scoticanae: The Succession of Ministers in the Parish Churches of Scotland, from the Reformation, A.D. 1560, to the Present Time.* 8 vols. Edinburgh, 1867- .

Scott, Thomas. *The Force of Truth: An Authentic Narrative.* London, 1779; reprint, Edinburgh, 1984.

———. *Sermons, Preached in London, at the Formation of the Missionary Society, September 22, 23, 24, 1795.* London, 1795.

Sibree, James. *London Missionary Society: A Register of Missionaries, Deputations, etc. from 1796 to 1923.* 4th ed. London, 1923.

Simeon, Charles, ed. *Memorial Sketches of the Rev. David Brown.* London, 1816.

[Anon.]. *South Sea Islands,* edited by Frederic Shoberl. 2 vols. London, n.d.

Steel, Robert. *The New Hebrides and Christian Missions.* London, 1880.

Stewart, James. *The Educated Kafir, An Apology and Industrial Education: A Sequel.* Lovedale, 1880.

Teignmouth, Lord. *Memoir of the Life and Correspondence of John Lord Teignmouth. By his son, Lord Teignmouth.* 2 vols. London, 1843.

Telford, John, ed. *Wesley's Veterans: Lives of Early Methodist Preachers Told by Themselves.* 7 vols. London, 1912-14.

Turner, George. *Nineteen Years in Polynesia: Missionary Life, Travels and Researches in the Islands of the Pacific.* London, 1861.

Tyerman, Daniel, and George Bennett. *Journal of Voyages and Travels.* London, 1841.

Venn, John. *Life and . . . Letters of the Late Rev. Henry Venn.* 2nd ed. London, 1835.

Wardlaw, Ralph. *The Early Success of the Gospel an Evidence of its Truth, and an Encouragement to Zeal for its Universal Diffusion . . .* London, 1823.

Waterhouse, Joseph. *The King and People of Fiji.* London, 1866.

Wheeler, Daniel. *Extracts.* London, 1839.

Whittingham, Richard, ed. *The Works of the Rev. John Berridge . . . with an Enlarged Memoir of his Life.* London, 1838.

Wilberforce, R. I., and S. Wilberforce. *The Life of William Wilberforce.* 5 vols. London, 1838.

Wilberforce, S., ed. *Journals and Letters of the Rev. Henry Martyn, B.D.* 2 vols. London, 1837.

Wilder, S. V. S. *Records from the Life of S. V. S. Wilder.* New York, 1865.

Wilkes, Charles. *Narrative of the United States Exploring Expedition.* 5 vols. Philadelphia, 1845.

Williams, D., ed. *The Journals and Selected Writings of the Reverend Tiyo Soga.* Cape Town, 1983.

Williams, John. *A Narrative of Missionary Enterprises in the South Sea Islands.* 1st U.S. ed. New York, 1837.

Williams, Thomas. *Fiji and the Fijians,* vol. 1 of *The Islands and Their Inhabitants,* edited by George Stringer Rowe. 2nd ed. London, 1860.

B. Printed Secondary Sources

Aagaard, Johannes. *Mission, Konfession, Kirche: Die Problematik ihrer Integration.* Bd. 2. Lund, 1967.

Abbey, Charles J., and John H. Overton. *The English Church in the Eighteenth Century.* 2 vols. London, 1878.

Ajayi, J. F. Ade. *Christian Missions in Nigeria, 1841-1891: The Making of a New Elite.* London, 1965.

Allan, David. *Virtue, Learning and the Scottish Enlightenment: Ideas of Scholarship in Early Modern History.* Edinburgh, 1993.

Anderson, G. H., ed. *Biographical Dictionary of Christian Missions.* New York, 1998.

Anstey, R. T. *The Atlantic Slave Trade and British Abolition, 1760-1810.* Basingstoke, 1975.

Axtell, James. *The Invasion Within: The Contest of Cultures in Colonial North America*. New York, 1985.

Ballhatchet, Kenneth. "The East India Company and Roman Catholic Missionaries." *Journal of Ecclesiastical History* 44.2 (April 1993): 273-88.

———. *Caste, Class, and Catholicism in India, 1789-1914*. London, 1998.

Bebbington, D. W. *Evangelicalism in Modern Britain: A History from the 1730s to the 1980s*. London, 1989.

———. "Evangelical Christianity in the Enlightenment." *Crux* 25.4 (December 1989): 29-36. Also published (slightly revised) in *The Gospel in the Modern World,* edited by M. Eden and D. F. Wells, 66-78. Leicester, 1991.

———. "Revival and Enlightenment in Eighteenth-century England." In *Modern Christian Revivals,* edited by Edith L. Blumhofer and Randall Balmer, 17-41. Urbana and Chicago, 1993.

———. "Evangelical Conversion, c. 1740-1850." North Atlantic Missiology Project Position Paper No. 21. Cambridge, 1996.

Berger, Peter. *The Sacred Canopy*. New York, 1967.

Berkhofer, Robert F., Jr. "Protestants, Pagans, and Sequences among the North American Indians, 1760-1860." *Ethnohistory* 10 (1963): 201-32.

Berning, M., and S. Fold. "Scottish Missionaries on the Frontier." *Annals of the Grahamstown Historical Society* 17 (1987): 4-12.

Bernstein, Richard J. "Are We beyond the Enlightenment Horizon?" In *Knowledge and Belief in America: Enlightenment Traditions and Modern Religious Thought,* edited by William M. Shea and Peter A. Huff, 335-45. Washington, D.C., and Cambridge, 1995.

Bianquis, J. *Les Origines de la Société des Missions Evangéliques de Paris, 1822-1929*. Paris, 1930.

Binney, Judith. *The Legacy of Guilt: A Life of Thomas Kendall*. Christchurch, New Zealand, 1968.

———. "Christianity and the Maoris to 1840: A Comment." *New Zealand Journal of History* 3 (1969): 143-65.

Bosch, David J. *Transforming Mission: Paradigm Shifts in Theology of Mission*. Maryknoll, N.Y., 1991.

Bowden, Henry Warner. *American Indians and Christian Missions: Studies in Cultural Conflict,* edited by Martin E. Marty. Chicago History of American Religion. Chicago, 1981.

Boxer, C. R. *The Christian Century in Japan, 1549-1650*. Berkeley, Calif., 1976.

Bränström, Olaus. *Peter Fjellstedt: Mångsidig Men Entydig Kyrkoman*. Uppsala, 1994.

Brauer, Jerald C. "Conversion: From Puritanism to Revivalism." *Journal of Religion* 58 (1978): 227-43.

Brock, S. "James Stewart and Lovedale: A Reappraisal of Missionary Attitudes and African Response in Eastern Cape, South Africa, 1870-1905." Ph.D. thesis. University of Edinburgh, 1974.

Brown, S. J., ed. *William Robertson and the Expansion of Empire.* Cambridge, 1997.

Brunner, Daniel L. *Halle Pietists in England: Anthony William Boehm and the Society for Promoting Christian Knowledge.* Göttingen, 1993.

Burridge, Kenelm. *In the Way: A Study of Christian Missionary Endeavours.* Vancouver, 1991.

Calder, James M. *Scotland's March Past: The Share of Scottish Churches in the London Missionary Society.* London, 1945.

Caldwell, Patricia. *The Puritan Conversion Narrative: The Beginnings of American Expression.* Cambridge, 1983.

Cameron, N. M. de S., ed. *Dictionary of Scottish Church History and Theology.* Edinburgh, 1993.

Carson, P. S. E. "Soldiers of Christ: Evangelicals and India, 1784-1833." Ph.D. thesis. University of London, 1988.

Chadwick, Owen. *The Secularization of the European Mind in the Nineteenth Century.* Cambridge, 1975.

Chidester, David. *Savage Systems: Colonialism and Comparative Religion in Southern Africa.* Charlottesville, Va., and London, 1996.

Chitnis, A. *The Scottish Enlightenment.* London, 1976.

Christophers, Brett. *Positioning the Missionary: John Booth Good and the Confluence of Cultures in Nineteenth-Century British Columbia.* Vancouver, 1998.

Clark, I. D. L. "From Protest to Reaction: The Moderate Regime in the Church of Scotland, 1752-1805." In *Scotland in the Age of Improvement,* edited by N. T. Phillipson and R. Mitchison, 200-24. Edinburgh, 1970.

Clarke, W. K. Lowther. *A History of the SPCK.* London, 1959.

Cohen, William B. *The French Encounter with Africans: White Response to Blacks, 1530-1880.* Bloomington and London, 1980.

Comaroff, Jean, and John Comaroff. *Of Revelation and Revolution,* vol. 1: *Christianity, Colonialism, and Consciousness in South Africa.* Chicago and London, 1991.

———. *Ethnography and the Historical Imagination.* Boulder and Oxford, 1992.

Comaroff, John L., and Jean Comaroff. *Of Revelation and Revolution,* vol. 2: *The Dialectics of Modernity on a South African Frontier.* Chicago and London, 1997.

Congar, Yves M.-J. *A History of Theology.* New York, 1968.

Cracknell, Kenneth. *Justice, Courtesy and Love: Theologians and Missionaries Encountering World Religions, 1846-1914.* London, 1995.

Crocker, Lester G. "Introduction." In *The Blackwell Companion to the Enlightenment,* edited by John W. Yolton. Oxford, 1991.

Currie, David A. "The Growth of Evangelicalism in the Church of Scotland, 1793-1843." Ph.D. thesis. University of St. Andrews, 1990.

Dalferth, I. U. *Theology and Philosophy.* Oxford, 1988.

Davidson, Allan K. "The Development and Influence of the British Missionary

Movement's Attitudes to India, 1786-1830." Ph.D. thesis. University of Aberdeen, 1973.

Davie, G. E. "The Scottish Enlightenment." In *The Scottish Enlightenment and Other Essays*, edited by G. E. Davie. Edinburgh, 1991.

de Kock, L. *Civilising Barbarians: Missionary Narrative and African Textual Response in Nineteenth-Century South Africa.* Johannesburg, 1996.

Don, Alexander. *Peter Milne (1834-1924) Missionary to Nguna, New Hebrides.* Dunedin, 1927.

Drummond, A. L., and J. Bulloch. *The Church in Victorian Scotland, 1843-1874.* Edinburgh, 1975.

Duviols, Pierre. *La lutte contre les religions autochtones dans le Pérou colonial: "l'extirpation de l'idolâtrie" entre 1532 et 1660.* Lima, n.d.

Edmond, Rod. *Representing the South Pacific: Colonial Discourse from Cook to Gauguin.* Cambridge, 1997.

———. "Translating Missionary Cultures: William Ellis and Missionary Writing." In *Science and Exploration in the Pacific: European Voyages to the Southern Oceans in the Eighteenth Century,* edited by Margarette Lincoln. Woodbridge, Suffolk, 1998.

Elder, J. R., ed. *Marsden's Lieutenants.* Dunedin, 1934.

Elliott, J. H. *The Old World and the New, 1492-1650.* Cambridge, 1992; first published, 1970.

Elliott-Binns, L. E. *The Early Evangelicals: A Religious and Social Study.* London, 1953.

Embree, A. T. *Charles Grant and British Rule in India.* London, 1962.

Enklaar, Ido Hendricus. *Life and Work of Dr. J. Th. Van Der Kemp, 1749-1811: Missionary, Pioneer and Protagonist of Racial Equality in South Africa.* Cape Town, 1988.

Eze, Emmanuel C. *Race and the Enlightenment: A Reader.* Oxford, 1996.

Fieldhouse, D. K. *The Colonial Empires: A Comparative Study from the Eighteenth Century.* 2nd ed. London, 1982.

Ferguson, M. *Subject to Others.* London, 1992.

Finney, Ben. "James Cook and the European Discovery of Polynesia." In *From Maps to Metaphors: The Pacific World of George Vancouver,* edited by Robin Fisher and Hugh Johnston. Vancouver, 1993.

Fisch, Jörg. "A Pamphlet War on Christian Missions in India, 1807-1809." *Journal of Asian History* 19.1 (1985): 22-70.

Fisher, Robin. "Henry Williams' Leadership of the CMS Mission to New Zealand." *New Zealand Journal of History* 9 (1975): 142-53.

Flynn, P. *Enlightened Scotland.* Edinburgh, 1992.

Frei, Hans W. *The Eclipse of Biblical Narrative.* New Haven, 1974.

———. "The 'Literal Reading' of Biblical Narrative." In Hans Frei, *Theology and Narrative: Selected Essays,* edited by G. Hunsinger and W. Placher, 117-52. New York, 1993.

Frykenberg, R. E. "Constructions of Hinduism at the Nexus of History and Religion." *Journal of Interdisciplinary History* 23.3 (1993): 523-50.

Fyfe, Christopher. *A History of Sierra Leone*. Oxford, 1962; reprint, Aldershot, 1993.

Garrett, John. *To Live Among the Stars: Christian Origins in Oceania*. Geneva and Suva, 1982.

Gascoigne, John. *Cambridge in the Age of the Enlightenment*. Cambridge, 1989.

Gordon, Grant. *From Slavery to Freedom: The Life of David George, Pioneer Black Baptist Minister*. Hansport, Nova Scotia, 1992.

Gunson, Niel. *Messengers of Grace: Evangelical Missionaries in the South Seas, 1797-1860*. Oxford and Melbourne, 1978.

Gusdorf, Georges. "Conditions and Limits of Autobiography." In *Autobiography: Essays Theoretical and Critical*, edited by James Olney, 28-48. Princeton, N.J., 1980.

Hair, P. E. H. *The Early Study of Nigerian Languages: Essays and Bibliographies*. Cambridge, 1967.

Haller, William. *The Rise of Puritanism*. 1st ed., 1938; reprint, New York, 1957.

Hambrick-Stowe, Charles E. *The Practice of Piety: Puritan Devotional Disciplines in Seventeenth-Century New England*. Chapel Hill, N.C., 1982.

Hardy, Daniel W. *God's Ways with the World*. Edinburgh, 1996.

Harran, Marilyn J. *Luther on Conversion*. Ithaca, N.Y., 1983.

Harris, Harriet A. *Fundamentalism and Evangelicals*. Oxford, 1998.

Hempton, David. *The Religion of the People: Methodism and Popular Religion c. 1750-1900*. London, 1996.

Hennell, M. M. *John Venn and the Clapham Sect*. London, 1958.

Herbert, Christopher. *Culture and Anomie: Ethnographic Imagination in the Nineteenth Century*. Chicago and London, 1991.

Hewat, E. G. K. *Vision and Achievement, 1795-1956*. London, 1960.

Hilton, Boyd. *The Age of Atonement: The Influence of Evangelicalism on Social and Economic Thought, 1785-1865*. Oxford, 1988.

Hinchliff, Peter. "Whatever Happened to the Glasgow Missionary Society." *Studia Historia Ecclesiastica* 18.2 (1992): 104-20.

Hindmarsh, Bruce. "The Olney Autobiographers: Evangelical Conversion Narrative in the Mid-eighteenth Century." *Journal of Ecclesiastical History* 49 (1998): 61-84.

Hogg, Garry. *Pathfinders in New Zealand*. London, 1963.

Holsten, W. *Johannes Evangelista Gossner: Glaube und Gemeinde*. Göttingen, 1949.

Höpfl, H. M. "From Savage to Scotsman: Conjectural History in the Scottish Enlightenment." *Journal of British Studies* 17 (1978): 19-40.

Howe, K. R. "The Maori Response to Christianity in the Thames-Waikato Area, 1833-1840." *New Zealand Journal of History* 7 (1973): 28-46.

————. *Where the Waves Fall: A New South Sea Islands History from First Settlement to Colonial Rule.* Sydney, 1984.

Hull, E. R. *Bombay Mission History: The Padraodo Question.* 2 vols. Bombay, 1927.

Hunsberger, George R. *Bearing the Witness of the Spirit: Lesslie Newbigin's Theology of Cultural Plurality.* Grand Rapids, 1998.

Hurtado, Larry W. "Convert, Apostate or Apostle to the Nations: The 'Conversion' of Paul in Recent Scholarship." *Studies in Religion* 22 (1993): 273-84.

Hutchison, W. R. *Errand to the World: American Protestant Thought and Foreign Missions.* Chicago and London, 1987.

Im Hof, Ulrich. *The Enlightenment,* translated by William E. Yuill. Oxford, 1994.

Ingham, K. *Reformers in India, 1793-1833.* Cambridge, 1956.

Jenkins, Paul. "The Church Missionary Society and the Basel Mission: An Early Experiment in Inter-European Co-operation." In *The Church Mission Society and World Christianity, 1799-1999,* edited by Kevin Ward and Brian Stanley, 43-65. Grand Rapids, 2000.

Jeyaraj, Daniel. *Inkulturation in Tranquebar: der Beitrag der frühen dänisch-halleschen Mission zum Werden einer indisch-einheimischen Kirche (1706-1730).* Erlangen, 1996.

Kidd, C. "Gaelic Antiquity and National Identity in Enlightenment Ireland and Scotland." *English Historical Review* 109.2 (1994): 1197-214.

King, E. H. *James Beattie.* Boston, 1977.

Kings, Graham. "A Corresponding Theology of Mission: Letters between Max Warren and Roger Hooker, 1965-1977." NAMP Position Paper no. 89. Cambridge, 1998.

Kool, A. M. *God Moves in a Mysterious Way: The Hungarian Protestant Foreign Mission Movement, 1756-1951.* Zoetermeer, 1993.

Krüger, Bernhard. *The Pear Tree Blossoms: A History of Moravian Mission Stations in South Africa, 1737-1869.* Genadendal, 1967.

Laird, M. A. *Missionaries and Education in Bengal, 1793-1837.* Oxford, 1972.

Lennox, Cuthbert. *James Chalmers of New Guinea.* 2nd ed. London, 1902.

Lewis, D. M., ed. *Blackwell Dictionary of Evangelical Biography.* 2 vols. Oxford, 1995.

Lovegrove, Deryck W. "English Evangelical Dissent and the European Conflict, 1789-1815." In *The Church and War,* edited by W. J. Sheils, 263-76. Studies in Church History, vol. 20. Oxford, 1983.

————. *Established Church: Sectarian People: Itinerancy and the Transformation of English Dissent, 1780-1830.* Cambridge, 1988.

Luker, David. "Revivalism in Theory and Practice: The Case of Cornish Methodism." *Journal of Ecclesiastical History* 37 (1986): 603-19.

McGrane, Bernard. *Beyond Anthropology: Society and the Other.* New York, 1989.

MacIntyre, Alasdair. *After Virtue: A Study in Moral Theory.* 2nd ed. London, 1985.

Mascuch, Michael. *Origins of the Individualist Self: Autobiography and Self-Identity in England, 1591-1791.* Cambridge, 1997.

Marshall, P. J., and Glyndwr Williams. *The Great Map of Mankind: British Perceptions of the World in the Age of Enlightenment.* London, 1982.

Marshall, P. J., ed. *Problems of Empire: Britain and India, 1757-1813.* London,
1968.

Maxwell, I. D. "Alexander Duff and the Theological and Philosophical Background to the General Assembly's Mission in Calcutta to 1840." Ph.D. thesis. University of Edinburgh, 1995.

————. "Enlightenment and Mission: Alexander Duff and the Early Years of the
General Assembly's Institution in Calcutta." North Atlantic Missiology
Project Position Paper No. 2. Cambridge, 1996.

May, Henry F. *The Enlightenment in America.* New York, 1976.

Miles, A. H. *The Poets and Poetry of the Century,* vol. 10. London, n.d.

Miller, Char, ed. *Missions and Missionaries in the Pacific.* New York and Toronto,
1985.

Mitchell, William. "Language and Conquest in Early Colonial Peru: The Ambiva-
lent Dialectic of the Appropriation of the Andean Language." In *From
Christendom to World Christianity,* edited by L. Sanneh and A. F. Walls.
Forthcoming.

Morris, Henry. *The Life of Charles Grant.* London, 1904.

Murdoch, A., and R. B. Sher. "Literary and Learned Culture." In *People and Society in Scotland,* vol. 1: *1760-1830,* edited by T. Devine and R. Mitchison,
127-42. Edinburgh, 1988.

Murray, David. "David Brainerd and the Gift of Christianity." *European Review of
Native American Studies* 10.2 (1996): 23-29.

Neill, Stephen. *A History of Christianity in India, 1707-1858.* Cambridge, 1985.

Nenadic, S. "The Rise of the Urban Middle Classes." In *People and Society in Scotland,* vol. 1: *1760-1830,* edited by T. Devine and R. Mitchison, 109-26. Edinburgh, 1988.

Newbigin, Lesslie. *The Gospel in a Pluralist Society.* London, 1989.

Noll, Mark A. *Princeton and the Republic, 1768-1822: The Search for a Christian
Enlightenment in the Era of Samuel Stanhope Smith.* Princeton, 1989.

————. *A History of the Churches in the United States and Canada.* Grand Rapids
and London, 1992.

————. "Revolution and the Rise of Evangelical Social Influence in North Atlantic Societies." In *Evangelicalism: Comparative Studies of Popular Protestantism in North America, the British Isles, and Beyond, 1700-1990,* edited by
Mark A. Noll, David W. Bebbington, and George A. Rawlyk, 113-36. New
York, 1994.

————. "The Rise and Long Life of the Protestant Enlightenment in America." In
*Knowledge and Belief in America: Enlightenment Traditions and Modern Re-
ligious Thought,* edited by William M. Shea and Peter A. Huff, 88-124.
Washington, D.C., and Cambridge, 1995.

————. "The Americanization of Christian Theology in the Evangelical Surge,

1790-1840." Unpublished paper read at the Anglo-American Conference of Historians, 1996.

Nuttall, Geoffrey F. "Northamptonshire and the Modern Question: A Turning-point in Eighteenth-century Dissent." *Journal of Theological Studies* n.s. 16 (1965): 101-23.

———. "Methodism and the Older Dissent: Some Perspectives." *United Reformed Church History Society Journal* 2 (1981): 259-74.

O'Brien, Susan. "A Transatlantic Community of Saints: The Great Awakening and the First Evangelical Network, 1735-55." *American Historical Review* 91 (1986): 811-32.

———. "Eighteenth-century Publishing Networks in the First Years of Transatlantic Evangelicalism." In *Evangelicalism: Comparative Studies of Popular Protestantism in North America, the British Isles, and Beyond, 1700-1990,* edited by M. A. Noll, D. W. Bebbington, and G. A. Rawlyk. New York, 1994.

Oddie, Geoffrey A. "The Protestant Missionary Movement as a Factor in the Hindu Construction and Refashioning of 'Hinduism.'" In *Missionary Challenges in India since 1700,* edited by R. E. Frykenberg. Curzon Press, forthcoming.

Owens, J. M. R. "Christianity and the Maoris to 1840." *New Zealand Journal of History* 2 (1968): 18-40.

Packer, J. I. "Orthodoxy." In *Evangelical Dictionary of Theology,* edited by W. A. Elwell, 808. Basingstoke, 1984.

———. "Puritanism as a Movement of Revival." In *Among God's Giants: The Puritan Vision of the Christian Life,* 41-63. Eastbourne, 1991.

Pagden, Anthony. *The Fall of Natural Man: The American Indian and the Origins of Comparative Ethnology.* Cambridge, 1982.

———. *European Encounters with the New World: From Renaissance to Romanticism.* New Haven and London, 1993.

Pailin, David A. *Attitudes to Other Religions: Comparative Religion in Seventeenth- and Eighteenth-Century Britain.* Manchester, 1984.

Parsonson, G. S. "The Literate Revolution in Polynesia." *Journal of Pacific History* 2 (1967): 39-57.

Payne, Ernest A. *The Church Awakes: The Story of the Modern Missionary Movement.* London, 1942.

Pearce, R. H. *Savagism and Civilization: A Study of the Indian and the American Mind.* Baltimore, 1965.

Penny, Frank. *The Church in Madras.* 3 vols. London, 1904-22.

Pettit, Norman. *The Heart Prepared: Grace and Conversion in Puritan Spiritual Life.* New Haven, 1966.

———. "Editor's Introduction." In *The Life of David Brainerd,* edited by Norman Pettit. *The Works of Jonathan Edwards,* vol. 7. New Haven, 1985.

Piggin, F. Stuart. *Making Evangelical Missionaries, 1789-1858: The Social Back-*

ground, Motives and Training of British Protestant Missionaries to India. Abingdon, 1984.

Pinnington, J. "Church Principles in the Early Years of the Church Missionary Society: The Problem of the 'German' Missionaries." *Journal of Theological Studies* n.s. 20.2 (1969): 523-32.

Pocock, J. G. A. "Enlightenment and Revolution: The Case of English-speaking North America." In *Transactions of the Seventh International Congress on the Enlightenment,* 249-61. Oxford, 1989.

Porter, Andrew N. "'Commerce and Christianity': The Rise and Fall of a Missionary Slogan." *Historical Journal* 28.3 (1985): 597-621.

———. "Scottish Missions and Education in Nineteenth-century India: The Changing Face of 'Trusteeship.'" *Journal of Imperial and Commonwealth History* 16 (1988): 35-57.

———. "Religion and Empire: British Expansion in the Long Nineteenth Century, 1780-1914." *Journal of Imperial and Commonwealth History* 20.3 (1992): 370-90.

Potts, E. Daniel. *British Baptist Missionaries in India, 1793-1837.* Cambridge, 1967.

Pratt, Mary Louise. *Imperial Eyes: Travel Writing and Transculturation.* London and New York, 1992.

Raboteau, Albert J. *Slave Religion: The "Invisible Institution" in the Antebellum South.* New York, 1978.

———. "The Black Experience in American Evangelicalism: The Meaning of Slavery." In *The Evangelical Tradition in America,* edited by Leonard I. Sweet. Macon, Ga., 1984.

Rambo, Lewis R. *Understanding Religious Conversion.* New Haven, 1993.

Rawlyk, G. A. *The Canada Fire: Radical Evangelicalism in British North America, 1775-1812.* Kingston, Ontario, 1994.

Rivers, Isabel. "'Strangers and Pilgrims': Sources and Patterns of Methodist Narrative." In *Augustan Worlds,* edited by J. D. Hilson, M. M. B. Jones, and J. R. Watson, 189-203. Leicester, 1978.

Robertson, Bruce. *Raja Rammohan Ray: The Father of Modern India.* Delhi, 1995.

Rooy, Sidney H. *The Theology of Missions in the Puritan Tradition.* Grand Rapids, 1965.

Rosman, Doreen M. *Evangelicals and Culture.* Aldershot, 1992; first published, 1984.

Ross, Andrew. *John Philip (1775-1851): Missions, Race and Politics in South Africa.* Aberdeen, 1986.

Roxborogh, John. "Thomas Chalmers and the Mission of the Church with Special Reference to the Rise of the Missionary Movement in Scotland." Ph.D. thesis. University of Aberdeen, 1978.

Shea, Daniel B., Jr. *Spiritual Autobiography in Early America.* Princeton, 1968.

Sher, Richard B. *Church and University in the Scottish Enlightenment: The Moderate Literati of Edinburgh.* Edinburgh, 1985.

Sloan, Douglas. *The Scottish Enlightenment and the American College Ideal.* New York, 1971.

Smith, Bernard. *European Vision and the South Pacific.* 2nd ed. New Haven and London, 1985.

Smith, George. *The Life of John Wilson, DD, FRS.* London, 1879.

Smith, Thomas. *Alexander Duff DD, LLD.* London, 1883.

Smith, Vanessa. *Literary Culture and the Pacific: Nineteenth-Century Textual Encounters.* Cambridge, 1998.

Stanley, Brian. *The Bible and the Flag: Protestant Missions and British Imperialism in the Nineteenth and Twentieth Centuries.* Leicester, 1990.

———. *The History of the Baptist Missionary Society, 1792-1992.* Edinburgh, 1992.

Stendahl, Krister. "The Apostle Paul and the Introspective Conscience of the West." In *Paul Among the Jews and Gentiles and Other Essays,* edited by Krister Stendahl, 78-96. Philadelphia and London, 1976.

Stock, Eugene. *The History of the Church Missionary Society: Its Environment, Its Men and Its Work.* 4 vols. London, 1899, 1916.

Stoeffler, F. Ernst. *The Rise of Evangelical Pietism.* Studies in the History of Religions, 9. Leiden, 1971.

Stoever, William K. B. *"A Faire and Easie Way to Heaven": Covenant Theology and Antinomianism in Early Massachusetts.* Middletown, Conn., 1978.

Stuart, Doug. "'Of Savages and Heroes': Discourses of Race, Nation and Gender in the Evangelical Missions to Southern Africa in the Early Nineteenth Century." Ph.D. thesis. University of London, 1994.

Stunt, Timothy C. F. *From Awakening to Secession: Radical Evangelicals in Switzerland and Britain, 1815-1835.* Edinburgh, 2000.

Taylor, Charles. *Sources of the Self.* Cambridge, 1992.

Thomas, Nicholas. *Colonialism's Culture: Anthropology, Travel and Government.* Cambridge, 1994.

Tippett, Alan R. "Conversion as a Dynamic Process in Christian Mission." *Missiology* 5.2 (April 1977): 203-21.

Turner, Mary. *Slaves and Missionaries: The Disintegration of Jamaican Slave Society, 1787-1834.* Urbana, 1982.

Valenze, Deborah. *Prophetic Sons and Daughters: Female Preaching and Popular Religion in Industrial England.* Princeton, 1978.

Van der Veer, Peter, ed. *Conversion to Modernities: The Globalization of Christianity.* New York and London, 1996.

Van Rooden, Peter. "Nineteenth-century Representations of Missionary Conversion and the Transformation of Western Christianity." In *Conversion to Modernities: The Globalization of Christianity,* edited by Peter van der Veer, 65-87. New York and London, 1996.

Viswanathan, Gauri. *Masks of Conquest: Literary Study and British Rule*. London, 1990.

Voges, Friedhelm. "Moderate and Evangelical Thinking in the Later Eighteenth Century: Differences and Shared Attitudes." *Records of the Scottish Church History Society* 22.2 (1985): 141-57.

Volf, Miroslav. *Exclusion and Embrace: A Theological Exploration of Identity, Otherness, and Reconciliation*. Nashville, 1996.

Walls, Andrew F. "A Christian Experiment: The Early Sierra Leone Colony." In *The Mission of the Church and the Propagation of the Faith*, edited by G. J. Cuming, 107-29. Studies in Church History, vol. 6. Cambridge, 1970.

―――. "A Colonial Concordat: Two Views of Christianity and Civilisation." In *Church Society and Politics*, edited by Derek Baker, 293-302. Studies in Church History, vol. 12. Oxford, 1975.

―――. "Missions." In *Dictionary of Scottish Church History and Theology*, edited by N. M. de S. Cameron et al., 567-94. Edinburgh, 1993.

―――. "The Evangelical Revival, the Missionary Movement, and Africa." In *Evangelicalism: Comparative Studies of Popular Protestantism in North America, the British Isles, and Beyond, 1700-1990*, edited by Mark A. Noll, David W. Bebbington, and George A. Rawlyk, 310-30. New York, 1994.

―――. "Mission VI." In *Theologische Realenzyklopädie*, 4-Auflage, Bd. XXIII, 40-50. Berlin, 1994.

―――. "Christianity in the Non-Western World: A Study in the Serial Nature of Christian Expansion." *Studies in World Christianity* 1.1 (1995): 1-25.

―――. "Introduction: African Christianity in the History of Religions." In *Christianity in Africa in the 1990s*, edited by C. Fyfe and A. F. Walls, 1-16. Edinburgh, 1996.

―――. *The Missionary Movement in Christian History: Studies in the Transmission of Faith*. Edinburgh and Maryknoll, N.Y., 1996.

―――. "Black Europeans — White Africans." In *The Missionary Movement in Christian History: Studies in the Transmission of Faith*, 102-10. Edinburgh and Maryknoll, N.Y., 1996.

―――. "Romans One and the Missionary Movement." In *The Missionary Movement in Christian History: Studies in the Transmission of Faith*, 55-67. Edinburgh and Maryknoll, N.Y., 1996.

Walsh, J. D. "The Yorkshire Evangelicals in the Eighteenth Century with Special Reference to Methodism." Ph.D. thesis. University of Cambridge, 1956.

Walsh, John, Colin Haydon, and Stephen Taylor, eds. *The Church of England, c. 1689–c. 1833: From Toleration to Tractarianism*. Cambridge, 1993.

Walsh, John, and Ronald Hyam. *Peter Peckard: Liberal Churchman and Anti-Slave Trade Campaigner*. Magdalene College Occasional Papers No. 16. Cambridge, 1998.

Ward, W. R. "Introduction." In *The Works of John Wesley*, vol. 18: *Journal and Di-*

aries I (1735-38), edited by W. R. Ward and Richard P. Heitzenrater, 1-119. Nashville, 1988.

———. *The Protestant Evangelical Awakening.* Cambridge, 1992.

———. "Enlightenment in Early Moravianism." In W. R. Ward, *Faith and Faction*, 95-111. London, 1993.

———. "Orthodoxy, Enlightenment and Religious Revival." In W. R. Ward, *Faith and Faction*, 16-37. London, 1993.

Watkins, Owen, *The Puritan Experience: Studies in Spiritual Autobiography.* London, 1972.

Wessels, Anton. *Europe: Was It Ever Really Christian?* translated by John Bowden. London, 1994.

Whaley, Joachim. "The Protestant Enlightenment in Germany." In *The Enlightenment in National Context,* edited by Roy Porter and Mikuláš Teich, 106-17. Cambridge, 1981.

White, Gavin. "'Highly Preposterous': Origins of Scottish Missions." *Records of the Scottish Church History Society* 19.2 (1976): 111-24.

Whiteman, Darrell L. *Melanesians and Missionaries: An Ethnohistorical Study of Social and Religious Change in the Southwest Pacific.* Pasadena, 1983.

Wilcox, Peter. "Restoration, Reformation and the Progress of the Kingdom of Christ: Evangelisation in the Thought and Practice of John Calvin, 1555-1564." D.Phil. thesis. University of Oxford, 1993.

Willey, Andrew. "Transforming Heroes: Seventeenth-century Puritan Missions to Native Americans." M.Phil. thesis. University of Birmingham, 1998.

Williams, D. "The Missionaries on the Eastern Frontier of the Cape Colony, 1799-1853." Ph.D. thesis. University of the Witwatersrand, 1959.

Willmer, Haddon. "Evangelicalism, 1785-1835." Hulsean Prize Essay. University of Cambridge, 1962.

Witherington, Donald J. "What Was Distinctive about the Scottish Enlightenment?" In *Aberdeen and the Enlightenment: Proceedings of a Conference Held at the University of Aberdeen,* 9-19. Aberdeen, 1987.

Wood, A. S. *Thomas Haweis, 1734-1820.* London, 1957.

Wright, Harrison M. *New Zealand, 1769-1840: Early Years of Western Contact.* Cambridge, Mass., 1959.

Yarwood, A. T. *Samuel Marsden, The Great Survivor.* Carlton, Victoria, 1977.

Young, R. F., and S. Jebanesan. *The Bible Trembled: The Hindu-Christian Controversies of Nineteenth-Century Ceylon.* Vienna, 1995.

Young, R. F., and G. P. V. Somaratna. *Vain Debates: The Buddhist-Christian Controversies of Nineteenth-Century Ceylon.* Vienna, 1996.

Index